Anonymous

Naismith's Hamilton Directory for 1878-79

Including Bothwell, Blantyre, Uddingston, Motherwell, and Larkhall to which is

added, A history of Hamilton and neighbourhood

Anonymous

Naismith's Hamilton Directory for 1878-79
Including Bothwell, Blantyre, Uddingston, Motherwell, and Larkhall to which is added, A history of Hamilton and neighbourhood

ISBN/EAN: 9783337370527

Printed in Europe, USA, Canada, Australia, Japan

Cover: Foto ©ninafisch / pixelio.de

More available books at **www.hansebooks.com**

NAISMITH'S HAMILTON DIRECTORY,

FOR

1878-79,

INCLUDING

BOTHWELL, BLANTYRE, UDDINGSTON,

MOTHERWELL, AND LARKHALL,

TO WHICH IS ADDED

A HISTORY OF HAMILTON

AND NEIGHBOURHOOD.

HAMILTON:
PRINTED AND PUBLISHED BY W. NAISMITH,
"ADVERTISER" OFFICE.

PREFACE.

The first Directory of Hamilton was issued by us in 1847, our firm at the time being Brown & Naismith. Other three issues, the last in 1859, have since made their appearance, and have long been out of print.

The present publication has been loudly called for, the wonderful growth of the Burgh in population, wealth, and commercial importance during the past few years, causing the want of a good, reliable local Directory to be felt more and more. We have exerted every effort to supply the desideratum; and for any shortcomings and inaccuracies which may appear we have to crave the indulgence and forbearance of the public.

With the Directory is issued a Handbook of Hamilton and neighbourhood, the aim of the compiler of which has been to supply natives at home and abroad with a historical memorial of the district, past and present, and strangers with what does not exist at present—a handy guide to its many and varied objects of interest. The information has been derived from all available sources, including several that have not previously been drawn upon. In the course of the passage of the Handbook through the press, the compiler has become cognisant of many defects and omissions, which it will be his anxious desire to rectify and supply in the event of a re-issue being demanded.

January 15, 1879.

CONTENTS.

	Page.
ALMANAC, 1879, WITH CALENDAR OF LOCAL EVENTS,	10
CALENDAR, 1879,	9
LANARKSHIRE:—	
ACTING JUSTICES OF THE PEACE,	22
COMMISSIONERS FOR PROPERTY AND INCOME TAX, &c.,	25
COMMISSIONERS OF SUPPLY,	22
COUNTY POLICE,	25
COURTS OF JUSTICE—SHERIFF, COMMISSARY, AND J.P.,	24
EAST AND WEST LANARKSHIRE ROAD TRUST,	25
EXCISE OFFICE,	25
HAMILTON PRISON,	25
INLAND REVENUE,	25
LIEUTENANCY,	22
POPULATION,	25
SHERIFF OFFICERS AND CONSTABLES,	25
SOCIETY OF SOLICITORS,	24
VALUATORS OF LANDS AND HERITAGES,	25
HAMILTON:—	
BANKS,	61
BURGH AND PARISH ROAD TRUSTS,	52
BURGH POLICE COURT,	51
CLERGY,	52
COMBINATION POORHOUSE,	52
COMMISSIONERS,	50
COMPANIES, SOCIETIES, &c,,	56
CO-OPERATIVE SOCIETIES,	58
COUNCILLORS SINCE 1834,	51
CRICKET AND FOOTBALL CLUBS,	59
FAIRS AND CATTLE MARKETS,	62-63

CONTENTS—*Continued.*

Fast-Days,	61-62
Free Gardeners,	58
Free Masons,	58
Gas Works,	51
Good Templar Lodges,	60
Hamilton Directory,	27-49
Insurance Agencies,	61
Letter Carriers,	64
Magistrates and Town Council,	50
Markets,	61
Omnibuses,	64
Parochial Board,	52
Population,	63
Post Office,	64
Presbyteries,	53
Rifle Volunteers, 16th L.R.V.,	54
School Boards,	55
Seminaries and Teachers,	55
Surgeons,	60
Trade Societies,	59
Voters—1st Ward,	65
,, 2d Ward,	73
,, 3d Ward,	81
,, 4th Ward,	88
,, Extended Burgh,	93
Water Works,	52

BLANTYRE (High and Low):—

Churches,	104
Clergy,	104
General Directory,	98-104
Schools and Teachers,	104
Societies,	104

BOTHWELL:—

Banks, &c.,	108
Churches,	108
Clergy,	108
General Directory,	105-108
Post Office,	108
Schools and Teachers,	108
Societies,	108

CONTENTS—*Continued.*

UDDINGSTON:—

BANKS, &c.,	115
CHURCHES,	115
CLERGY,	115
GENERAL DIRECTORY,	109–114
POST OFFICE,	115
SCHOOLS, AND TEACHERS,	115
SOCIETIES,	115

MOTHERWELL:—

CHURCHES,	123
CLERGY,	123
GENERAL DIRECTORY,	116–123
PAROCHIAL BOARD,	123
POLICE COMMISSIONERS,	123
SCHOOLS AND TEACHERS,	123
SOCIETIES, BANK, &c.,	124

LARKHALL:—

CHURCHES,	129
GENERAL DIRECTORY,	125–129
PAROCHIAL BOARD,	130
SCHOOL BOARDS,	129
SCHOOLS AND TEACHERS,	129
SOCIETIES, BANK, &c.,	130

ADVERTISEMENTS:—

ANDERSON, Miss, Ladies' Outfitter, 13 Townhead Street,	i.
ANNAN, THOMAS & ROBERT, Photographers, Bothwell Road,	ii.
BEGBIE'S PURE FLUID MAGNESIA—Globe Company, Glasgow,	(1).
BELLEVUE ESTABLISHMENT (Young Ladies),	xvi.
BURNBANK COFFEE HOUSE AND READING ROOMS,	xiv.
CAMERON, ALLAN, Plumber, Uddingston,	xx.
CAMERON, WILLIAM, Grocer, Quarry Street,	iii.
CARLTON HOUSE SCHOOL, Uddingston,	xx.
CINNAMOND, JAMES, Hatter, Cadzow Buildings,	xiii.
CLYDESDALE COLLEGE,	xv.
CLYDE HOTEL, Bothwell,	xxi.
CRAWFORD, THOMAS W., Watchmaker, 296 Argyle St., Glasgow,	(1).
CROSS, GAVIN, Tailor and Clothier, 79 Quarry Street,	ii.
CURRIE & WILSON, Plasterers, Quarry Street,	viii.
DAVIDSON, ROBERT, Joiner and Timber Merchant, Blantyre,	xix.
DOBBIE, JOHN, Grocer and Wine Merchant, Burnbank Road,	iii.
EDUCATIONAL INSTITUTE, Rosemount, Uddingston,	xx.

CONTENTS—Continued.

FAIRLEY, JAMES, Ironmonger, 23 Townhead Street, ... xi.
GRANT, ALEXANDER & CO., Cabinetmakers, Glasgow, .. xxiv.
HAMILTON ACADEMY, ... xvi.
HAMILTON & MOFFAT, Joiners and Timber Merchants, Bent Road, viii.
HAZELS, JAMES, Tinsmith and Plumber, High Blantyre, .. xix.
JACK, THOMAS, Accountant and Sheriff-Officer, Motherwell, xxiii.
JOHNSTON, JOHN, Painter, 11 Muir Street, ... ix.
KEITH, JAMES, Grocer and Wine Merchant, 86 Cadzow Street, iv.
LIGHTBODY, JOHN, Baker, 58 Cadzow Street and 4 Duke Street, vi.
MACKIE, WILLIAM, Saddler, Duke Street, ... ii.
MACKILL, R. C., Chemist, 56 Cadzow Street and 10 Brandon St., vii.
MERRYLEA SEMINARY, Bothwell. .. .. xxi.
MITCHELL, DAVID, 20 Hope St., Glasgow—Old Irish Whisky, &c., (2).
MOCHRIE, ROBERT, Grocer and Wine Merchant, Burgh Buildings, iii.
M'GHIE, J., Photographer, ... viii.
M'NAUGHTON, DAVID, Wine Merchant, Blantyre and Holytown, xviii.
M'QUEEN, NORMAN, Surgeon-Dentist, 33 Townhead Street, xiv.
NAISMITH, GAVIN, Ironmonger, 21 Cadzow Street, .. xii.
PARKER, A., Umbrella-Maker, Brandon Street, ... ii.
PATENT OFFICE AND DESIGNS REGISTRY, Glasgow and Edinr., (2).
PATON, ROBERT A., Ironmonger, 36 Cadzow Street, ... x.
RAPLOCH ARMS HOTEL, Larkhall, ... xxii.
RITCHIE, JAMES, Ironmonger, Strathaven, ... xxiii.
RITCHIE, THOMAS, Ironmonger, Larkhall, ... xxiii.
ROYAL ARMS HOTEL, Larkhall, ... xxii.
SHARP, Photographer, 7 and 9 Low Patrick Street, .. viii.
SIMPSON, JOHN M., 60 Great Clyde Street, Glasgow, .. (4).
SOMMERVILLE & KINNEAR, Drapers, 14 and 16 Cadzow Street, vii.
STAFFORDSHIRE FIRE INSURANCE COMPANY—R. Muir, Glasgow, (3).
STEWART, JOHN, Chemist, 8 Cadzow Street, ... iii.
STEWART, ROBERT, Slater, &c., High Blantyre, ... xix.
STRUTHERS, JAMES B., Wine Merchant, Kirkton, H. Blantyre, xviii.
TORRANCE, THOMAS, Boot and Shoemaker, 70 Cadzow Street, viii.
THOMSON, W. C., General Outfitter, Glasgow, ... xxv.
VICTORIA HOTEL, Larkhall, ... xxii.
WALKER, THOMAS, Chemist, Uddingston, ... xix.
WALLACE, WILLIAM, Carriage-Hirer and Funeral Undertaker, xvii.
WISEMAN, JAMES, Watchmaker, 46 and 48 Cadzow Street, .. ii.
YOUNG, A. T., General Draper, 69 Quarry Street, ... i.

CALENDAR, 1879.

JANUARY.

```
S.  ..  5 12 19 26
M.  ..  6 13 20 27
Tu. ..  7 14 21 28
W.   1  8 15 22 29
Th.  2  9 16 23 30
F.   3 10 17 24 31
S.   4 11 18 25 ..
```

FEBRUARY.

```
S.  ..  2  9 16 23
M.  ..  3 10 17 24
Tu. ..  4 11 18 25
W.  ..  5 12 19 26
Th. ..  6 13 20 27
F.  ..  7 14 21 28
S.   1  8 15 22 ..
```

MARCH.

```
S.  ..  2  9 16 23 30
M.  ..  3 10 17 24 31
Tu. ..  4 11 18 25 ..
W.  ..  5 12 19 26 ..
Th. ..  6 13 20 27 ..
F.  ..  7 14 21 28 ..
S.   1  8 15 22 29 ..
```

APRIL.

```
S.  ..  6 13 20 27
M.  ..  7 14 21 28
Tu.  1  8 15 22 29
W.   2  9 16 23 30
Th.  3 10 17 24 ..
F.   4 11 18 25 ..
S.   5 12 19 26 ..
```

MAY.

```
S.  ..  4 11 18 25
M.  ..  5 12 19 26
Tu. ..  6 13 20 27
W.  ..  7 14 21 28
Th.  1  8 15 22 29
F.   2  9 16 23 30
S.   3 10 17 24 31
```

JUNE.

```
S.   1  8 15 22 29
M.   2  9 16 23 30
Tu.  3 10 17 24 ..
W.   4 11 18 25 ..
Th.  5 12 19 26 ..
F.   6 13 20 27 ..
S.   7 14 21 28 ..
```

JULY.

```
S.  ..  6 13 20 27
M.  ..  7 14 21 28
Tu.  1  8 15 22 29
W.   2  9 16 23 30
Th.  3 10 17 24 31
F.   4 11 18 25 ..
S.   5 12 19 26 ..
```

AUGUST.

```
S.  ..  3 10 17 24 31
M.  ..  4 11 18 25 ..
Tu. ..  5 12 19 26 ..
W.  ..  6 13 20 27 ..
Th. ..  7 14 21 28 ..
F.   1  8 15 22 29 ..
S.   2  9 16 23 30 ..
```

SEPTEMBER.

```
S.  ..  7 14 21 28
M.   1  8 15 22 29
Tu.  2  9 16 23 30
W.   3 10 17 24 ..
Th.  4 11 18 25 ..
F.   5 12 19 26 ..
S.   6 13 20 27 ..
```

OCTOBER.

```
S.  ..  5 12 19 26
M.  ..  6 13 20 27
Tu. ..  7 14 21 28
W.   1  8 15 22 29
Th.  2  9 16 23 30
F.   3 10 17 24 31
S.   4 11 18 25 ..
```

NOVEMBER.

```
S.  ..  2  9 16 23 30
M.  ..  3 10 17 24 ..
Tu. ..  4 11 18 25 ..
W.  ..  5 12 19 26 ..
Th. ..  6 13 20 27 ..
F.  ..  7 14 21 28 ..
S.   1  8 15 22 29 ..
```

DECEMBER.

```
S.  ..  7 14 21 28
M.   1  8 15 22 29
Tu.  2  9 16 23 30
W.   3 10 17 24 31
Th.  4 11 18 25 ..
F.   5 12 19 26 ..
S.   6 13 20 27 ..
```

JANUARY, 1879.

1	W.	Coal Mines Inspection Act came into operation, 1861, and Explosives Act, 1876.
2	Th.	Dr. Livingstone presented with Freedom of Burgh, 1857.
3	F.	Mr Shaw resigned Rectorship of Grammar School, 1845.
4	S.	Rev. John Hart appointed colleague to Rev. James Naismith, Parish Church, 1653.
5	S.	Present Parish Church first opened, 1732.
6	M.	Prince Charlie Stuart (the Pretender) at Hamilton Palace, 1745.
7	T.	Sheep Market instituted in Old Muir, 1736.
8	W.	Great Curling Match (north and south of Clyde) at Lochwinnoch, 1864.
9	Th.	William Leighton, Chamberlain to the Duke of Hamilton, died, 1857.
10	F.	Prince Alfred (Duke of Edinburgh) visited Hamilton Palace and Wishaw House, 1864.
11	S.	Banquet to Duke of Hamilton in Town Hall, 1867. William, second Duke of Hamilton, born 1616; died 1651.
12	S.	Rev. Jas. Proctor, minister of Congregational Church, died, 1860.
13	M.	Visit of H.R.H. the Prince of Wales to Hamilton Palace, 1878.
14	Tu.	Francis Hamilton appointed Burgh Fiscal, 1856.
15	W.	Soiree and Presentation to the late Lieut.-Col. Simpson, 1864.
16	Th.	Great Pugilistic Meeting at Chapelton (1000 Glasgow roughs) 1871.
17	F.	William Henderson, Town Clerk, died 1865.
18	S.	James, sixth Duke of Hamilton, born 1724; died 1758.
19	S.	Enactment of Council that all vents in town be swept three times yearly, at 1d each, 1740.
20	M.	Town-Criers first appointed, at 1d for each notice, 1754.
21	Tu.	Dr Barr, of Silvertonhill, died 1867.
22	W.	Adoption of "Police and Improvement Act, 1862," 1863.
23	Th.	James, first Duke of Chatelherault, died 1575. Home Farm Colliery flooded, and great subsidence, 1877.
24	F.	Lanark Co-Operative Society formed, 1862.
25	S.	Mr Clawson resigned Rectorship of Grammar School, 1786.
26	S.	Motherwell formed into a burgh, 1865.
27	M.	Oldest date in Hamilton Parochial Register 1650.
28	Tu.	Rev. John Inglis appointed Minister of Established Church, 1656.
29	W.	The Grand Duchess Stephanie of Baden (mother of Dowager Duchess of Hamilton), died 1860.
30	Th.	Mr Findlater admitted second minister of Hamilton, 1695.
31	F.	Newarthill Board School opened by Col. Hozier, 1876.

FEBRUARY.

1	Sa.	Cash credit granted by British Linen Bank to burgh for £2000, 1835.
2	S.	Edward P. Dykes appointed to the office of Town-Clerk, 1865.
3	M.	Coal found in No. 2 Cadzow Colliery, 1878.
4	Tu.	Strathaven Railway opened, 1863.
5	W.	Postal Telegraphs opened for business in Hamilton and district, 1870.
6	Th.	Mrs Simpson's Mortification, of £40 yearly, to the poor, 1867.
7	F.	Kennedies School opened, 1859.
8	Sa.	Church (now Free Church) erected in Duke Street, 1835.
9	S.	Mr Hamilton. of Dalzell, moved Address in House of Commons in reply to Queen's Speech, 1871.
10	M.	Neil Livingstone (aged 67), father of Dr Livingstone, died, 1856.
11	Tu.	Aikman's Hospital endowed, 1775.
12	W.	Auchingramont Church organ finished, 1866.
13	Th.	Mr Ramsay elected M.P. for Falkirk Burghs, and Sir W. C. J. C Anstruther, Bart., for South Lanarkshire, 1874.
14	F.	James Rodger and John Cooper to take charge of fire-engine, at a salary of 20s per annum each, 1791.
15	Sa.	Lady Susan Hamilton (sister of the late Duke), visited Hamilton Palace, 1871.
16	S.	Archibald, ninth Duke of Hamilton, born 1740; died 1819.
17	M.	Rev. P. W. Robertson inducted to St. John's Free Church, 1870.
18	Tu.	Terrible fire in Barrie's Close, 1744.
19	W.	Mr Ramsay, M.P., addressed his supporters in Town Hall, 1874.
20	Th.	Commercial Bank Branch opened in Wishaw, 1874.
21	F.	Complimentary dinner in Holytown to Mr M'Donald, M.P., 1874.
22	Sa.	Complimentary dinner in Wishaw to Sir W. C. Anstruther, M.P., 1874.
23	S.	Cadzow Street and bridge opened 1836.
24	M.	Mr Houldsworth, of Coltness, presented to the Prince of Wales at St James' Palace, London, 1871.
25	Tu.	J. G. Chancellor and H. F. M'Lean, appointed Deputy-Lieutenants of county, 1862. John Naismith, leather merchant, aged 84, died, 1866.
26	W.	John Leslie (Sheriff-Clerk-Depute from 1825) died 1868.
27	Th.	Closing of Blackswell Church (after being used 110 years), 1872.
28	F.	Muir Street Old Relief Church built, 1761.

MARCH.

1	Sa.	Corporation and Consumers' Gas Coy.'s first meeting, 1868.
2	S.	Alexander Baird of Ury died, 1862.
3	M.	William Dickson, Rector of Hamilton Academy, died, 1863. Formation of Hamilton Skating and Curling Club, 1871.
4	Tu.	Walter Cook Spens appointed successor to Sheriff Veitch, 1870.
5	W.	William Dickson appointed as registrar of the burgh, 1855.
6	Th.	Part of Muir Street feued to Government as Barracks, 1795.
7	F.	Rev. T. R. Anderson ordained colleague and successor to Rev. John Inglis, 1871.
8	Sa.	James Holmes, of Cornsilloch, presented with painting of himself, 1878.
9	S.	James, first Duke of Hamilton, beheaded in Palace yard, Westminster, 1649; and James, fifth Duke, died, 1743.
10	M.	First entertainment in Town Hall, 1863.
11	Tu.	At County Police inspection, the force numbered 50 in 1859.
12	W.	Birthday of present Duke of Hamilton, 1845. Rejoicings at coming of age, 1866.
13	Th.	Rev. Thomas Struthers, Chapel Street U.P. Church, died, 1864. School opened at Beechfield, 1876. Power granted to feu glebe, 1876
14	F.	Archibald, Duke of Hamilton, appointed Archibald Hamilton as Town Clerk, 1801.
15	Sa.	First letter from Dr Livingstone after Stanley's departure, 1872.
16	S.	James, third Earl of Arran, died 1609.
17	M.	Two weavers and a tailor are made burgesses for rescuing the Bailies from the violence of the Duke's servants, 1743.
18	Tu	Rev. E. L. Thompson inducted to Second Charge, 1875.
19	W.	Dr Livingstone born at Blantyre, 1813.
20	Th.	Minerals of Burgh of Lanark let on exploring lease, 1862.
21	F.	John Patrick of Woodcroft, died, 1852. Rejoicings—Marriage of Marquis of Lorne to Princess Louise, 1871.
22	Sa.	James, second Marquis of Hamilton, born 1589; died 1625.
23	S.	Bailies and Council agree to allow 10s to boys in Grammar School who behave best, 1743.
24	M.	Hamilton Factory commenced operations, 1862.
25	Tu.	Public presentation to Rev. John Inglis, 1846.
26	W.	Mr Ramsay, M.P., re-elected, 1874.
27	Th.	Duke of Hamilton appointed Colonel of Queen's Own Yeomanry Cavalry, 1866.
28	F.	Jas. Cullen, St. Ninians, elected master of Grammar School, 1742.
29	Sa.	Marriage of J. G. C. Hamilton, of Dalzell, to Lady Emily Eleanor Leslie, daughter of the Earl of Leven and Melville, 1834.
30	S.	Opening of the Glasgow, Bothwell, Hamilton and Coatbridge Railway, 1878.
31	M.	Feu-duties due the burgh in 1853, £108 11s 6½d.

APRIL.

1	Tu.	Ferniegair and Motherwell Branch Railway opened, 1868.
2	W.	Visit of Prince Alfred (Duke of Edinburgh) to Hamilton Palace, 1864. Memorial Organ in Town Hall in memory of Provost J. Dykes, 1871.
3	Th.	William Moffat appointed Registrar of Births, &c., 1863.
4	F.	St. Mary's Episcopal Church opened in Trades Hall, 1842. Collegiate Church, with steeple, erected, and George de Graham appointed Provost, 1462.
5	Sa.	Kennedies School taken over by Hamilton Parish School Board, 1874.
6	S.	Dr. John Shirley, Lanark, died, aged 76, 1862.
7	M.	Negotiations by James Baird & Co. to work Mineral around Bothwell Castle, 1874.
8	Tu.	Fountain at Hamilton Palace completed, 1862.
9	W.	Boiler Explosions at Mossend (five boilers burst, 10 men killed, 1873), and at Greenfield Colliery (4 lives lost, 1874).
10	Th.	Rev. Charles Hope, of Lamington, died, 1862.
11	F.	James, 4th Duke of Hamilton and 1st Duke of Brandon born [1658, died 1712. British Workman's Public House opened, 1878.
12	Sa.	New Court-Houses at Wishaw opened, 1860.
13	S.	Explosion at Allanton Colliery, 1877.
14	M.	John, Marquis of Hamilton, born 1589, died 1604. [died 1853.
15	Tu.	Rev. Wm. Patrick, author of "The Flora of Lanarkshire," &c., Soldiers' Home and Institute opened in Almada Street, 1878.
16	W.	James Merry, M.P., presented with Freedom of Burgh, 1857.
17	Th.	Formation of a Hamilton Traction Engine Company, 1871.
18	F.	Funeral of Dr. Livingstone in Westminster Abbey, 1874.
19	Sa.	Rev. M. P. Johnstone ordained to Cadzow Church, 1877.
20	S.	Sir Norman Macdonald Lockhart, Bart., of Lee, died, 1870.
21	M.	Wellhall Mansion House purchased by Alex. M'Donald, M.P., 1874.
22	Tu.	Bailies summoned before Lords of Council to pay for meal stolen by a mob, 1741.
23	W.	Fire at No. 1 Pit, Ferniegair Colliery, 1878.
24	Th.	Petition for Abolition of Patronage by Hamilton Established Presbytery, 1871.
25	F.	Biggar New Bowling Green completed, 1874.
26	Sa.	Disastrous Fire at Hamilton Factory, 1870.
27	S.	Acceptance of call by Rev. T. S. Trench to Chapel St. U.P. Ch., 1875. Mrs Livingstone, wife of the African explorer, died, 1863.
28	M.	Larkhall Free Church opened, 1861.
29	Tu.	First meeting as to School Board and Burgh Extension, 1878.
30	W.	William, 12th Duke of Hamilton, presented with Freedom of Burgh, 1877.

MAY.

1	Th.	Streets of Hamilton first named and numbered, 1847.
2	F.	Wm. Beckford of Fonthill (donor of Beckford Library in Palace), died 1844.
3	Sa.	Burnbank Free Church opened, 1875.
4	S.	Dr Livingstone died in Central Africa, 1873.
5	M.	Barncluith Gardens constructed by John Hamilton, 1583.
6	Tu.	First boring operations for Coal in Town Lands, in full operation, 1838.
7	W.	Public Dinner to Mr J. Guthrie Smith, 1875.
8	Th.	Foundation-stone of Bellshill Relief Church laid, 1846. Second Directory for Hamilton published by James Brown, 1855.
9	F.	Foundation-stones of E.U. Church and Masons' Hall at Stonefield, Blantyre, laid, 1878.
10	Sa.	Mary Fielding, Duchess of James, first Duke of Hamilton, died, 1638.
11	S.	Blackswell Church (Anti-burgher) built, 1761.
12	M.	The Palace Gardens enlarged, 1862.
13	Tu.	Rev. J. S. Memes, D.D. (second charge), died 1858.
14	W.	Robert Wylie admitted Minister of Hamilton, 1692.
15	Th.	Pontage for foot passengers taken off Clyde Bridge, 1847.
16	F.	Rev. R. Paterson, B.A., inducted to Glassford Parish Church, 1871.
17	Sa.	Police Office first transferred to Burgh Buildings, 1862.
18	S.	Ground broken for Greenfield Colliery, by Provost Nisbet, 1853.
19	M.	Hector F. M'Lean, of Carnwath, installed as P.G.M. of Upper Ward, 1868.
20	Tu.	James Wingate of Linnhouse died, 1877.
21	W.	Public Dinner and Presentation to R. Bruce, teacher, Uddingston, 1875.
22	Th.	East Kilbride opened its first Co-Operative Store, 1862.
23	F.	Dr Heatherington, assistant in Hamilton to Dr Meek, and Professor of Systematic Theology, died 1865.
24	Sa.	Wm. Frazer of Tweedale, rector of Cadzow, 1273.
25	S.	Jubilee Dinner in Edinburgh to late Rev. Dr Wylie, Carluke, 1868.
26	M.	Fifth Enlargement of *Hamilton Advertiser*, 1864.
27	Tu.	Susanna Euphemia, wife of Alexander, 10th Duke of Hamilton, died 1859.
28	W.	J. G. C. Hamilton of Dalzell presented with Freedom of Burgh, 1857.
29	Th.	Lair-Owners and their Families to have access to the Cemetery on Sabbaths, 1864.
30	F.	Presentation, by Mr Wardrop and Mr Renwick, of Drinking Fountains to Burgh of Wishaw, 1862.
31	Sa.	Assessment for Poor levied at £3457, ending Whitsunday, 1863.

JUNE.

1	S.	Battle of Drumclog, 1679. Gas-works taken over by Corporation. 1868.
2	M.	Foundation Stone of Allanshaw House laid, 1871.
3	Tu.	Rev. J. S. Trench inducted to Chapel Street U.P. Church, 1875.
4	W.	Foundation Stone of Kirkmuirhill U.P. Church laid, 1863.
5	Th.	Charter of Town's Lands by Anne, Duchess of Hamilton, 1670.
6	F.	Foundation Stone of New U.P. Church, Stonehouse, laid, 1878.
7	Sa.	Foundation Stone of E.U. Church, Motherwell, laid, 1875.
8	S.	Baillie's Causeway widened and footpath made, 1859.
9	M.	Dowager Duchess of Hamilton interred in Mausoleum, 1859.
10	Tu.	Foundation Stone of Hamilton New Prison laid, 1834.
11	W.	Duke of Hamilton took his seat as British Peer (Duke of Brandon) in Parliament, 1782.
12	Th.	Commercial distress amongst weavers in Strathaven, Chapelton, &c., 1863.
13	F.	Farmers' Society of East Kilbride established, 1816.
14	Sa.	Deputation on Roads and Bridges Bill to Home Secretary, 1876.
15	S.	Mr Hamilton, M.P., Maiden Speech in House of Commons, 1870.
16	M.	Committee of Council report favourably as to selling of coal in Town's Lands, 1859.
17	Tu.	James Blacklock appointed Rector of Hamilton Academy, 1863.
18	W.	Agnes Hunter, mother of Dr Livingstone, died 1865, aged 82.
19	Th.	Terrible Dynamite explosion at Burnbank, 1876.
20	F.	"The Hamilton Declaration" drawn up by the moderate Covenanters, 1679.
21	Sa.	Rev. W. Buchan of Free St. John's died (39 years a minister) 1860. James, 3d Marquis and 1st Duke of Hamilton, born 1606, died 1649.
22	S.	Battle of Bothwell Bridge, 1679. Freedom of Burgh and Banquet to Lieut.-Col. Campbell M'Intyre, C.B., 78th Highlanders, 1860.
23	M.	Hamilton Industrial Co-operative Society commenced, 1862.
24	Tu.	Heavy fall of rain—streets and houses flooded in Carluke, 1863.
25	W.	Decided by Road Trust to add footpaths to Hamilton Bridge, 1863.
26	Th.	Young Men's Christian Association first met in their own Hall, Church Street, 1860.
27	F.	Cadzow Pit on Fire, 1877.
28	Sa.	A workman named Thomson fatally assaulted in Bothwell Road, 1875.
29	S.	Fifty Shillings awarded to eight persons for capturing a thief who broke out of Prison, 1788.
30	M.	Major Paterson, of the "Queen's Own," died, 1874.

JULY.

1	Tu.	Foundation Stone of School at Jackton, East Kilbride, laid, 1875.
2	W.	Hamilton Co-Operative Society, instituted 1861.
3	Th.	William, 11th Duke of Hamilton, born 15th February, 1811, died 1863.
4	F.	First issue of *The Hamilton Advertiser*, 1856.
5	Sa.	Rejection by Town Council of proposal to maintain pump wells, 1871.
6	S.	First Interment in Hamilton Cemetery (Ord, aged 7, son of Ord Adams, coalmaster), 1853.
7	M.	James George, 7th Duke of Hamilton, born 18th February, 1755, died, 1769.
8	Tu.	Bronze Doors for Mausoleum arrived at Palace, 1856.
9	W.	Volunteer Sham Fight at Barrhead, 1862.
10	Th.	Revival Meetings in connection with Scottish Evangelistic Association, 1863.
11	F.	First Show of Hamilton Horticultural Society, 1856.
12	Sa.	Interdicts obtained against angling on Bonnington, 1862.
13	S.	Presentation to Dr Gloag, Blantyre, of Greyfriars' Ch. & Par. 1863. Opening of Hamilton Central Railway Station, C.R., 1876.
14	M.	Mr Merry re-elected for Falkirk Burghs, 1865.
15	Tu.	William Alexander Anthony Archibald, 11th Duke of Hamilton, died at Paris, 1863.
16	W.	Great Flooding of Houses in Holytown, 1862.
17	Th.	Foundation Stone of New Methodist Chapel, Shieldmuir, Wishaw, laid by Lady Belhaven, 1871.
18	F.	George Gillies, Inveraray, chosen rector of Grammar School, 1786.
19	Sa.	Lieutenant-Colonel Simpson died, 1869. New Established Church opened at Blantyre, 1863.
20	S.	Thomas Dykes, of Woodside, died 1876.
21	M.	Proposal to divide Burgh into Wards adopted, 1870.
22	Tu.	Cadzow Church opened, 1877.
23	W.	Funeral of the 11th Duke of Hamilton, 1863.
24	Th.	Purse of Sovereigns presented to Rev. John T. M'Farlane, 1856. Douglas, 8th Duke of Hamilton, born 1756, died 2d Aug., 1799.
25	F.	Standard Weights and Measures introduced, 1801.
26	Sa.	Opening of New Parish Church at Blantyre, 1863. [1856. Marquis of Clydesdale and Cousins visited Avon Bridge Coalpit,
27	S.	Daring Burglary at Crossbasket Mansion-House, 1862.
28	M.	Inspection around Hamilton of Rivers Pollution Commissioners, 1870.
29	Tu.	James Cullen appointed Inspector of Weights and Measures, 1862.
30	W.	House Property to the value of about £6000 erected in Hamilton, 1856.
31	Th.	Hamilton Cemetery opened 1853 (2795 interments up till 1870).

AUGUST.

1	F.	238 Paupers on poor's roll, at a cost of £800 per annum, 1837.
2	Sa.	Alexander, 10th Duke of Hamilton, born 3d Oct., 1767, died 1852
3	S.	Commissioners agreed to supply water free for drinking fount 1858.
4	M.	Enlargement of pipes at Wishaw Gas Works, 1862.
5	Tu.	Heating apparatus introduced into old Parish Church, 1863.
6	W.	Auchingramont new Established Church opened, 1860.
7	Th.	Fire at Summerlee Colliery, Dykehead (12 men killed), 1861.
8	F.	St. Mary's Episcopal Church, Auchingramont, opened consecrated 6th), 1847.
9	Sa.	John Dykes, Provost of Hamilton, died, 1869.
10	S.	Strathaven Railway Bill received Royal assent, 1857.
11	M.	Rev. Thomas Miller ordained to Lamington Parish Church, 1862
12	Tu.	Great floods in Rivers Avon and Clyde, 1861.
13	W.	Bowling Green renewed, and match with Shotts, 1846.
14	Th.	Flood and destruction of property in old town, 1871.
15	F.	Formation of Hamilton Troop of "Queen's Own" Yeomanry Cavalry, 1862.
16	Sa.	Prince Napoleon visited Hamilton (incog.), 1864.
17	S.	Marriage of Lord Dunglass to Miss Grey, 1870.
18	M.	Dr. William Naismith, of Auchincampbell, died, 1875.
19	Tu.	Rev. T. M. B. Paterson ordained to Burnbank Free Church 1875.
20	W.	City of Glasgow Bank branch opened in Hamilton, 1857.
21	Th.	Proposed railway survey from Hamilton to Quarter, 1856.
22	F.	James, 1st Earl of Arran (created), 1503.
23	Sa.	The Rev. Dr. Hamilton, of London, preached in Stonehouse, 1863
24	S.	W. A. Dykes appointed Provost, 1869. Installation of J. C. Forrest, as P.G.M., 1877.
25	M.	U. P. Church, Motherwell, opened, 1866.
26	Tu.	Hamilton Combination Poorhouse opened, 1867.
27	W.	Valedictory sermon of the late Rev. John M'Farlane, Saffronhall Church, 1871.
28	Th.	Mr Merry's horse "Buckstone" sold for £4,500, 1863.
29	F.	Truck Commission commenced its 12 days' sitting in Hamilton 1870.
30	Sa.	Contract entered upon for Chapelton Gas-works, 1856.
31	S.	First omnibus ran from Hamilton to Motherwell Station, 1856.

CALENDAR OF LOCAL EVENTS.

SEPTEMBER.

1	M.	Clydesdale Bank Branch opened in Hamilton, 1865.
2	Tu.	The Dykes Memorial Organ placed in Town Hall, 1871.
3	W.	The Gospel Hall opened in Baillie's Causeway, 1871.
4	Th.	Marriage of Sir W. C. J. C. Anstruther, Bart., M.P., 1872.
5	F.	Foundation-stone of Uddingston New Parish Church laid, 1872.
6	Sa.	Bailies and Council allow £15 to repair and maintain Burgh Clock for 7 years, 1801.
7	S.	Opening of British Linen Co.'s Bank Branch in Hamilton, 1821.
8	M.	Lady Belhaven and Stenton died, 1873.
9	Tu.	Assize appointed to watch Bakers because of deficient weight, 1785.
10	W.	First Fire-Engine procured for Burgh, 1748.
11	Th.	Foundation-stone of Auchingramont U.P. Church laid, 1866.
12	F.	John Hamilton of Fairholm died, 1867. [to Second Charge, 1858.
13	Sa.	(12) Rev. Mr Robertson first preached in Par. Ch. after presentation The Right Hon. the Earl of Lincoln pr. with F. of B., 1835.
14	S.	Opening of the Trial of Jessie M'Lachlan for Murder, 1862.
15	M.	Foundation-stone of Railway Viaduct at Barncluith laid (by P. G. Master J. C. Forrest), 1874.
16	Tu.	Death of the Rev. Wm. Anderson, D.D., at Uddingston, 1872, and Police Act adopted, 1857.
17	W.	Notice as to Building of a New Bridge over Burn at Miln Port to be proclaimed by Town-Crier, 1793.
18	Th.	Oldest date in Hamilton Presbytery Records, 1687.
19	F.	Accident at Maryville Colliery, Uddingston, 1876.
20	Sa.	Hamilton divided into 11 districts and visited by T. C. for sanitary purposes, 1853. [Joyce Stokes, Leicestershire, 1858.
21	S.	Marriage of H. H. R. Aikman, of Ross and Bromelton, to Mary Lady M. H. D. Hamilton mar. to H.S.H. Pr. Alb. of Monaco, 1869.
22	M.	Rev. H. M. Hamilton inducted to Second Charge of the Parish, 1864, and Rev. Dr Bowman to E.U. Church, Uddingston, 1878.
23	Tu.	Marriage of W. G. Fitzgerald, Esq., to Miss Macdonald Lockhart, 1862.
24	W.	Magistrates and Council agree to charge 1d per day for use of ladders borrowed from Corporation, 1793.
25	Th.	Fire at Murdostoun Castle, 1858.
26	F.	Foundation-stone of New Burgh Buildings laid, 1861.
27	Sa.	Entertainment to Employés of Earnock Colliery on occasion of finding coal, 1878.
28	S.	Upper Ward Valuation, £207,168 15s, excl. of railways, 1862.
29	M.	Merryton converted into a Model Farm by Duke of Hamilton, under charge of Mr Drew, 1862.
30	Tu.	New Holder erected at Gasworks, 1863.

OCTOBER.

1	W.	First sale of cattle at Merryton, 1867.
2	Th.	Principal Cunningham baptised in Muir Street Church, 1805.
3	F.	Stoppage of the City of Glasgow Bank, 1878.
		Right of way dispute as to Avon Sands (Aikman v. Duke of Hamilton) settled, 1833.
4	Sa.	Visit of Prince and Princess Christian to Dalzell House, 1875.
5	S.	First record of Town Council business, 1701.
6	M.	Opening of E. U. Church at Blantyre, 1878.
7	Tu.	Hamilton made a Collegiate charge, 1451.
8	W.	First Directory for Hamilton, published by Brown & Naismith and statistical account by Rev. Wm. Patrick, 1847.
9	Th.	Rev. J. M. Killen inducted to Established Church, Bellshill, 1878.
10	F.	Rev. James A. Campbell, A.M., ordained to Quarter Church, 1872.
11	Sa.	Rev. P. C. Duncanson inducted to Muir Street U. P. Church, 1864.
12	S.	Consecration of High Altar in St. Mary's R. C. Chapel, 1856.
13	M.	Robert G. Baillie, of Culteraller, D.L. and J.P., aged 75, died, 1862.
14	Tu.	Rev. G. Wallace inducted to St. John's Free Church, 1875.
15	W.	Centenary of North U. P. Church, Biggar, 1861.
16	Th.	Town's Lands acquired from James, Lord Hamilton, 1474.
17	F.	Royal Bank branch opened in Hamilton, 1854.
18	Sa.	Detachment of Hussars called out to quell riot at Carfin, 1856.
19	S.	W. G. Dickson, Sheriff-Principal, died, 1876.
20	M.	Prospectuses issued to form a Gaslight Company for High Blantyre, 1862.
21	Tu.	Social Reform concerts in Town Hall, 1863.
22	W.	Robert Graeme, of Wellhall, died, 1870, and explosion at High Blantyre Colliery (212 killed), 1877.
23	Th.	Picture gallery in Palace fitted up for private theatricals, 1856.
24	F.	H. M. Stanley presented with freedom of Burgh, 1872.
25	Sa.	First slaughter-house erected with regulations, 1795.
26	S.	Rev. Daniel Craig ordained to E. U. Church, 1871.
27	M.	Fire at Dalzell House (left wing destroyed), 1868.
28	Tu.	Street lamps first introduced into Hamilton, 1737.
29	W.	Dixon Vallance, a Waterloo veteran, died at Carluke, 1876.
30	Th.	Rev. Dr. Keith, minister of first charge, died, 1874.
31	F.	Revenue of Burgh of Hamilton for year 1878, £4,366 16s 1¼d.

NOVEMBER.

1	Sa.	First Municipal Election after division into Wards, 1870.
2	S.	Police Assessment reduced to 7d per £, 1871.
3	M.	Formation of 52d L.R.V. (now B Company), 1859.
4	Tu.	Charge for Burgh of Hamilton, for year ending November 1736, £4190 11s. [Provost, 1875.
5	W.	Resignation of Provost Dykes, and election of J. C. Forrest as First Election in Fifth Ward—M'Alpine, Clark, and Thomson
6	Th.	James, 1st Lord Hamilton, died, 1479. [returned, 1878. Commercial Bank Branch opened in Hamilton, 1832.
7	F.	The late Lord Belhaven appointed Lord-Lieutenant in room of Duke of Hamilton, 1863.
8	Sa.	Dinner to A. B. Cochrane, M.P., at Lanark, 1871.
9	S.	John Dykes elected Provost, 1860.
10	M.	Roman Catholic Chapel in Lanark opened, 1859.
11	Tu.	James Mackie appointed Town Treasurer, 1858.
12	W.	Great Flood on Clyde, 1760. Hamilton Water Commissioners ceased to exist, 1878.
13	Th.	New Bridge over Clyde at Edinburgh Road opened, 1780.
14	F.	Motion to proceed with Water Bill carried by Town Council, 1853.
15	Sa.	[14] Rev. Alex. Stewart, LL.D., Douglas, died, aged 81, 1862.
16	S.	Clyde Bridge completed, 1780.
17	M.	Cromwell sent five regiments to overawe Covenanters, 1650. Ann, Duchess of Hamilton, born 1636, succeeded 1651, died 1716.
18	Tu.	Requiem Mass in R.C. Chapel for killed at Blantyre Explosion, 1877.
19	W.	Dr John Dykes, of Woodside, died 1863.
20	Th.	Third Directory for Hamilton published by W. Naismith, 1859.
21	F.	Election of Sir T. E. Colebrooke, as M.P. for North Lanarkshire, 1868.
22	Sa.	Rev. Walter R. Paton inducted to Free Church, Chapelton, 1876.
23	S.	Rev. John Pagan appointed minister of Bothwell, 1865.
24	M.	Opening of Auchingramont U.P. Church, 1867.
25	Tu.	Mr Hamilton of Dalzell elected M.P. for South Lanarkshire, 1868
26	W.	Rev. H. M. Hamilton appointed minister of 1st Charge, 1874.
27	Th.	Empress of the French visited Hamilton Palace, 1860.
28	F.	Number of Interments in New Cemetery from opening till 1878, £3000 given by Magistrates to build Clyde Bridge, 1778. [8040.
29	Sa.	Geo. Mackay appointed 1st Chief-Con. of Lanarkshire, 1857. St Mary's R.C. Church opened by Right Rev. Dr Murdoch, 1846.
30	S.	Old Churchyard closed for Burials, 1861. Lord Belhaven and Stenton married to Georgina, fourth daughter of John Watson, Esq. of Earnock and Neilsland, 1877.

DECEMBER.

1	M.	Lesmahagow Branch Railway opened, 1866. First election of Town Council under "Municipal Reform Act," 1868.
2	Tu.	Rev. John M'Farlane, Saffronhall Church—Jubilee, 1870.
3	W.	The Burgess ticket to be charged five guineas, 1787.
4	Th.	Rev. Mr Robertson (Parish Church) died at sea, 1863.
5	F.	Society of Procurators formed, 1862.
6	Sa.	Rev. Thos. Struthers, Chapel Street U. P. Church—Jubilee, 1862.
7	S.	Bank of Scotland succeeded to Western Bank, 1857. Execution of the four martyrs whose heads are in Hamilton churchyard, 1666.
8	M.	Boats and boathouse customs let for 19 years for £20, 1760.
9	Tu.	Cadzow Colliery on fire, 1876.
10	W.	Marriage of His Grace the Duke of Hamilton to Lady Mary Montague, 1873.
11	Th.	James Gillies, for "stooking his corn on Sabbath," rebuked by session, 1648.
12	F.	Fire at Merryton Colliery, 1875.
13	Sa.	Rev. Ivie M'Lachlan inducted to new Free Church, Uddingston, 1877.
14	S.	Sheriff Spens removed to Glasgow (presentation and address), 1876.
15	M.	James Veitch, upwards of 30 years Sheriff-substitute, died at Edinburgh, 1873.
16	Tu.	M. Kossuth presented with freedom of Burgh, 1856.
17	W.	Hamilton Academy declared a higher-class school, 1875.
18	Th.	Public dinner to Provost John Dykes, 1863.
19	F.	The Right Hon. Lord Stanley presented with Freedom of Burgh, 1834.
20	Sa.	Rev. A. C. M'Phail appointed first minister of Quarter, 1861.
21	S.	Proposal for Drainage of Hamilton rejected, 1861.
22	M.	Lord Belhaven and Stenton died, 1868.
23	Tu.	Wm. Guthrie, as first skinner and breachmaker in town, made burgess, 1753.
24	W.	Lord William Douglas, 3d Duke of Hamilton, born 1634, died 18th April, 1694.
25	Th.	Subscription in Lanark for Unemployed Weavers, 1862.
26	F	7000 Veils manufactured weekly in Hamilton and neighbourhood, 1846.
27	Sa.	Duchess of Hamilton born, 1854.
28	S.	Hamilton Penny Savings Bank established, 1874.
29	M.	James S. Cullen appointed Superintendent of Police, 1859.
30	Tu.	Police, under Burgh Act, first perambulated the streets, 1858, and Bellshill Established Church opened, 1877.
31	W.	Rev. M. R. Battersby resigned Muir Street Church, 1863.

ACTING JUSTICES OF THE PEACE—UPPER WARD.

LIEUTENANCY OF LANARKSHIRE.

Lord Lieutenant, Sir Thomas Edward Colebrooke, of Crawford, Bart., M.P.
Vice-Lieutenants, John Glencairn Carter Hamilton, of Dalzell
Clerk of Lieutenancy, Edward Pellew Dykes, Hamilton

COMMISSIONERS OF SUPPLY.

Convener, William Wallace Hozier, of Mauldslie
Clerk of Supply, Wm. Alston Dykes, Hamilton

Collectors—Biggar District, Adam Pairman, Biggar; Lanark District, John Smith; Hamilton District, John C. Forrest; Strathaven District, Thomas Tennent; Airdrie District, James Russell; Lower Ward and Hillhead Districts, Archibald Tennent, 30 John Street, Glasgow

ACTING JUSTICES OF THE PEACE FOR LANARKSHIRE.

NOTE.—This list includes only such as have been qualified as Acting Justices.

UPPER WARD.

Alston, John Stirling, of Stockbriggs
Alston, William
Anstruther, Sir W. C. J. C., Bt., M.P., of Anstruther and Carmichael
Baillie, James W., of Cultcrallers
Bertram, William, of Kersewell
Brown, James, of Orchard
Carmichael, M. T., of Eastend
Collyer, W. D., of Cormiston
Cranstoun, C. E. H. E., of Corehouse
Cunninghame, W. C. S., of Auchlochan
Darling, John, of Climpy
Denholm, Robert, factor, Carmichael
Forrest, James, Bellfield
Gibb, John, Lesmahagow
Gibson, John, of Toftcombs
Gilchrist, James, of Gillfoot
Gillespie, R., of Springhill, Douglas
Greenshields, J. Blackwood, of Kerse
Hozier, W. W., of Newlands & Mauldslie
Hamilton, Gavin, of Auldtown
Hamilton, J. Stevenson, of Fairholm
Harvey, William, of Brownlie
Johnstone, Ronald, of Sunnyside
Kay, Alexander, of Cornhill
Lindsay, C., of Ridgepark, Lanark
Lockhart, W. E., of Cleghorn
Lockhart, Sir Simon M'Donald, of Lee and Carnwath, Bart.
Lockhart, Lt.-Col., of Milton Lockhart
Logan, James, of Eastshield
Mackenzie, John Ord, of Dolphinton
Martin, James, Carluke
Matthews, Thomas, banker, Carluke
Mitchell, William G., of Carwood
Mosman, Hugh, of Auchtyfardle
Murray, John Lamb, of Heavyside
M'Kirdy, J. G., of Birkwood
M'Lean, H. F., w.s., Carnwath House
Neilson, James, of Biggar Park
Newton, James Ewan, of Linnbank
Paterson, James, of Carmacoup
Paterson, Robert, of Birthwood
Paul, John, of Cambuswallace
Scott, Sir W. M., of Stonebyres, Bart.
Smith, Andrew, factor, Douglas
Smith, John, of Birkhill
Somerville, Robert, of Cormiston
Steel, Gavin, of Holmhead
Stein, John, of Kirkfield
Stein, A. H., yr., of Kirkfield
Stodart, David, banker, Lanark
Vassie, John, of Croftonhill
Walker, Charles, New Lanark
Watson, Sir James, Milton-Lockhart
Watson, Thomas, of Wheatpark
Waugh, John, of St. John's Kirk
Wilson, John, of Westsidewood
The Provost of Lanark, and
The Dean of Guild of Lanark
The Sheriff-Substitute for the Upper Ward of the County of Lanark

PUBLICANS' CERTIFICATE (SCOTLAND) ACT.

Licensing Committees.—Upper Ward.
Chairman, Andrew Smith.

Brown, James	Matthews, Thomas	Stein, A. H.
Darling, John	M'Lean, H. F.	Vassie, John
Gilchrist, James	Neilson, James	Waugh, John
Greenshields, J. B.	Smith, Andrew	Wilson, John

JOINT COMMITTEE FOR BURGH OF LANARK.—JUSTICES.

Forrest, James	Lindsay, Charles	Stodart, David

MAGISTRATES.

Hislop, James	Lamb, William	Muir, George

ACTING JUSTICES OF THE PEACE—MIDDLE WARD.

JUSTICES OF THE PEACE FOR THE MIDDLE WARD.

Addie, Alex., of Braidhurst
Addie, James, Wester Moffat, Airdrie
Addie, John, of Viewpark
Aitken, Andrew, Airdrie
Aikman, H. R. H., of Ross
Alexander, A. J., of Airdrie House
Alexander, J., Gartsherrie Iron Works
Alison, William, of Dunavon
Alston, J. Patrick, of Muirburn
Auchinvole, D., banker, Uddingston
Austine, John, Oak Lodge, Hamilton
Bannatyne, Lt.-Col. J. Millar
Buchanan, Andrew, Greenfield
Buchanan, D. C. R. C., of Drumpellier
Cassels, Robert, Glasgow
Clark, John, of Parkhead
Colt, George F. R., of Gartsherrie
Cochrane, Thomas, of Walsley
Colquhoun, W. Campbell, of Clathic
Colville, David, Motherwell
Deedes, Henry C., Airdrie House
Dixon, William S., of Govanhill
Downie, Alexander
Duncan, Thomas, Larkhall
Dunlop, Colin R., of Quarter
Dunlop, Colin, jun., Quarter
Ferrie, William, Calderbank, Airdrie
Forrest, John Clark, of Auchenraith
Forrest, Peter, of Hairmyres, Shotts
Fraser, Maj.-Gen. Simon, of Overton
Gebbie, Fran., of Shawtonhill, Adv.
Gerard, Archibald, of Rochsoles
Grant, Alexander, Hamilton
Hamilton, Douglas, Hamilton
Hamilton, James, of Bogside
Hamilton, John G. C., of Dalzell
Hamilton, Andrew, of Drumclog
Hamilton, William H. M., of Raploch
Hamilton, James S., of Fairholm
Hamilton, James, of Colinhill
Hamilton, Robert, Airdrie
Harrington, Major, of Torrance House
Hastie, Thomas, of Braehead
Hendrie, John, of Larbert
Holmes, James, of Cornsilloch
Houldsworth, James, of Coltness
Houldsworth, Walter J., of Coltness
Hunter, James, Coltness Iron Works
Jackson, Thomas, Coats Iron Works
Jardine, Geo. Charles, of Hallside
King, William, Motherwell House
Kirkpatrick, Alex., of Allanshaw
Leadbetter, James G., Alderbank
Lennox, Dr. W. W., Hamilton
Lockhart, Major-General, of Cambusnethan, C.B.
Loudon, Dr. James, Hamilton
Marshall, Dr. John, of Burnhouse
Marshall, James, of Sandyford
Maxwell, John, of Baillieston
Meek, John, of Fortisset, Hamilton
Michie, Thos. S., banker, Hamilton
Miller, David C., of Avonbank
Miller, James, factor, Wishaw
Mitchell, David, banker, Airdrie
Montgomery, John B. H., of Newton
Moore, John W., of Greenhall
Murray, Francis, Monkland House
M'Callum, George, Cambuslang
MacKenzie, John Munro, Wishaw
M'Pherson, John, of Blantyre Farm
Napier, John S., of Lethame
Neilson, John, Carnbroe House
Neilson, James, Thankerton House
Neilson, W., Summerlee Ironworks
Neilson, Wm., of Mossend Ironworks
Ormiston, Jn. W., Shotts Ironworks
Osborne, Robert, of Thorntonhall
Osborne, James, Thorntonhall
Paterson, Thomas, Hamilton
Pollok, George, of Rhindmuir
Rankine, Patrick, M D, Airdrie
Reid, James, Blantyre Works
Rintoul, Peter, of Bothwellbank
Robertson, D. S., of Lindsaylands
Robertson, Stewart S., London
Robertson, Dr., Airdrie
Robertson, James, Glasgow
Roberton, James, of Lauchope
Rodger, R. M., banker, Airdrie
Russell, James, of Crosshouse
Russell, James, banker, Airdrie
Shaw, William, Elmwood, Bothwell
Simpson, George, of Viewfield
Stair, Earl of
Steuart, Sir H. J. S., of Allanton and Touch, Bart.
Stewart, Dr. Robert, Coatbridge
Stirling, W., late of Drumpellier
Stirling, Walter, of Faskin
Struthers, James, of Avonholm
Tennent, Thomas, of Ryeland
Thomson, J., Calder Ironworks
Thomson, James, architect, Airdrie
Thomson, John, Avonhead, Airdrie
Thomson, George, banker, Airdrie
Thomson, Dr. Samuel, Jerviston
Wallace, John, banker, Airdrie
Watson, John, of Earnock
Whitelaw, Alex., Gartsherrie, M.P.
Wilson, Dr. Robert, Coatbridge
Wilson, James, coalmaster, Airdrie
The Sheriff-Substitute of Hamilton
The Sheriff-Substitute of Airdrie
The Provost of Hamilton
The Senior Bailie of Hamilton
The Provost of Airdrie
The Senior Bailie of Airdrie
The Senior Magistrate of Wishaw
The Senior Magistrate of Motherwell
James Naismith, Depute Clerk of the Peace at Hamilton
James Gebbie, Clerk of the Peace at Strathaven
Robert Watt, Depute Clerk at Airdrie

COURTS OF JUSTICE, SOCIETY OF SOLICITORS, &c.

LICENSING COMMITTEE FOR HAMILTON DISTRICT OF THE MIDDLE WARD.

Alston, John P.	Hamilton, James S	Lockhart, Maj.-Gen.
Austine, John	Harington, J.	Meek, John
Forrest, John C.	Holmes, James	Reid, James
Hamilton, John G. C.	Hunter, James	Watson, John

LICENSING COMMITTEE FOR THE MIDDLE WARD.
Chairman, Thomas Jackson.

Hozier, Lt.-Col. W. W.	Robertson, Dr. John	Pollok, George
Buchanan, Col. D.C.R.C.	Forrest, Peter	Roberton, James
Colt, G. F. R.	Simpson, George	Aitken, Andrew
Wilson, Dr. Robert	Maxwell, John	Jackson, Thomas

COURTS OF JUSTICE.

SHERIFF COURT.

Held in County Buildings, Almada Street, for Ordinary Business, every Tuesday, at 11 a.m. and Friday at 12 noon ; and for Small Debt and Debts Recovery Business, Friday at 12 noon during Session

Sheriff, Francis Wm. Clark, Advocate *Sheriff-Sub.*, John Black Leslie Birnie, Advocate

Honorary Sheriff-Subs., John Austine, Oak Lodge, and Alex. Grant, Rose Villa

Small Debt Circuit Court, held every third Thursday, at Noon, at Wishaw
Sheriff-Clerk, Geo. Sillar, Glasgow
Sheriff-Clerk-Depute, Wm. Paterson, County Buildings
Proc.-Fiscals for the Sheriff Court, James Alston Dykes and *Depute* John Miller
Auditor, William Paterson

COMMISSARY COURT.

Com., Francis William Clark, Advocate *Com.-Dep. at Hamilton*, John Black Leslie Birnie, Advocate

Clerk, Thomas Donald, Glasgow

JUSTICE OF PEACE COURT.

Sits every Monday, in the Ordinary Sheriff-Court, County Buildings, at 12 Noon
Judges, the Acting Justices *J.P Clerk*, James Gebbie, Strathaven
J.P. Clerk Depute, James Naismith ; Office, James Street ; House, John Street
Procurator-Fiscals, James A. Dykes and John Miller, County Buildings

SOCIETY OF SOLICITORS.
The following are resident and practising :—
OFFICE-BEARERS.
Dean, Wm. Brown.   *Secretary*, J. C. Kay.   *Treasurer*, David Patrick.

Archibald, Robert, N P,	1869	Gebbie, James, Strathaven,	1863
Bairnsfather, J. H. M.,	1876	Keith, Patrick	1863
Barclay William	1867	Kay, James Cunningham	1869
Barrie, John, N P, Strathaven,	1857	Livingstone, W., S S C, Wishaw,	1870
Brown, William, N P,	1858	Miller, David, N P,	1876
Campbell, William, N P,	1868	Naismith, James	1814
Christie, John, N P,	1850	Paterson, John, N P, Wishaw,	1868
Christie, G. Fyffe, Glasgow,	1854	Patrick, David, N P,	1865
Dunlop, Robert	1865	Pollok, William, N P,	1863
Dykes, William Alston	1854	Soutter, J. B.,	1874
Dykes, Edward Pellew	1862	Stratton, William, Motherwell,	1873
Fairley, John D., Motherwell,	1876	Torrance, John, N P,	1828

Officer and Librarian—William Wilson

TAYLOR & HENDERSON,

Ironfounders, Engineers, & Blacksmiths,

GREENFIELD FOUNDRY,

HAMILTON.

REPAIRS PROMPTLY EXECUTED.

ESTIMATES FURNISHED.

LACHLAN TAYLOR,

Plumber and Brass Founder,

HAMILTON BRASS FOUNDRY,

CHAPEL STREET,

Manufacturer of Safety Lamps, and all kinds of Engineer's Brass Work.

SHERIFF OFFICERS AND CONSTABLES.

George Kemp, 16 Almada Street
Andrew Sandilands, 17 Nisbet's Bldgs
James Young, 1 Quarry Street
William Wilson, County Buildings
Ebenezer Leslie, 1 Tuphall Road
William Thomson, Young Street, Wishaw
Edward Gorman, Wishaw
Robert Wiseman, Strathaven
Thomas Cassels, Bellshill

COUNTY POLICE—Head Quarters, Beckford Street

Clerk to Commissioners, Wm. A. Dykes
Chief Constable, W. B. M'Hardie, R.N.
Superintendent, John Dewar, Wishaw
Inspector of Weights and Measures for County District, Peter Carmichael,
Inspector of Police, County Police Office
Inspector of Weights and Measures, (Hamilton District) P. Carmichael
Collector, J. Clark Forrest
Medical Officer, Dr W. W. Lennox
Inspector under Contagious Diseases (Animals) Act, Peter M'Kay
Inspector under Gunpowder Act, Peter Carmichael

HAMILTON PRISON.

Governor, George Mackay *Chaplain*, Rev. James A. Campbell, M.A., Quarter
Surgeon, Dr. W. W. Lennox
Chief Warder, James England *Junior Do.*, John Potter and James Dunlop
Matron, Miss M'Gregor.

POPULATION.

	Males	Females	Total
Population in 1861	304,151	327,415	631,566
Do., 1871	377,739	387,540	765,379

Parliamentary Constituency in 1877-78.
North Lanarkshire, ... 9,686 | South Lanarkshire, ... 3,513

Member of Parliament for Northern Division of the County, Sir Thomas Edward Colebrooke, of Crawford, Bart. (L)

Do., for Southern Division, Sir Windham Charles James Carmichael Anstruther, of Anstruther and Carmichael, Bart. (C)

EAST AND WEST LANARKSHIRE ROAD TRUST.

Clerk, William A. Dykes *Treasurer*, John Martin *Surveyors*, Matthew Hamilton, Stonehouse, and John Miller, Wishaw

COMMISSIONERS FOR PROPERTY AND INCOME AND INHABITED HOUSE DUTY TAX FOR MIDDLE WARD.

Alston, John P., of Muirburn
Buchanan, D. C. R. C., of Drumpellier
Hamilton, John G. C., of Dalzell
Hozier, W. W., of Mauldslie
Meek, John, of Fortissct
Moore, John W., of Greenhall
Steuart, Sir H. J. S., of Allanton, Bt.
Spens, W. C., Sheriff-Substitute

Assessor, David Patrick, Hamilton *Clerk*, W. A. Dykes
Surveyors, T. M. Black, Hamilton; James S. Miller and John Airth, Glasgow

TAX OFFICE—*Collector*, William Kelman, Glasgow
    Sub-Collector—James Annan, 72 Cadzow Street

INLAND REVENUE—*Distributor of Stamps*, James Annan, 72 Cadzow Street

EXCISE OFFICE—*Collector*, James Smith, Linlithgow
    Sub-Collector—James Annan, 72 Cadzow Street
    Supervisor, Wishaw District, James Deans
    Officer—James Ferguson, Waddiefield, Baillie's Causeway

VALUATORS OF LANDS AND HERITAGES.

For Landward part of Middle Ward, T. M. Black, Hamilton; James S. Miller and John Airth, Glasgow
For Burgh of Hamilton, T. M. Black, Hamilton

GENERAL DIRECTORY.

HAMILTON.

Abercrombie, William, contractor, 40 Almada street
Adam, M., shoemaker, Tainsh's buildings, Gateside street
Adams, James, joiner, 23 Holmes street
Adams, James, weaving manufacturer, 23 Lamb street
Adams, John, chimney-sweeper, 21 Church street
Adams, John, schoolmaster, Bellevue Terrace, Clydesdale street
Aikman, Alex., Hollandbush
Aiton, Mrs, dressmaker, 18 Quarry street
Alexander, Samuel, fruiterer, Docherty's buildings, Burnbank
Allan, Robert, boot and shoemaker, 33 Burnbank
Allan, Robert, builder, Orchard place
Allan, William, of Wylie, Dunlop, & Allan, merchants, 28 Cadzow street
Allison, Miss, 35 Almada street
Alston, Robert L., ship-owner, Newfield, Burnbank road
Alston, Thomas, grocer, 90 Townhead street
Alston, Mrs, Glenlee
Anderson, Alexander, gardener, 4 Tuphall road
Anderson, Daniel M'A., agent, 1 Holmes street
Anderson, David, gardener, Whiteford's buildings, Low Quarry
Anderson, David, manager, Oakbank, Windmill road
Anderson, James, agent, 1 Holmes street
Anderson, Miss, ladies' outfitter, and agent for J. Pullar & Sons, Dyers to the Queen, Perth
Anderson, Mrs, 2 Earnock View, Union street
Anderson, Rev. T. R., Bothwell street
Annan, James, stamp office and collector of Inland Revenue, 72 Cadzow street
Annan, T. & R., photographers, Montreal House, Bothwell road
Archibald & Kay, writers, Bank of Scotland, Cadzow street
Archibald, Robert, of Archibald & Kay, house—Burnside House
Arnott, A., commercial traveller, M'Naughton's buildings, Almada street
Armit, Cornes, & Co., lessees of Earnock quarry
Austine, John, coalmaster, Oak Lodge, Almada street

Baillie, John, grocer and joiner, 28 and 30 Union street
Bain, David, plasterer, 18 Hope street
Bain, J. F., & Son, musicsellers, 38 Townhead street
Baird, Archibald, ironmonger, Hopeton Cottage, Park road
Baird, E., fruiterer and confectioner, Burnbank
Bairnsfather, John Hugh M'Intosh, solicitor, 29 Almada street, house—Zambese cottage
Bannatyne, Andw., accountant, Douglas Lodge, Clydesdale street

Barclay, John, general dealer, 2 Victoria place, Greenfield
Barclay, William, writer, Bothwell street
Barr, Christina, contractor, 83 Almada street
Barr, Duncan C., cashier, Gavinbank Cottage, Park road
Barrie, Andrew, tanner, 11 Haddow street
Barrie, David, flesher, 10 Gateside street
Barrie, William, clerk, Low-waters
Baxter, Thomas, flesher, 63 Almada street
Begg, Alexander, grocer, 6 Back-o'-barns, and 38 Church street, house—5 Bothwell road
Beith, Robert, colliery manager, Bothwell street
Bell, James, late carrier, 76 Townhead street
Bell, James, postmaster, Springbank House, Windmill road
Bell, John, grain-dealer, 16 and 18 Gateside street
Bell, Mrs, draper, 71 Cadzow street
Bell, Peter, carrier, 12 Lamb street
Bell, Peter, 12 Leechlee street
Bell, Rev. George, M.A., Portland park
Bell, Thomas S., draper, 31 Cadzow street, house, 76 Townhead st
Bell, Walter, potato-merchant, Turner's buildings, Portland pl.
Bell, William, fruit merchant, Royal buildings, Duke street
Bent Coal Company, colliery—Bent road
Bentley, William, hairdresser, 9 Almada street
Bertram, John, flesher, Victoria place, Greenfield
Bertram, William, farmer, Greenfield
Beveridge, James, accountant, 9 Union street
Beveridge, James, pit engineer, 2½ Low Patrick street
Binning, Hugh, plumber, 7 Muir street
Binning, James, broker, 49 Castle street
Binning Robert (asthma cure), 45 Townhead street
Birnie, J. B. L., Sheriff-Sub. of Lanarkshire, Haxton, Bothwell
Bishop, Thos. G., tea merchant, Craven Cottage, Windmill road
Black, David, Portland park
Black, Mrs, Ladies' School, Forestview, Portland Park
Black, T. M., assessor, house—Woodcroft, Townhead street
Blacklock, James, rector, Hamilton Academy, Hope street
Blaney, John, sergeant-major, the Armoury, Muir street
Blyth, Alexander, flesher, Tainsh's buildings, Butterburn place
Blyth, Archibald, manager, Bent colliery
Bowie, Mrs, bookseller, 74 Cadzow street
Bowman, Thomas, manufacturer, Bellevue, Clydesdale street
Boyd, Archibald, chimney sweep, Back-o'-barns
Boyes, Mrs, Orchardhill Cottage
Boyle, Adam, contractor, 59 Almada street
Brackenridge, William, merchant, 87 Muir street
Brakenridge, David, Portland park
Bridges, John, stationmaster, G. B. H. and C. Railway, house—Saffronhall crescent
Briton, Misses, Waddiefield Cottage
Brock, Thomas, Beckford street

Brodie, Robert, licensed grocer, Royal Buildings
Brown, David, dealer, Greenfield place
Brown, James, builder, of Brown & Henderson, house—Portland place
Brown & Henderson, builders, Portland place
Brown, John, joiner, Ellengowan Cottage, Park road
Brown, John, of Brown Bros., painters, 44 Townhead street, house—8 Orchard street
Brown, John, spirit dealer, 55 Townhead street
Brown, Mrs J. Kay, Avongrange, Crescent
Brown, Mrs, Roslin Place, Windmill road
Brown, Mrs Thomas, 1 Quarry street
Brown, Robert, tinsmith, 1 Quarry street, house—36 Castle street
Brown, Thomas, of Brown Bros., painters, 44 Townhead street, house—5 Brandon street
Brown, William, builder, Orchard place
Brown, William, of Brown Bros., painters, 44 Townhead street, house—29 Gateside street
Brown, William, tinsmith, 36 Castle street
Brown, William, solicitor, house—Townfield, Clydesdale street
Brown, William, & Co., solicitors, Currie House, Almada street
Brownlie, Claud, cowfeeder, Low-waters
Brownlie, James, bricklayer, 52 Union street
Brownlie, Miss, dressmaker, 19 Hope street
Brownlee, Thomas, baker, 11 Almada street
Bruce, James, fruiterer, 35 Cadzow street
Bruce, John, spirit merchant, Postgate
Bruce, Mrs, dressmaker, Burnbank terrace
Buchan, Alexander G., grocer, 65 Almada street
Buchanan, Andrew, manufacturer, 21 Low Patrick street
Buchanan, James, plasterer, 3 Ann street
Buchanan, James, plasterer, 28 Leechlee street
Buchanan, Mrs, 4 Bothwell road
Buchanan, Peter, wine merchant, Viewfield, Burnbank road
Buist, Miss, Netherlea, Union street
Bulloch, William, spirit retailer, 25 Campbell street
Burns, Misses, 28 Almada street

Caird, Alexander, contractor, 1 Oriel buildings, Beckford street
Cairncross, Alexander, of J. & A. Cairncross, florists, &c., 23 Cadzow street, house—5 Beckford street
Cairncross, James, of J. & A. Cairncross, florists, 23 Cadzow street, house—Spencerside
Cairns, James, tobacconist, Church street, house—Cairnlea, Clydesdale street
Cairns, John, portioner, 5 Church street
Cameron, Duncan, lace agent, 6 Holmes street
Cameron, James, lathsplitter, 69 Townhead street
Cameron, John, Dunmore cottage, Clydesdale street
Cameron, John, eating-house keeper, 47 Townhead street

Cameron, William, grocer, Brown's buildings, Quarry street
Campbell, Ananias, poultry merchant, Castle street, house—28 Campbell street
Campbell, Captain, adjutant 16th L.R.V., Clydesdale Cottage, Clydesdale street
Campbell, John, baker, 14 Townhead street
Campbell, Misses, 46 Muir street
Campbell, Rev. James A., Eddlewood House
Campbell, William, of Campbell & Taylor, plumbers, 3 Chapel st
Campbell, William, writer, 14 Almada street, house—20 Almada street
Carlyle, John Edminston, clerk, Park road.
Carmichael, Peter, police inspector, 13 Society buildings, Beckford street
Carnagan, Captain, ship captain, 5 Bothwell road
Cassells, Thomas B., tailor and Burgh School Board Officer, 46 Quarry street
Cassells, William, spirit merchant, Low-waters
Cassels, Mrs, 28 Almada street
Cassels, Andrew, of D. & J. Cassels, merchants, Sommerville place, house—Gowanlee Cottage, Park road
Cassels, John, of D. & J. Cassels, merchants, Sommerville place, house—Auchingramont
Cassels, D. & J., wholesale grocers and wine merchants, Sommerville place, Quarry street
Cassels, William, junior, clerk, Silverray, Portland park
Cassels, William, spirit merchant, 37 Castle street
Chalmers, David, tinsmith, 2 Church st., house—18 Low Patrick street
Chalmers, John, bootmaker, 7 Miller street
Chalmers, Thomas, shoemaker, 29 Duke street
Chalmers, William, beadle, Auchingramont U.P. church
Chalmers, William, spirit dealer, 4 Quarry street
Chassells, Mirrlees, builder, Portland place
Chassels, John, clothier, Brown's buildings, Quarry street
Chassels, William, cowfeeder, 97 Almada street
Cherrie, Thomas, saddler, 4 Townhead street, house—Glengyle Cottage, Portland place
Christie, Charles, clothier, 7 Cadzow buildings, house—36 Muir st.
Christie, James C., teacher, Beckford school
Christie, John, writer, Orchard place, Bothwell road
Christie, Mrs, spirit retailer, 20 Muir street
Cinnamond, James, hatter, 10 Cadzow buildings, house—Orchard place
Clark, James D., C.E. and surveyor, Sommerville place, Quarry street
Clark, John, blacksmith, 53 Quarry street
Clark, Peter, grocer, 61 Quarry street
Clark, Thomas, of Clark & Brownlee, brickbuilders,[Shakespere place, Park road

Clarke, Daniel, Linnview, Auchingramont
Clarkson, John, fruiterer, Brown's buildings, Quarry street
Clelland, James, grazier, Portland cottage, Portland place
Coats, John, fruiterer, 73 Cadzow street
Clyde Coal Co. (Limited), Townlands ; Wm. Granger, commercial manager
Cochrane, Alexander, portioner, Bellfield house, M'Ghie street
Cochrane, Misses, Orchardhill
Cochrane, Nathaniel, shoemaker, Sommerville place, Quarry st.
Cockburn, Wm., stationer, M'Alpine's buildings, Beckford st.
Coffee House, Burnbank—George Moffat, manager
Coghill, Major, adjutant Yeomanry, Gilmourhill, Windmill road
Combe, Robert, licensed grocer, Fleming's buildings, Almada street—house, 50 Cadzow street
Constable, George, grocer, 57 Cadzow street
Consumers' Tea Company, tea shop, 7 Quarry street
Cooper, John, 1 Bothwell road
Cooper, Mrs Robert, fruiterer, 50 Quarry street
Cooper, Peter, sergeant, Burgh police, 4 Quarry place
Cooper, Richard, weaving agent, 26 High Patrick street
Cooper, Thomas, 1 Bothwell road
Cooper, Wm., tailor, 82 Cadzow street
Corbet, Robert, shoemaker, 51 Townhead street
Cossar, John, draper and clothier, 1 Cadzow buildings
Cowan, Hope, goods porter, 6 John street
Cowan, James, tailor, M'Alpine's buildings, Beckford street
Cowan, Miss, ladies' nurse, 20 Cadzow street
Cowan, Thomas, spirit merchant, 16 and 18 Burnbank
Cowan, William, grocer and confectioner, Mackie's buildings, Quarry street
Craig, Alexander, farmer, Udston
Craig, John, farmer, Udston
Craig, Robert, of Craig & Findlay, plasterers, Baillie's Causeway, house—9 Brandon street
Craig, William, farmer, Udston
Crawford, Alexander, weaving agent, 9 Woodside walk
Crawford, Dr Christopher, Auchenarden
Crawford, James, commercial traveller, 9 Woodside walk
Crawford, John, clerk, Robin's buildings, Portland park
Crawford, Joseph, of Crawford & Grindall, coachbuilders, 19 Church street, house—19 Church street
Crichton, James, contractor, Turner's buildings, Portland place
Cross, David, spirit-retailer, 89 Quarry street
Cross, Gavin, tailor and clothier, 79 Quarry st., house—Orchard pl.
Cross, George, tailor, 4 Chapel street
Cross, Thomas, licensed grocer, 18 and 20 Union street
Cross, William, tailor, 18 Townhead street
Cruickshanks, Francis, of Cromar & Co., drapers, 3 Cadzow street, house—Victoria Cottage, Orchard place
Cullen, James S., superintendent of burgh police, 77 Quarry st.

Cunningham, Alexander, chimney-sweeper, 24 Church street
Cunningham, Peter, shoemaker and house factor, M'Laren's buildings, Portland place
Cunningham, Robert, corkcutter, Sommerville place, Quarry st.
Cunninghame, Mrs, grocer, etc., 16 Muir street
Cunninghame, William, goods clerk, 7 John street
Currie, William, gardener, 2 Edinburgh road

Dalglish, Henry, mill-owner, Hilton Bank, Wellhall road
Dalziel, Gavin, bill-poster, 7 Union street
Dalziel, John, shoemaker, 5 Quarry street, house—1 Orchard st.
Dalziel, William, town-officer, 58 Townhead street
Danaher, Rev. James, Chapel house, Cadzow street
Davidson, James, contractor, 41 Campbell street
Davidson, Thomas, grocer, Burnbank
Davidson, Thos., pipe manufacturer, Brandon Villa, Bothwell rd.
Dawson, Mrs, dressmaker, 30 Church street
Devaney, James, pipe maker, 3 Back-o'-barns
Dick, Charles, mason, 2 Woodside walk
Dick, James, of J. & W. Dick, wood-merchants, Baillie's Causeway, house—12 Low Patrick street
Dick, John, flesher, 75 Cadzow street
Dick, John, grocer, 1 Victoria place, Greenfield
Dick, John, tobacconist, 2 Cadzow street, house—6 Quarry street
Dick, Robert W., printer and stationer, 9 Cadzow buildings and Royal buildings, Duke street
Dick, Thomas, flesher, 12 Duke street
Dick, William, wood merchant, Rockview Cottage, Low quarry
Dickson, Mrs, spirit merchant, Peacock cross
Dixon, Peter Watson, Tuphall
Dobbie, John, grocer, Burnbank road
Docherty, Thomas, broker, 53 Castle street
Doherty, William, spirit-dealer, 45 Cadzow street and County Court Restaurant, Almada street
Donald, Robert, portioner, Portland park
Donald, William, plumber, Greenfield place
Downie, Robert, builder, Portland place
Doyle, Hugh, broker, 42 Townhead street
Doyle, James, draper, Chassells' buildings, Portland place
Duncan, Hugh, timber merchant, Bellevue terr., Clydesdale st.
Duncan, William, grocer, Nisbet's buildings
Duncanson, Rev. Peter C., U.P. Manse, Auchingramont
Dunlop, Colin, jun., Oakenshaw
Dunlop, James, of Wylie, Dunlop, & Allan, grocers, 28 Cadzow street, house—30 Cadzow street
Dunlop, Mrs, Bellevue House, Clydesdale street
Dunlop, Robert, writer, Cadzow street, house—Ardenlea, Park rd.
Dunlop, Wm., engineer, 1 Campbell street
Dunn, William, Park road
De Vine, Captain, Almabank, Castlehill Crescent

Dykes, Douglas, Auchingramont
Dykes, Edward P., town clerk, house—Woodburn
Dykes, James A., procurator-fiscal, house—Alstonville
Dykes, John Joseph, Woodside cottage
Dykes, T. J. & W. A., writers and agents, Royal bank
Dykes, William Alston, writer, house—The Orchard, Auchingramont

Eden, Captain, 26th Cameronians, Catherine Bank, Muir street
Edwards, George, 21 Almada street
Elder, Mrs, Gleniffer Villa, M'Ghie street
Ewing, John, meter-examiner, Gas Works

Fairbairn, Thomas, artist, 10 Union street
Fairley, George, ironmonger, Townhead street, house—Rosehill Cottage, Almada street
Fairley, John D., writer, Sommerville place, Quarry street
Fairley, John, smith, Low-waters
Fairley, Miss, furnishing shop, Low-waters
Fairley, Robert, upholsterer, 69 Cadzow st., house—52 Almada st.
Fegan, Patrick, bootmaker, Burnbank
Ferguson, Andrew, teacher, Saffronhall crescent
Ferguson, David, tailor and clothier, 17 Cadzow street, house—9 Brandon street
Ferguson, James, inland revenue officer, Waddiefield cottage, Baillie's causeway
Ferrie, Richard, upholsterer, 59 Cadzow street, house—Muirbrow House, Muir street
Findlay, James, mason and dairyman, 21 Lamb street
Findlay, John, of Craig & Findlay, plasterers, house—32 Brandon street
Finlayson, Alexander, grocer, 63 Townhead street
Finlayson, Matthew, carrier, 21 Chapel street
Fisher, Duncan, hatter, 10 Cadzow street
Fisher, James, joiner, Portland park
Fisher, John, cooper, 23 Gateside street
Fisher, John, grocer, Sommerville place, Quarry street, house—26 Brandon street
Fisher, John, joiner, Portland park
Fisher, Joseph, grocer and provision merchant, 39 & 41 Burnbank
Fleming, Gavin, spirit-retailer, 34 Gateside street
Fleming, George, hairdresser, 6 Quarry street
Fleming, George, jun., hairdresser, Marybank place, Quarry st.
Fleming, James, cattle-dealer, 28 Gateside street
Fleming, John, grain dealer, Almada street
Fleming, Thomas, draper, 7 Townhead st., house—30 Cadzow st.
Fletcher, George, of Mason & Fletcher, licensed grocers, 41 Cadzow street, house—Turner's buildings, Portland place
Fletcher, William, of Templeton & Fletcher, licensed grocers, Townhead street, house—Portland park

c

Forgie, James T., manager, Allanshaw Colliery, house—Saffronhall place
Forgie, Mrs, Saffronhall place
Forrest, Alexander, smith, Quarry road, house—23 Portland park
Forrest, John Clark, Muir House
Forrest, Mrs, Bellevue, Clydesdale street
Forrest, Samuel, joiner, 34 Portland place
Forrest, William, farmer, Allanton
Forsyth, Miss, 3 Bothwell road
Forsyth, James, spirit merchant, 4 Church street
Frame, David, baker, Tainsh's buildings, Butterburn place
Frame, Gavin, clerk, 4 Almada street
Frame, John, cowfeeder, 44 Low Quarry
Frame, Robert, cowfeeder, 10 Lamb street
Frame, Robert, grocer, 10 Castle street
Frame, Thomas, teacher, 14 M'Ghie street
Frame, William, grocer, 21 Duke street
Fraser, Alexander, tailor, 11 Townhead street
Freebairn, Charles, rope-spinner, 34 Quarry street
Freebairn, Misses, 2 Hope street
Freer, Robert, grocer, 19 Almada street and Burnbank road
French, Henry, millwright, 7 M'Ghie street
French, Richard T., draper, 33 Burnbank
Frew, J. & J., ironfounders, Burnbank road
Frew, James, ironfounder, Burnbank road
Frew, John, ironfounder, Dunrod cottage, Burnbank road
Frew, Robert, ironfounder, Russell's buildings, Burnbank road
Frew, Thomas, ironfounder, 22 Burnbank road
Frew & Aikman, drapers, Mackie's buildings, Quarry street

Galbraith, James, grocer, Tainsh's buildings, Gateside street
Gall, George W., engineer, 5 St. John's lane
Gardiner, Henry, tobacconist, Marybank place, Quarry street
Gardiner, James Waterston, cooper, &c., 2 Castle street
Gardiner, John, cowfeeder, 12 Miller street
Gardiner, Mrs James, Whitehill Farm, Burnbank
Gardiner, William, gardener, 20 High Patrick street
Gardiner, William, gardener, 25 Low Patrick Street
Geddes, Thomas, junior, spirit-dealer, Eddlewood buildings, Low-waters
Gibb, Robert, Bothwell street
Gibson & Gillon, leather merchants, Postgate
Gibson, James, weaver, 19 Muir street
Gibson, Mrs, Woodlands
Gibson, John, of Gibson & Gillon, Postgate, house—23 Union st.
Gibson, Thomas, baker, 3 Church street
Gibson, William, spirit-dealer, Low-waters
Giffen, Mrs, furnishing shop, 7 Cadzow buildings
Gilchrist, Archibald, grocer, Sommerville place, Quarry street
Gilchrist, Archibald, licensed grocer, 1 Union street

Gilchrist, James, manager, Earnock collieries, Burnbank terrace
Gilchrist, John, flesher, Turner's buildings, Portland place, and 3 Cadzow buildings
Gilchrist, Samuel, baker, 26 Castle street
Gillon, James, of Gibson & Gillon, house—40 Union street
Gilmour, James, Gilmourhill, Windmill road
Gilmour, Mrs, Saffronhall house, Windmill road
Gilmour, William, portioner, Hepziebah Lodge, Park road
Glass, James, beamer, 14 Low Patrick street
Goodwin, John, contractor, Burnbank farm
Gow, Adam L., clerk, 11 Barrack street
Gowans, Alexander, builder, Gowans' buildings, Low-waters
Gowans, Brothers, builders, 12 Gateside street
Gowans, Peter, joiner, Gowans' buildings, Low-waters
Gowans, Walter, joiner, Low-waters
Gowans, William, of Gowans Bros., builders, house—12 Gateside street
Graham, William, grocer, Low-waters
Grainger, Wm., cashier, Bothwell street
Granger, James, lace-manufacturer, 13 John street
Grant, Alexander, Rose Villa, Brandon street
Grant, William, grocer, 11 Burnbank
Gray, Richard, M'Alpine's Buildings, Beckford street
Green, Robert, blacksmith, Paterson's buildings, Barrack street
Greenfield Station, G. B. H. & C. Railway Coy.—station master, John M'Donald
Grindall, William, of Crawford & Grindall, coachbuilders, 13 Church street, house—19 Church street

Haddow, James, mason, Beechwood Cottage, Portland place
Haley, James, draper, Marybank place, Quarry street
Haley, James, pawnbroker, 25 Castle street
Halliday, A., shoemaker, 15 Castle street
Hamilton, Alexander, builder, 11 Woodside walk
Hamilton, Andrew, Castlehill crescent
Hamilton, Andrew, dairyman, 71 Almada street
Hamilton, Andrew, saddler, 55 Cadzow s.t, house—36 Union st.
Hamilton, Clement M., bricklayer, 21 Almada street
Hamilton & Co., brickmakers, Greenfield
Hamilton Coal Coy., Greenfield colliery. Cashier—Peter M'Callum; manager, James Hastie; Glasgow office—54 St Enoch sq.
Hamilton, Daniel, superintendent of markets, Park road
Hamilton, Elizabeth, dairy, 3 M'Ghie street
Hamilton Estate Office, Muir street
Hamilton, James, auctioneer, 11 Campbell street
Hamilton, James F., grocer, 2 Townhead street, house—Orchard Villa
Hamilton, James, flesher, Royal buildings, house—22 Brandon st.
Hamilton, James, grocer, 24 Brandon street
Hamilton, James, watchmaker, 21 Campbell st. house—6 Ann st.

Hamilton, John, china merchant, 34 Cadzow street, and lace agent, 23 Lamb street, house—91 Almada street
Hamilton, John, greengrocer, 31 Duke street
Hamilton, John, shoemaker, Springwell place, Low-waters
Hamilton, John, tailor and clothier, 32 Townhead street
Hamilton, Joseph, dealer, 14 Baillie's causeway
Hamilton, Major George, adjt., 1st R. L. Militia, Burnbank house
Hamilton, Miss, dressmaker, 11 Campbell street
Hamilton, Miss Henrietta, Viewfield cottage, Burnbank road
Hamilton, Miss, Woodlands
Hamilton, Mrs John, Woodlands
Hamilton, Mrs, Orchard villa, Orchard place
Hamilton, Rev. Henry Monteith, Muirhall
Hamilton, Robert, bricklayer, 29 Almada street
Hamilton, Robert, joiner, Gowan's buildings, Low-waters
Hamilton, Thomas, clerk, Portland park
Hamilton, Wm., & Co., stationers, M'Crone's bdgs., Brandon st.
Hamilton, William, grocer, 28 Townhead street
Hamilton, William, joiner, Bent road
Hamilton, William, law clerk, 6 St. John's lane
Hamilton, William, teacher, Portland park
Hanline, James, grocer, Robin's buildings, Portland park
Harcus, Sinclair, of Robertson & Harcus, joiners, house—Robertson's buildings, Woodside walk
Hardie, David, grocer, Low-waters
Hargrave, Joseph, clerk, Hawthorn villa, Portland park
Harley, William, flesher, Fairley's buildings, Low-waters
Harvie, Mrs, Almada cottage, Almada street
Hastie, Miss, milliner and draper, Burnbank
Haughie, Hugh, hawker, 56 Townhead street
Hay, Robert, flesher, 1 Cadzow street, house—Garvald villa, Portland park
Heatherington, William, blacksmith, Whitehill road
Henderson, Alexander, grocer, 40 Cadzow Street—house, Wharrie house, 44 Muir street
Henderson, Charles Greenhall, clergyman, Parsonage, Auchingramont
Henderson, John, merchant, Linnview, Auchingramont road
Henderson, John, of Brown & Henderson, builders, house—Portland place
Henderson, Miss, Shawburn
Henderson, Thomas, Auchingramont
Henderson, Walter, sawyer, M'Ghie street, house—62 Almada st.
Hendry, David, tobacconist, 42 Cadzow street
Hendry, Mrs, Bent road
Hendry, William, licensed grocer, 1 Hope street
Henry, Andrew, clerk, 6 Quarry road
Hepburn, James, Chantingrove
Higgans, Hugh, dairyman, 26 Brandon street
Higgins, James, engineer, Park road

Hill, John, shoemaker, 6 Beckford street
Hillan, Hugh, restaurant, 16 and 18 Quarry street
Hinds, John, grocer, 31 Church street
Hobbs, Captain, paymaster, 59th Brigade; house—1 Earnock View, Union street
Hogg, John Thomas, druggist, 23 Almada st., house—Bothwell st.
Hogg, Robert, greengrocer, Low-waters
Hood, James, spirit retailer, 1 Castle street
Hood, William, organist, 119 Almada st.
Howie, John, contractor, 56 Muir street
Hunter, Edward, spirit retailer, 36 Quarry street
Hunter, James, Royal Hotel, Quarry street
Hunter, Matthew, police constable, 8 Hope street
Hunter, Mrs, 66 Cadzow street
Hutcheson, Mrs, 2 Bothwell road

Inglis, Charles, agent, Bellevue terrace, Clydesdale street
Inglis, Rev. John, Manse, Blackswell

Jack, Andrew II., tailor, 9 Nisbet's buildings, Baillie's causeway
Jackson, Daniel, clergyman, Windsor terrace
Jackson, Daniel, cowfeeder, 16 James street
James, Mrs E. D., Shawburn
Jamieson, Alexander, Fairview, Hollandbush
Jeffrey, Thomas, grocer, 11 Beckford street
Johanson, J. L., timber merchant, Dovre Villa, Clydesdale street
Johnston, John, painter, 11 Muir street
Johnstone, James, contractor, 19 Burnbank road
Johnstone, Rev. M. P. minister of Cadzow Church; house, Park road
Johnstone, Robert, tailor, 14 M'Ghie street
Johnstone, Alexander, joiner, Whiteford's buildings, Low Qry.
Jones, Charles, shoemaker, Shakspere place, Park road

Kane, Dennis, hawker, 34 Church street
Kay, Andrew, plasterer, 13 Hope street
Kay, James Cunninghame, agent, Bank of Scotland, Cadzow street, of Archibald & Kay, solicitors
Kay, John A., teacher, Mackie's buildings, Quarry street
Keith and Patrick, writers, Clydesdale Bank, Cadzow street—D. Patrick, agent
Keith, Henry, Huttonbank, Townhead street
Keith, James, licensed grocer, 84 Cadzow street, house—Marionfield, Castlehill crescent
Keith, Mrs Dr, Auchingramont
Keith, Patrick, writer, Clydesdale Bank; house, Auchingramont
Kelly, James, broker, 59 Castle street
Kemp, Charles, painter, 28 Chapel street
Kemp, George, auctioneer, Baillie's causeway, house—16 Almada street

Kemp, James, Silverwells
Kemp, John, of J. & S. Kemp, painters, 75 Quarry street
Kemp, Simon, of J. & S. Kemp, painters, house—Mackie's buildings, Quarry street
Kellar, Alexander Bent cottage, Bent road
Kelly, Edward, beadle, 52 Union street
Keogh, Jeremiah, grocer, Paterson's buildings, Barrack street
Kergan, Robert, china merchant, 9 Burnbank
Kerr, James, portioner, 48 Union street
Kinmond, D. G., of Clydesdale College, Windsor terrace, Bothwell street
Kirk, David F., printer, Brevier cottage, Portland park
Kirkland, Mrs Robert, Waddellbank, Quarry street
Kirkland, Robert, weigher, 6 Lamb street
Kirkpatrick, Alexander, of Allanshaw
Kirkpatrick, Robert, station-master, C.S., house—Templehall
Kirkpatrick, Roger, cashier, Closeburnville, Auchingramont
Kyle, James, tailor, Gowans' buildings, Low-waters
Kyle, Miss A., flock and bedding warehouse, Docherty's Buildings, Burnbank

Laidlaw, Archibald, accountant, Brown & Henderson's buildings, Portland place
Laird, James, auctioneer, Bourtreehill, Cadzow street
Lang, David, law-clerk and house factor, 17 Barrack street
Lang, John, tobacconist and hairdresser, 15 Burnbank
Leadbetter, John, carter and contractor, 8 M'Ghie street
Lee, William, spirit merchant, 17 Campbell street
Leggate, Robert, joiner, 56 Almada street
Leishman, John, inspector, Brown & Henderson's buildings, Portland place
Lennox, Walter Walker, M.D., Auchenarden, Cadzow st.
Liddell, Robert, coalmaster, Bothwell street
Lightbody, John, baker, 58 Cadzow street and 4 Duke street
Lightbody, Thomas, engineer, Turner's buildings, Portland pl.
Lindsay, Archibald, baker, 12 and 14 Union street, and Restaurant, Castle street
Lindsay, J. C., shoemaker, 63 Cadzow street; house, Barnfield cottage, Low-waters
Little, Misses, Allan's villa, Park road
Livingstone, Misses, Alva Cottage, Burnbank road
Livingstone, Robert, law-clerk, 2 Saffronhall crescent
Lochhead, James, baker, M'Alpine's buildings, Beckford street, house—8 Muir street
Lochore, Mrs, Gilmourhill, Windmill road
Lockhart, Mrs, Bellevue terrace, Clydesdale street
Loudon, James, M.D., Linnwood, Union street
Loudon, John, grocer, 8 Low Patrick street
Lynas, Joseph, pawnbroker, Burnbank
Lytle, Robert, warehouseman, Herbertfield, Burnbank road

Macdonald, Alexander, M.P., Wellhall
Macdonald, Donald, licensed grocer, 20 Castle street
Mackay, George, governor of prison, Beckford street
Mackenzie, J. F., writer, Cadzow street
Mackie, James, collector and Town Chamberlain, 5 Holmes st.
Mackie, James, junior, accountant, Royal buildings, Duke st.
Mackie, John, cowfeeder, 49 Townhead street
Mackie, Robert, gardener and church officer, 17 Miller street
Mackie, William, saddler, Royal buildings, Duke street
Mackill, Robt. C., druggist, 56 Cadzow street and 10 Brandon street
Mackintosh, Mrs, 43 Cadzow street
Mackintosh, Richard, druggist, 43 Cadzow street and Burnbank
Main, Robert, reporter, Purdie's buildings, Burnbank road
Marr, William C., tailor, 8 Castle street
Marshall, James, missionary, Bothwell street
Marshall, John S., M.D., Auchingramont
Marshall, Robert, contractor, 1 Barrack street
Martin, John, banker, Lochside cottage, Bent road
Martin, John, road surfaceman, 29 Orchard street
Martin, Thomas, merchant, 9 High Patrick street
Mason, James, of Mason and Fletcher, licensed grocers, 41 Cadzow street, house—Portland park
Mason, John, baker, 48 Church street
Massie, Mrs, 24 Almada street
Mather, James A., Spencerside, Townhead street
Mather, Janet, grocer, Low-waters
Mather, William, Townhead house, Townhead street
Maxwell and Green, blacksmiths, 50 Almada street
Maxwell, David, cork-cutter, 24 Campbell street
Maxwell, David, joiner, Mulberry cottage, Douglas street.
Maxwell, James, blacksmith, Paterson's buildings, Barrack st.
Maxwell, James, joiner, Rosehill cottage, Almada street
Maxwell, William, clerk, 99 Almada street
Meek, John, of Fortisset, Cadzow bank
Meickle, Robert, flesher, 28 Campbell street and Townhead st.
Meickle, Robert, junior, flesher, Spalding's buildings, Chapel st.
Meikle, Robert B., grocer, 23 Muir street
Menzies, Thomas, painter, Turner's buildings, Portland place
Menzies, Walter, green grocer, Allan's buildings, Portland place
Michie, Thomas S., Commercial Bank, Cadzow st.
Millar, John, clerk, 25 Almada street
Miller, A., fruiterer and confectioner, Burnbank
Miller, Archd., wood merchant, Bothwell street
Miller & Co., drapers, Gowans' buildings, Low-waters
Miller, David, writer, 1 Quarry street
Miller, J. H., artist, Montreal house, Bothwell road
Miller, Mrs, grocer, 88 Muir street
Miller, Mrs, Bourtreehill
Miller, Robert, joiner, 11 Sheilinghill

Miller, Robert, of R. Miller & Sons, coachbuilders, Baillie's Causeway, house—14 Orchard street
Miller, Robert, junior, saddler, 40 Townhead street
Miller, William, cooper, 16½ Campbell street
Miller, William, grocer, 11 John street
Mills, Miss, Bourtree villa, Cadzow street
Minto, Thomas, hotel keeper (Douglas and Clydesdale Hotel), Townhead street
Mirrlees, John R., grocer, Burnbank Terrace; house, Saffronhall crescent
Mitchell, Alexander, Ardenclutha
Mitchell, James, missionary, 13 Union street
Mitchell, John, flesher, M'Alpine's buildings, Beckford street
Mitchell, Peter B., Isla Cottage, Bent road
Mitchell, William, plumber, 28 Chapel street
Mitchell, William, plumber, 22 Quarry street
Mochrie, Robert, grocer, 79 and 81 Quarry street
Moffat, John, joiner, Bent road
Moffat, William, architect, 19 Cadzow st., house—Auchingramont
Monteith John, carter, 33 Almada street
Monteith, Misses, dressmakers, 33 Almada street
More, Miss, dressmaker, 42 Brandon street
Morris, Mrs Wm., fruiterer, Brown's buildings, Quarry street
Mossman, Mrs, Bay horse hotel, Bothwell road
Mowbray, John, portioner, Brandon Cottage, Orchard place
Muir, Alexander, restaurant, 11 Quarry street
Muir, Joseph, baker, Gowan's buildings, Low-waters
Muir, Robert, furnishing shop, Brown and Henderson's buildings, Portland place
Murphy, H. & C., furniture sale shop, 31 Burnbank
Murphy, William, eating house, 28 Castle street
Murray, Francis, jun., Bellridden cottage, Park road
Murray, Henry, restaurant keeper, Brown's buildings, Quarry place, Quarry street
Murray, John, tailor, 8 Beckford street
Murray, Robert, dyer, 9 Cadzow buildings
Myres, David, architect and measurer, Cross park, M'Ghie st.
M'Allister, Mrs, Windsor terrace, Bothwell street
M'Alpine, Robert, contractor; house, Udston House; office, 1 Whitehill terrace; factor's office, 3 Whitehill terrace, Thomas Brock, factor
M'Auslin, Mrs James, carter and contractor, 7 M'Ghie street
M'Brain, James, insurance agent, Park road
M'Cabe, John, teacher, Brevier cottage, Portland park
M'Call, Archibald, of A. & J. M'Call, joiners, 33 Campbell street, house—13 Church street
M'Call, Henry, watchmaker, 28 Brandon street
M'Call, James, of A. & J. M'Call, joiners, Campbell street, house—6 Ann street
M'Call, Mrs, spirit merchant, 17 Church street

M'Call, Mrs, The Yews, Burnbank road
M'Clements, John, spirit-dealer, 20 Brandon street
M'Cormick, William, baker, 21 Burnbank
M'Cowan, David, shoemaker, 42 Fore row, Muir street
M'Crone, Mrs Margaret, dairy, 63 Muir street
M'Culloch, Allan, grocer, 31 Portland place
M'Donald, Alexander, Foreman joiner, 6 Tuphall road
M'Evoy, James, commission agent, 25 Castle street
M'Farlane, Rev. John T., Spencerfield
M'Geechan, Charles, tailor, 17 Townhead street
M'Geechan, John, tailor, Chassells' buildings, Portland place
M'Ghie, Gavin, baker, Taylor's buildings, Chapel street
M'Ghie, John, photographer, Quarry street
M'Ghie, Thomas, joiner, 13 Union street
M'Ghie, William, slater and plasterer, 4 Woodside walk
M'Ginlay, Charles, spirit dealer, 33 Castle street
M'Ginnis, Michael, carter, 9 Leechlee street
M'Gourlick, John, miner, 16 Lamb street
M'Gregor, John, quarrier, 9 Tuphall road
M'Gregor, Mrs, Mountaden, Park road
M'Guiness, Joseph, miner, 8 Leechlee street
M'Hardy, Commander Wallace Bruce, R.N., Bothwell street
M'Indoe, Mrs James, spirit merchant, 50 Brandon street
M'Kay, George, Violetbank, Auchingramont
M'Kay, Lewis, clerk, Brandon Cottage, Orchard Street
M'Kay, Peter, police inspector, Society buildings, Beckford st.
M'Kenna, Patrick, fruiterer and coal dealer, John st., Greenfield
M'Kenzie, John, clerk, Foundry House, Burnbank road
M'Kenzie, Arch., blacksmith, Muirbank Cottage, Windmill road
M'Kerrow, William Henry, Zambesi Cottage, Burnbank road
M'Kinnes, James, gardener, 14 Hope street
M'Laren, John, painter, &c., 26 Castle street and 7 Cadzow st., house—Portland park
M'Laren, Mrs James, Allan's villa, Park road
M'Laren, Robert, joiner, Misses M'Laren, Hope cottage, Hope st.
M'Lauchlan, Mrs, dairy and refreshment rooms, 25 Burnbank
M'Laughlin, John, greengrocer, Springwell place, Low-waters
M'Lay, Alexander, oil and grease manufacturer, Auchingramont Cottage
M'Leish, John, grocer, 7 Burnbank
M'Lintock, William, china merchant, 15 Gateside street
M'Nair, Duncan, grocer, M'Alpine's buildings, Beckford street
M'Naughton, John, spirit retailer, 27 Almada street
M'Nish, Joseph, barber, 20 Quarry street
M'Phail, Matthew, carrier, 49 Townhead street
M'Pherson, John, police inspector, Society buildings, Beckford st.
M'Queen, Norman, dentist, 33 Cadzow street
M'Taggart, Godfrey, carriage hirer, 74 Almada street
M'Tavish, John, coal merchant, Burnbank
M'Whinnie, Miss, milliner, Ferguson's buildings, Bent road

Naismith, Gavin, tinsmith, gasfitter, &c., 21 Cadzow street, house—Portland park
Naismith, James, Justice of the Peace clerk, 25 James street, house—Patrickcroft
Naismith, J. & S., tanners, Greenside, Sheilling hill
Naismith, John, of J. & S. Naismith, tanners; house, Maryfield, Low-waters
Naismith, Miss, Saffronhall place
Naismith, Mrs Archibald, Park road
Naismith, Mrs Dr., Auchincampbell
Naismith, Samuel, of J. & S. Naismith, tanners, Windmill Cottage, Windmill road
Naismith, Wm., publisher, 38 Cadzow street, house—The Priory
Napier, Mrs, washer and dresser, 3 Bothwell road
Neilson, William, joiner, M'Ghie st., house—Saffronhall crescent
Nelson, Miss, Boarding school, Bellevue terrace, Clydesdale st.
Nicol, Andrew, spirit-merchant, 2 Lamb street
Nicol, James, broker, 47 Castle street
Nicol, James, green-grocer, 27 Duke street
Nicol, John, spirit merchant, 27 and 29 Gateside street
Nicol, Thomas, Beechfield, Bothwell road
Nicol, William, cowfeeder, 13 Brandon street
Nimmo, David, draper, 19 Duke street
Orr, William, toy shop, Lawrie place, Duke street
O'Neill, James, fruiterer, Greenfield place, Greenfield
O'Neil, Robert, eating-house, 21 Castle street

Park, Dougald, draper, 29 Burnbank
Park, Wm., tailor and clothier, 61 Cadzow st., house—10 Miller st.
Parker, Absalom, draper, 12 Brandon street
Passmore, Mrs, grocer, 89 Almada street
Paterson, Gavin, calenderer, Lochside House, Bent road
Paterson, George, master of works, 1 Edinburgh Road
Paterson, James, draper, 33 Townhead street
Paterson, James, fruiterer, Tainsh's buildings, Gateside street
Paterson, James, quarrymaster, Duke street
Paterson, James, spirit dealer, 8 Young street
Paterson, James, spirit merchant, Lilybank, Wellhall road
Paterson, John, agent, Glasgow Friendly Society, 11 Campbell st.
Paterson, John, painter, 6 Hope street
Paterson, John, quarrier, 14 Quarry road
Paterson, John, tinsmith, Sommerville place, Quarry street
Paterson, Miss Mary, 41 Almada street
Paterson, Miss, Park road
Paterson, Rev. T. M. B., Greenbank, Wellhall road
Paterson, Thomas, grocer, 49 Low Quarry
Paterson, Thomas, Hillside, Auchingramont
Paterson, William, blacksmith, 36 Townhead street
Paterson, William, builder, Park road
Paterson, William, Sheriff-clerk-depute, 119 Almada street

Paton, Robert A., ironmonger, 36 Cadzow street
Patrick, David, of Keith & Patrick, writers, house—Woodview
Paul, Robert, dairyman, 47 Almada street
Peat, John G, architect, 9 Cadzow street, house—Portland park
Peebles, James, clerk, Crosspark, M'Ghie street
Penman, George, grocer, 39 Quarry road
Penman, Matthew, of Turner & Penman, builders, house—Turner's buildings, Portland place
Pollock, James F. spirit merchant, Marybank place, Quarry st.
Pollock, James, smith, Wellhall road
Pollock, John, M.R.C.V.S., Peacock cross
Pollok, William, writer, 11 Campbell street, house—Park road
Pomphrey, John, carriage hirer, Commercial Stables, Townhead street, house—Quarry street
Prentice, John, contractor, 52 Quarry street
Prentice, John, pit manager, Robertson's bdgs., Portland place
Preston, Mrs, confectioner, 37 Burnbank
Purdie, John, builder, Burnbank road
Purdie, W., builder. quarry, Greenfield, house—Almada street
Queen, Hugh, marble-cutter, 33 Muir street
Quinlon, Patrick, 2 Saffronhall crescent
Quinlon, Misses, teachers, R.C. School, house—2 Saffronhall cres.

Rae, John, tinsmith, 2 Brandon street, house—Brandon Lodge
Ramsay, James, bill-poster, 33 Church street
Rankin, J. & J., china merchants and cork manufacturers, 14 Castle street, and 16 and 17 Great Clyde street, Glasgow
Rankin, James, of J. & J. Rankin, cork manufacturers and china merchants, 14 Castle street, house—Pine Cottage
Rankin, John, of J. & J. Rankin, cork manufacturers and china merchants, house—16 Castle street
Rankin, Thomas, seedsman, 12 Castle street, nursery—Allanshaw
Reed, H. H., accountant, Saffron Villa
Reid, Archibald, commission agent, Burnbank road
Reid, Miss, 1 Hope terrace
Reid, Mrs, dairy, 4 Campbell street
Reid, Mrs Robert, 30 Almada street
Reid, Peter F., news-agent, &c., M'Laren's bdgs., Portland place
Reilly, Michael, eating-house keeper, 43 Castle street
Richmond, William, The "Mie-Mie," Auchingramont
Ritchie, George W., furnisher and colporteur, 61 Almada street
Ritchie, Mrs, dressmaker, 18 Almada street
Robb, Alexander, cattle-dealer, 19 Burnbank road
Robb, Allan, baker, 23 Duke street,
Robb, William, cattle-dealer, Parkview House, Clydesdale street
Robbie, James, confectioner, 51 and 53 Cadzow street, house—Windsor terrace, Bothwell street
Robertson, Archibald, slater and plasterer, 21 Barrack street
Robertson, George, hatter, 64 Cadzow street, house—Mayfield Cottage, M'Ghie street

Robertson, Brothers, slaters and plasterers, Barrack street
Robertson, James, joiner, 20 Miller street, workshop, James st.
Robertson, John, oil merchant, 6 Clydesdale street
Robertson, Matthew, spirit dealer, 5 Castle street
Robertson, Robert, plasterer, 8 Almada street
Robertson, Robert Thim Craig, M.D., Bent road
Robertson, William, of Robertson & Harcus, joiners, house—Barleath cottage, Gateside street
Robin, Robert, Castlehill
Robinson, Miss, stationer, Post Office, Burnbank
Rocks, John, broker, 57 Castle street
Rodger, Mrs, spirit merchant, 18 Young street
Rodgers, David, greengrocer, 25 Almada street
Rogers, George, grocer and spirit merchant, 29 Chapel street
Rose, David, manufacturer of export clothing, Park road
Ross & Paton, photographers, Wellhall road
Ross, Hugh, police inspector, Society buildings, Beckford street
Ross, Miss, straw hat maker, 38 Brandon street
Rowan & Jolly, grocers, Ferguson's buildings, Bent road
Roxburgh, Miss, Muirside cottage, Muir street
Russell, Andrew, tailor, 29 Duke street
Russell, Gavin, draper, 31 Almada street, house—Clydesdale st.
Russell, George, teacher, Montreal House, Bothwell road
Russell, Henry, spirit dealer, King's Arms, Muir street
Russell, John, dairy, Victoria place, Greenfield
Russell, John, potato dealer, 30 Portland place
Russell, John, Woodside house
Russell, William, shaftmaker, Burnbank

Sandilands, Andrew, sheriff-officer, 17 Nisbet's buildings Baillie's Causeway
Sands, John, rag-dealer, 70 Castle street
Schröder, Henry, teacher, Saffronhall place, Muir street
Scotland, William, enginekeeper, 1 Saffronhall crescent
Scott, Adam, stationer, 44 Quarry street and 15 Almada street
Scott, Andrew, of T. & A. Scott, drapers, 41 and 43 Low qry., house—Portland place
Scott, George, Fairview, Hollandbush
Scott, James, gardener, 11 Church street
Scott, James, sculptor, 29 Duke street
Scott, John, contractor, 2 Parklea, Park road
Scott, John, cowfeeder, 49 Townhead street
Scott, John L., Thorn Villa, Clydesdale street
Scott, Miss, dressmaker, 91 Quarry street
Scott, Mrs, Bellvue terrace, Clydesdale street
Scott, Mrs, Cross Park, M'Ghie street
Scott, Mrs, spirit merchant, 84 Muir street
Scott, Robert, storekeeper, Lawrie place, Baillie's causeway
Scott, Thomas, of T. & A. Scott, drapers, 41 and 43 Low quarry, house—Brown & Henderson's buildings, Portland place

Selkirk, Thomas, wood merchant, 78 Townhead street
Sharp, Misses, Rosemount Quarry street
Sharp, Robert, shoemaker, M'Alpine's buildings, Beckford st.
Sharpe, James, veterinary surgeon, 43 Townhead street
Shearer, Agnes Fyfe, stationer, 3 Quarry street
Shearer, Robert, broker, 12 Lamb street
Shearer, Robert, late innkeeper, Spence's buildings, Quarry st.
Shearer, Robert, stationmaster, W.S., house—Clydesdale street
Sherry, Thomas, coal merchant, 65 Muir street
Simpson, James, carting contractor, 11 Hope street
Simpson, James C., coalmaster, Fernbank, Bothwell road
Simpson, James, flesher, 9 Duke street
Simpson, Samuel Ford, banker, The Grange, Auchingramont
Sinclair, George, commission agent, Park cottage, John street
Singer's Manufacturing Co. Sewing Machines, 32 Cadzow street
Siseman, John, dairyman, Chassells' buildings, Portland place
Sloan, Miss, milliner and dressmaker, 24 Castle street
Small, Joseph, pawnbroker, 9 to 17 Castle street, house—Campbell street
Small, Leonard, joiner, 4 Baillie's causeway
Small, Patrick, pawnbroker, 9 Castle street
Smart, Andrew, flesher, 27 Almada street
Smart, James, coalmaster, Angus lodge
Smellie, Lawson S., auctioneer, King's Arms, Muir street
Smellie, James, assistant road surveyor, 28 Portland place
Smellie, William, cowfeeder, 12 Hope street
Smith, Alexander L., inspector of poor, 11 Brandon street
Smith, Alexander, post-runner, 2 Quarry place
Smith & Son, Robert, drapers, 29 Cadzow street
Smith, Hamilton, colliery manager, Bent cottage
Smith, James B., merchant, Mackie's buildings, Quarry street
Smith, James, of J. & R. Smith, licensed family grocers, 24 Cadzow Street, house—Villa, Union street
Smith, John, broker, 65 Castle street
Smith, John, grocer, 9 Orchard street
Smith, John, fruiterer, Leggate's bdgs., Peacock Cross, Union st.
Smith, R. & J., licensed family grocers, 24 Cadzow street
Smith, Robert A., of R. Smith & Son, drapers, 29 Cadzow street, house—Castlehill crescent
Smith, Robert, of J. & R. Smith, licensed family grocers, 24 Cadzow street, house—Castlehill crescent
Smith, Robert, of R. Smith & Son, drapers, 29 Cadzow street, house—Leven Villa, Auchingramont
Smith, William, sen., agent, 5 Miller street
Soldiers' Home, 11 Almada street ; keeper, Private Madigan
Sommerville, James, cooper, 12 Quarry street, house—Portland pl.
Sommerville & Kinnear, drapers, 14 and 16 Cadzow street
Sommerville, Wm., ironmonger, 4 Castle street, house—Roseneath Cottage, Almada street.
Soutter, Joseph Brough, solicitor, Gleniffer Villa, M'Ghie street

Spalding, Colin, hotelkeeper, Commercial Hotel, Townhead st.
Speirs, William, watchmaker, 39 Cadzow street
Spence, Henry, lithographer, 87 Almada street
Spence, James, fruiterer, 4 Cadzow street, and 42 Quarry street
Spens, Walter C., sheriff-substitute, Bellevue, Clydesdale street
Steel, Hugh, commercial traveller, Muirbank House, 30 Muir st.
Steel, James, carting contractor, 10 Tuphall road
Steel, John G., grocer, Gowan's buildings, Low-waters
Steel, William, agent, 2 St. John's lane
Steven, George, house factor, 44 Townhead street
Stevenson, David, blacksmith, Burnbank
Stevenson, John, rope-spinner, 77 Townhead street
Stevenson, Mrs, Cadzow cottage, Union street
Stevenson, Thomas, of Freebairn & Stevenson, rope-spinners, house—1 Ann street
Stewart, Alexander, manufacturer, factory—Burnbank road, house—Fairfield House, Clydesdale st.
Stewart, Andrew, licensed grocer, Brown & Henderson's bdgs., Portland place.
Stewart, John, druggist, 8 Cadzow street, house—25 Townhead st.
Stewart, Malcolm, flesher, Docherty's buildings, Burnbank
Stewart, William, church-officer, 1 Chapel street
Stewart, William, gardener, 8 Union street
Stirling, Charles, of J. & C. Stirling, coachbuilders, Campbell street, house—5 Bothwell road
Stirling, John, junior, of J. & C. Stirling, coachbuilders, Campbell street, house— Fairburn cottage, Park road
Stirling, John, senior, coachbuilder, 3 Campbell street
Strachan, David, farmer, Laigh Stonehall
Strang, Robert, portioner, 35 Quarry street
Struthers, Andrew, cattle dealer, 2 Quarry place
Struthers, James, manufacturer, Chantinghall
Summers, Robert, confectioner, 5 Bothwell road
Symington, Andrew, greengrocer, Cadzow buildings

Tainsh, John, junior, 3 Holmes street
Tainsh, John, senior, confectioner, Quarryhall
Tait, Andrew Jack, bank clerk, 2 Muir street
Tait, John, baker, 4 Muir street
Tait, Mrs, M'Ghie street
Taylor, Alexander, mineral factor, Staneacre
Taylor, Alexander, plasterer, 6 Quarry place
Taylor, Alexander, slater (adjoining ropework) Baillie's causeway
Taylor & Henderson, ironfounders and engineers, Greenfield foundry. Manager—Mr Jas. Dunlop, Springwell, Blantyre
Taylor, Archibald, plumber, 18 Chapel street house—Bent road
Taylor, George A., 30 Almada street
Taylor, Lachlan, of Taylor & Henderson, ironfounders, &c., Greenfield, house—Craigview, Burnbank road
Taylor, Robert, plasterer, 44 Union street

Taylor, William, Mulberry cottage, Douglas street
Templeton, Archibald, of Templeton & Fletcher, licensed grocers, Townhead street, house—Sommerville place, Quarry street
Tennent, James, cattle-dealer, &c., 17 Brandon street
Thomas, William, dresser, 62 Almada street
Thompson, Rev. E. L. (second charge), Old Manse, Muir street
Thomson, Alexander, superintendent, cemetery, Bent road
Thomson, Anthony, mason, 24 Almada street
Thomson, David, grocer, 41 Gateside street
Thomson, George, shoemaker and house factor, 2 Duke street
Thomson, James, insurance agent, 5 Union street
Thomson, James, shoemaker, 11 Cadzow street
Thomson, John, farrier, Saffronhall crescent
Thomson, Misses, Roslin place Windmill road
Thomson, Misses, 33 Quarry street
Thomson, Mrs A., Netherfield, Auchingramont
Thomson, Robert, of R. & J. Thomson, drapers, 13 Cadzow street. house—Ivy Grove, Hollandbush
Thorburn, J. & T. confectioners, works—13 Muir street—shops 80 Cadzow street, and 8 Townhead street
Thorburn, Thomas, of J. & T. Thorburn, confectioners, house— The Hollies, Burnbank road
Thorburn, William, 13 Muir street
Toner, John, broker, 35 Castle street
Torrance, John, grain dealer, 6 Bothwell road
Torrance, John, writer, Cadzow villa
Torrance, John, shoemaker, Cadzow cottage, Windmill road
Torrance, Thomas, shoemaker, 70 Cadzow street
Trench, Rev. Thomas S., Bellfield House, M'Ghie street
Turner, George, architect, office—31 Almada street, house—14 Almada street
Turner, George, joiner, 46 Almada street
Turner, James, mason, Turner's buildings, Portland place
Turner, Mrs, 46 Almada street
Turner, Robert, mason, Turner's buildings, Portland place
Turner, Robert, M.D., 46 Almada street
Urquhart, John, Auchingramont house, Auchingramont
Urquhart, Misses, Auchingramont house, Auchingramont

Waddell, James, innkeeper, County Hotel, 22 Cadzow street
Walker, D., clergyman, Oakley house, Bothwell Road
Walker, James, engineer, Threshalea, Portland place
Walker, Miss, dressmaker, 55 Almada street
Walker, Mrs Janet, grocer, 55 Almada street
Walker, Mrs, Linnholm, Union street
Wallace, Rev. George, F.C. Manse, Union street
Wallace, William, carriage hirer, Cross, house—1 John street
Wardrop, David, of Wardrop & Young, carriage hirers, 20 Cadzow street, house—Baillie's causeway
Warnock, James, farmer, Auchingramont farm

Warnock, John, farmer, Auchingramont farm
Warnock, John, grocer, 58 Almada street
Warren, John, spirit dealer, 10 Campbell st., house—30 Cadzow st.
Watson, Charles, advertising agent, Beckford cottage, Clydesdale street
Watson, John, china merchant, 44 Church street
Watson John, dairyman, Russell's buildings, Burnbank road
Watson, John, of Earnock, Earnock house
Watson, Miss, music teacher, Beckford Cottage, Clydesdale st.
Watson, Mrs Alexander, grocer, 1 Orchard street
Watson, Mrs, Beckford cottage, Clydesdale street
Watson, Robert, water surveyor, 19 Cadzow street, house—Burgh buildings
Watt, Alexander, writer, Almada Hill
Watt, David, ironmonger, 13 Burnbank
Weir, Alex. L., grocer, Chassels' buildings, Portland place
Weir, James, spirit merchant, 10 Quarry street
Weir, Thomas W., grocer and joiner, Portland place
Welsh, John, fishmonger, 21 Castle street
Westwater, Andrew, draper, Greenfield place, Greenfield
Wheeling, William, keeper of club, Edinburgh road
Wheeling, James, of Paterson & Wheeling, builders and contractors, house—Duke street
Wheeling, Walter, cloth manufacturer, and spirit merchant, 12 Holmes street
White, Alexander, baker, 2 Campbell street
Whiteford, Adam, flesher, 50 Quarry street, house—Low quarry
Whiteford, Andrew, grocer, 54 Brandon street
Wilkie, Alexander, joiner, 21 Quarry st., house—Orchard place
Wilkie, James, joiner, 12 Orchard street
Wilkie, William, painter, Kingston cottage, Woodside walk
Wilkinson, Robert, grocer, 31 Castle street
Willans, Richard, cab driver and grocer, 11 Chapel street
Willmore, John, Saffron Villa, Windmill road
Wilson, Archibald, grocer, 12 Barrack street
Wilson, David, baker, 50 Townhead street
Wilson, Francis, wright and grocer, 25 Portland place
Wilson Henry, hairdresser, 12 Cadzow street
Wilson, James, weaver and grocer, 26 High Patrick street
Wilson, James, wright, Low-waters
Wilson, John Alexander, grocer, 36 Townhead street
Wilson, John, grocer, Bent road
Wilson, Mrs, keeper of County Buildings
Wilson, Mrs, umbrella-maker, 15 Cadzow street, house—Waddelbank, Quarry street
Wilson, William, bar officer, 18 Almada street
Wingate, Misses, Viewfield place, Burnbank road
Wingate, Mrs, Linnhouse
Winter, George, Captain 26th Cameronians, Portland park
Wiseman, James, watchmaker, 46 Cadzow st., house—Hope ter.

Wood, William, of Clydesdale College
Woodward, Thomas, fish merchant, Victoria place, Greenfield
Wotherspoon, Rev. J. H., Park road
Wotherspoon, Thomas, farmer, Hillhouse
Wright, Catherine M., stationer, 18 Cadzow street
Wright, James, joiner, 23 Church street
Wright, James H., bookseller, 37 Cadzow street
Wright, John, joiner, 22 Church street
Wright, Robert, carter, 53 Muir street
Wylie, Christina, cowfeeder, Low-waters
Wylie, John, of Wylie, Dunlop & Allan, grocers, Cadzow street, house—Garnocklea, Auchingramont
Wyper, Mrs, licensed grocer, 9 Campbell street

Young, David, flesher, Peacock cross
Young, Geo., silk manufacturer, Bellevue Cottage, Clydesdale st.
Young, James, sheriff-officer, 1 Quarry street
Young, James, spirit merchant, Peacock-cross
Young, John, junior, M.R.C.V.S., 24 Chapel street
Young, John, smith, 24 Chapel street
Young, Robert, grocer, Docherty's buildings, Burnbank
Young, Stephen, cowfeeder, M'Ghie street
Young, Thomas, bar-officer, 9 Holmes street
Young, Thomas, of Wardrop and Young, carriage-hirers, 20 Cadzow street—restaurant, 60 Quarry street

MAGISTRATES.

Provost, John Clark Forrest
Bailies, Andrew Cassels, Thomas Thorburn, James Cairns, and Gavin Paterson

TOWN COUNCIL.

James Keith	Gavin Cross	John Tainsh	John Clark
John Rae	Robt. Archibald	Jas. Sommerville	Robert Thomson.
		Robert M'Alpine	*

[* A vacancy was caused by the retirement of Mr James Mackie, on his appointment to the office of Chamberlain, which had not been filled up when this sheet went to press.]

Treasurer, James Keith   *Town Clerk,* Edward P. Dykes
Burgh Chamberlain—James Mackie
Procurator Fiscal, James Storrie Cullen
Collector of Burgh and Police Assessment, James Mackie, jun.
Registrar of Births, Deaths, and Marriages in Burgh, William Moffat, 19 Cadzow Street. *Assistant Do.,* T. H. Moffat
Billet Master, George Kemp, 16 Almada St. *Messenger-at-Arms,* George Kemp
Town Officer, William Dalziel, Townhead Street

LICENSING COMMITTEE.

Chairman, Provost Forrest; Bailie Cairns, Bailie Thorburn; John Austine, Oak Lodge; John Meek, of Fortisset; James Holmes, of Cornsilloch

TOWN COUNCIL COMMITTEES, 1878.

1.—*Property and Finance Commmittee*—Bailies Thorburn and Paterson, Treasurer Keith, Councillors Tainsh, Cross, and Clark. Bailie Paterson, convener.
2.—*Mortifications and Charities Committee*—Provost Forrest, Bailies Cassels and Thorburn, and Councillor Thomson. Provost Forrest, convener.
3.—*Assessments Committee*—Provost Forrest, Bailies Cassels and Thorburn, and Councillors Archibald and M'Alpine. Provost Forrest, convener.
4.—*Parliamentary Bills Committee*—Bailies Cairns and Paterson, Treasurer Keith, and Councillors Archibald Rae, and Tainsh. Councillor Archibald, convener.
5.—*Gas Committee*—Bailies Cassels and Paterson, and Councillors Sommerville, Archibald, and Clark. Bailie Cassels, convener.

POLICE COMMISSION COMMITTEES, 1878.

1.—*Street and Finance Committee*—Bailies Thorburn and Paterson, Treasurer Keith, and Messrs Tainsh, Cross, and Clark. Bailie Paterson, convener.
2.—*Sanitary Committee*—Bailies Cassels and Paterson, and Messrs Tainsh, Archibald, Rae, Thomson, and M'Alpine. Mr Archibald, convener.
3.—*Assessment Committee*—Provost Forrest, Bailies Cassels and Thorburn, and Messrs Archibald and M'Alpine. Provost Forrest, convener.
4.—*Police and Police Clothing Committee.*—Bailies Cairns and Paterson, and Messrs Tainsh, Rae, Cross, Sommerville, and Thomson. Mr Rae, convener.

WATER COMMITTEE, 1878.

Provost Forrest, Bailies Cassels, Thorburn, and Paterson, Treasurer Keith, Messrs M'Alpine and Archibald. Provost Forrest, convener.

DEAN OF GUILD COURT,

Dean, Bailie Paterson; *Deputy-Dean,* Bailie Thorburn; *Council,* Provost Forrest, Messrs Archibald and M'Alpine
First and Third Thursdays of each month at 11 a.m.

COUNCILLORS SINCE 1834.

James Henderson, banker........1834
James Bryson, surgeon............1834
Fergus Ferguson, Rosebank......1834
John Gowan, lace manufacturer..1834
James Hamilton, weaver..........1834
Walter Black, baker..............1834
James Miller, surgeon............1834
Joseph Rowatt, wood merchant..1834
Duncan Swim, residenter........1834
John Wingfield, writer...........1834
Thomas Anderson, bank agent....1834
James Naismith, writer...........1835
John Gowans 1837
Dugald MacCallum 1837
James Main, merchant...........1837
Andrew Henderson 1837
James Hamilton, grocer..........1837
Dan. MacArthur, lace man'fact'rer 1838
James Pile, lace manufacturer....1838
James Hamilton 1839
John Patrick.....................1839
John Brock, grocer...............1840
William Fairley, ironmonger......1840
William Paterson, mason.........1841
James Forrest, brewer............1841
James Thomson, grocer..........1841
William Aikman, banker.........1845
William Mowbray, ironmonger....1845
D. O. Marianski 1845
John Kirkland, weaving agent....1846
Thomas Allan, lace manufacturer 1846
James Smith, upholsterer 1847
William Fairley...................1847
John Cairns, grazier..............1848
Alexander Gibson, Castlehill......1849
John, M'Laren...................1850
John Dykes, writer...............1851
John Meek.......................1851
Samuel Finlator..................1851
James Nisbet....................1852
Alexander M'Intosh, druggist....1852
William Alston Dykes, writer.....1852
Alexander Currie, writer..........1853
Joseph Robertson, teacher........1854
Francis Hamilton.................1855
Alex. Kellar, Portland Cottage...1856
John Sommerville, Almada Hill..1856
James Barr, Silvertonhill.........1857
James Sommerville, cooper......1857
James Mackie, lace manufacturer 1857
Andrew Cassels, grocer...........1858
William Sage, carpenter..........1858
Thomas Thorburn, confectioner..1859
James Keith, grocer..............1859
Archibald Naismith, tinsmith....1860
James Cairns, tobacconist........1861
William Rankin, merchant........1862
William Brown, writer............1863
Edward Pellew Dykes, writer.....1865
John Clark Forrest, bank agent..1865
John Tainsh, confectioner........1866
John Rae, tinsmith 1869
William Mitchell, plumber........1869
Gavin Cross, tailor and clothier..1871
James Gillon, currier 1872
Gavin Paterson, calenderer.......1875
Robert Archibald, writer..........1875
John Clark, smith 1878
Robert M'Alpine, builder.........1878
Robert Thomson, draper..........1878

BURGH POLICE COURT.

Sits every day when necessary, in Burgh Buildings, Duke Street, at 11 a.m.

Judges, The Magistrates. *Procurator-Fiscal*, James S. Cullen
Clerk and Assessor, Edward Pellew Dykes
The *Procurators* as in the Sheriff Court

BURGH POLICE—*Office*, Burgh Buildings, Duke Street

Commissioners—The Town Council
Clerk to Commissioners, E. Pellew Dykes
Superintendent of Police, James S. Cullen
Inspector of Weights and Measures, J. S. Cullen
Inspector of Streets and Nuisances, Robt. Watson
Inspector of do. for Parish, John Blaney, Sergt.-Major, Muir Street
Medical Officer, Dr. Loudon

HAMILTON GAS WORKS.

Treasurer, James Mackie. *Manager*, John Johnstone
Collector, James Mackie, jun.

HAMILTON WATER WORKS.

Water Works Surveyor,	Robert Watson, 19 Cadzow Street
Collector of Water Rates,	James Peebles, Do.
Superintendent of Fire Brigade,	Robert Watson Do.

PARISH ROAD TRUST.

Clerk,	E. P. Dykes, Royal Bank
Surveyor,	William Bertram, Greenfield
Assistant do.,	James Smellie, Portland Place
Collector,	John Martin, British Linen Coy. Bank

BURGH ROAD TRUST.

Clerk,	Edward P. Dykes, The Town House
Surveyor,	Robert Watson, 19 Cadzow Street
Collector,	James Mackie, jun., 5 Holmes Street

PAROCHIAL BOARD—*Office*, 2 Chapel Street

Chairman, John Meek, of Fortisset.   *Inspector*, Alexander L. Smith
Medical Officer and Vaccinator, Dr. Marshall
Collector, James Mackie, Holmes Street

COMBINATION POORHOUSE,

For Parishes of Avondale, Blantyre, Cambuslang, Dalserf, Glassford, Hamilton, East Kilbride, and Stonehouse

Chairman, John Meek, of Fortisset
Governor and Secretary, George Edwards.   *Matron*, Mrs Edwards
Medical Officer, James Loudon, M D   *Chaplain*, Rev. John T. M'Farlane

CLERGY.

ESTABLISHED CHURCH, 1st Charge,	H. M. HAMILTON.
Do., 2d Charge,	E. L. THOMPSON.
CADZOW CHURCH,	M. P. JOHNSTONE, B.D.
CHAPEL OF EASE, QUARTER,	JAMES A. CAMPBELL.
ST. JOHN'S FREE CHURCH,	GEORGE WALLACE, M.A.
BURNBANK FREE CHURCH,	THOMAS M. B. PATERSON.
AUCHINGRAMONT U. P. CHURCH,	PETER C. DUNCANSON.
BRANDON STREET Do.,	J. T. M'FARLANE.
CHAPEL STREET, Do.,	T. S. TRENCH, M.A.
SAFFRONHALL, Do.,	JOHN INGLIS ; T. R. ANDERSON, M.A., *Colleague and Successor*.
ST. JAMES' CONGREGATIONAL CHURCH,	DANIEL JACKSON.
PARK ROAD E.U. CHURCH,	GEORGE BELL, M.A.
ST. MARY'S EPISCOPAL CHURCH,	CHARLES G. HENDERSON.
ST. MARY'S R. C. CHURCH,	JAMES DANAHER.

MISSIONARIES.

Established Church—Rev. George Stephen, H. J. Wotherspoon, M.A., James Mitchell (Lay)
Saffronhall U.P. Church—James Marshall
Burnbank Free Church—Rev W. C. M'Dougall

SESSION-CLERK—JAMES BLACKLOCK

U.P. AND ESTABLISHED PRESBYTERIES. 53

UNITED PRESBYTERIAN PRESBYTERY OF HAMILTON.
Clerk—Rev. JOHN T. M'FARLANE, Hamilton.

Place.	Ministers.	Ordinations.	Post-Towns.
Bellshill	John Wilson	1833	Bellshill
Cambuslang	William Baird	1876	Cambuslang
East Kilbride	James Bonnar	1841	East Kilbride
Hallside	R. J. Robson Cowan	1877	Cambuslang
HAMILTON—			
Auchingramont	Peter C. Duncanson	1859	Hamilton
Brandon Street	John T. M'Farlane	1842	....
Chapel Street	Thomas S. Trench	1867	....
Saffronhall	{ John Inglis	1834	....
	{ Thomas R. Anderson, M.A.	1871	....
Kirkmuirhill	John Meiklejohn, M.A.	1874	Lesmahagow
Larkhall	John Shearer	1840	Larkhall
Motherwell	James Dunlop, M.A.	1847	Motherwell
Newarthill	David Laughland	1844	Motherwell
Stonehouse	Henry A. Paterson, M.A.	1842	Stonehouse
Strathaven, 1st cong	Peter Leys	1851	Strathaven
.... East	Alex. W. Donaldson, B.A.	1864	....
.... West	Peter Morton	1873	....
Wishaw	Robert Stewart Bruce	1864	Wishaw

ESTABLISHED PRESBYTERY OF HAMILTON.
Clerk—JAMES STEWART JOHNSON, D.D., Minister of Cambuslang.

Parishes.	Pop. in 1871.	Ministers.	Ordinations.	Post Towns.
Airdrie (Q)	13,666	John Campbell, B.D.	1872	Airdrie
Avondale	5,460	Duncan Taylor	1864	Strathaven
Strathaven, East		James Allan	1869	....
Baillieston (Q)	4,924	Hugh Ramsay	1856	Baillieston
Bargeddie (Q)		Alex. T. Scott	1871	Bargeddie
Bellshill		James M. Killen, M.A.	1877	Bellshill
Blantyre	3,472	Stewart Wright	1855	Blantyre
Bothwell	9,193	John Pagan, M.A.	1861	Bothwell
Calderhead (Q)		Robert Dixon	1874	Shotts
Cambusnethan	8,631	R. S. Hutton, M.A.	1851	Wishaw
Cambuslang	3,740	James S. Johnson, D.D.	1843	Cambuslang
Newmains		Vacant	....	Wishaw
Chapelton, (Q)		John M'Gavin, M.A.	1864	Hamilton
Clarkston, (Q)	4,902	J. Brander, B.D.	1869	Airdrie
Meadowfield		Lockhart Dobbie	1878	Airdrie
Coats (Q)		George Alpine, B.D	1871	Coatbridge
Dalserf	2,009	William P. Rorison	1851	Carluke
Dalziel	9,175	David Scott, B.D.	1874	Motherwell
Chapel		Thomas Hislop	1877	....
Flowerhill (Q)		James Paton, B.A.	1867	Airdrie
Gartsherrie (Q)	10,041	Bryce Johnstone Bell	1846	Coatbridge
Calderbank		Robert S. Millar	1877	Airdrie
Garturk (Q)		John Robertson	1878	Coatbridge
Glassford	1,430	Robert Paterson	1859	Hamilton
Hamilton	16,803	Henry M. Hamilton	1862	....
2d charge		Edward Lytton Thompson	1869	....
Cadzow		M. P. Johnstone, B.D.	1877	....
Quarter		J. A. Campbell, M.A.	1872	....
Holytown, (Q)	10,099	John Wilkie	1843	Holytown
Kilbride, East	3,861	John Downs	1861	East Kilbride
Larkhall (Q)	5,332	John Crichton	1856	Larkhall
Monkland, New	4,886	Robert Archibald	1834	Airdrie
		John M'Gavin Boyd, A. & S.	1871	....
Greengairs		James Muir	1877	....
Monkland, Old	15,225	Peter C. Black	1862	Coatbridge
Overtown (Q)		George Burnett	1869	Wishaw
Shotts	7,651	William Martin Watt	1844	Shotts

FREE PRESBYTERY—VOLUNTEERS.

Cleland .... George Mackie .... 1878 Holytown
Harthill (Q) .... A. Watt .... 1877 ....
Stonehouse .... 3,177 James Dunn .... 1852 Stonehouse
Uddingston (Q) .... John Mackintosh, B.D. .... 1871 Uddingston
Wishaw (Q) ...... 11,695 Alexander Harper .... 1870 Wishaw

Those marked (Q) are *Quoad Sacra* parishes. Those in *italics* are Chapels of Ease.

FREE CHURCH PRESBYTERY OF HAMILTON.

Clerk—W. FINDLAY, M.A., Minister of Larkhall.

Place.	Ministers.	Ordinations.	Post-Towns.
Airdrie, High Church	R. W. Lawson	1846	Airdrie
West	Vacant	1870	....
Broomknoll	William Reid	1867	....
Graham Street	David Berry	1847	....
Baillieston	Alexander M'Millan	1869	Baillieston
Bellshill	William M'Donald	1874	Bellshill
Blantyre	Robert Macdonald	1860	Blantyre
Bothwell	Andrew Doak, M.A.	1872	Bothwell
Cambuslang	Henry George Shepherd, B.D.	1877	Cambuslang
Cambusnethan	Peter Gibson Millar	1854	Wishaw
Chapelhall	Hugh M. Mackenzie	1869	Airdrie
Chapelton	Walter R. Paton	1870	Hamilton
Coatbridge—			
Middle Church	Alexander Ogilvy, M.A.	1868	Coatbridge
East	John Dickson	1870	....
West	W. K. M'Killiam, M.A.	1877	....
Dalziel	David Ogilvy, M.A.	1854	Motherwell
East Kilbride	Thomas Pearson, M.A.	1877	East Kilbride
Greengairs	A. S. Houston	1874	Airdrie
Hamilton, St John's	George Wallace, M.A	1859	Hamilton
Burnbank	T. M. B. Paterson	1875	....
Holytown	Robert M'Gregor, M.A	1873	Holytown
Larkhall	William Findlay, M.A.	1861	Larkhall
Shotts	Robert Gilchrist	1861	Shotts
Stonehouse	W. K. Hamilton	1843	Stonehouse
Stonehouse,	James Laing, M.A.	1856	....
Strathaven	Alexander Rankin	1842	Strathaven.
Uddingston	Ivie M. Maclachlan	1862	Uddingston
Wishaw	David Brunton	1872	Wishaw

16TH LANARKSHIRE RIFLE VOLUNTEERS.

Headquarters, Hamilton. Orderly Room, Muir Street
Honorary Colonel, Duke of Hamilton. *Lieut.-Colonel*, John Austine
Majors, R. S. Harington and R. Jack. *Adjutant*, J. Campbell
Surgeons, James Loudon, M.D.; Bruce Goff, M.D.; W. Crawford, M.D.
Chaplain, Rev. John Pagan, M.A.

A Coy., Hamilton—*Capt.*, S. F. Simpson
B " Hamilton—*Capt.*, P. Keith. *Lieuts.*, J. C. Kay and J. A. Potter
C " Uddingston—*Capt.*, G. Walker. *Lieuts.*, J. Patterson and J. Martin
D " Blantyre—*Capt.*, J. C. Forrest. *Lieuts.*, J. Ness and J. Naismith
E " Bothwell—*Capt.*, T. B. Ralston. *Lieuts.*, A. Greig and P. Fisher
F " Wishaw—*Capt.*, T. E. Williams. *Lieut.*, J. Patterson
G " Newmains—*Capt.*, J. Scott. *Lieut.*, A. Kirkland
H " Motherwell—*Capt.*, J. Topping. *Lieuts.*, J. Colville and A. Wilson.
I " East Kilbride—*Capt.*, G. S. Robb. *Lieut.*, W. Strang
K " Strathaven—*Capt.*, J. Loudon. *Lieuts.*, J. Campbell and J. Donald
Sergt.-Major, J. Blaney

BURGH SCHOOL BOARD.

Chairman, Dr. Loudon

Anderson, Rev. T. R., A M
Cassels, John
Danaher, Rev. J.
Dunlop, James
Jackson, Rev. D.
Paterson, Gavin
Patrick, David
Simpson, S. F.

Clerk and Treas., Patrick Keith, Clydesdale Bank
Officer, T. B. Cassels, 46 Quarry Street

SCHOOLS.

Hamilton Academy—Rector, James Blacklock; Classical and Senior English Master, Andrew Ferguson, M.A., St. Andrews; Junior English, John A. Kay, University of Edinburgh; Commercial, Alex. Armstrong, University of Glasgow; German, H. F. Schröder; Drawing, R. L. Bain, Cert. Art Teacher; Drill, John Blaney, Sergt.-Major; Teacher of Elementary Section, Miss Bryson; Teacher of Pianoforte and Singing, Miss Austin.

Townhead Street—Master, John M'Cabe, A M,; *Assistant do.*, Thomas Frame: *Mistress*, Miss Hamilton

Beckford Street—Master, James C. Christie; *Assistant do.*, John S. Moyes; *Mistress*, Miss M. Fairley

PARISH SCHOOL BOARD.

Chairman, John Austine

Dunlop, Colin, jun.
Forrest, William
Hamilton, Rev. H. M.
Grieve, John
Taylor, Alexander
Watson, John

Clerk and Treas., William Brown, Writer, Almada Street
Officer, Sergeant-Major Blaney, Muir Street

SCHOOLS.

Greenfield—Master, R. Steel; *Mistress*, Miss Stewart

Ferniegair—Master, R. Thomson; *Mistress*, Miss Weaver

Quarter—Master, H. Jack; *Assistant do.*, J. K. Leitch; *Mistress*, Miss Stewart

Beechfield—Miss Smith

Low-waters—Master, Robert Muir; *Mistress*, Miss Montgomery

SCHOOLS NOT CONNECTED WITH THE SCHOOL BOARD.

St. John's Grammar School—Rector, John Adams, F S A; *Assistant Masters*, G. W. Russell, Wm. Fordyce, J. M. Calder; *Mistress*, Miss Crawford

QUARRY ROAD SCHOOL.

Pres., vacant *Vice-Pres.*, Rev. H. M. Hamilton and Rev. F. L. Thompson
Secy., W. A. Dykes *Treas.* Patrick Keith
Master, William Hamilton *Mistresses*, Miss Lindsay and Miss Jack

SEMINARIES AND TEACHERS.

Clydesdale College (Boarding and Day School)—Headmasters, William Wood, University of Edinburgh, D. G. Kinmond, M.A., Aberdeen; *Elocution*, H. Cooke; *French*, Albert Gempler breveti Berne, Normal School; *German*, H. Schröder; *Music, Piano, and Violin*, Charles Cornwall, Organist, Sandyford Church, Glasgow; *Drawing*, R. L. Bain, Certificated Art Teacher; *Gymnastics and Drill*, Thomas Lindsay

Bellevue (Boarding and Day School)—Miss Nelson.

Earnock View (Boarding and Day School)—Misses Spence.

Portland Park (Ladies' Boarding and Day School)—Mrs Black.

COMPANIES, SOCIETIES, &c.

HAMILTON BRITISH WORKMAN PUBLIC-HOUSE COY. (LIMITED)
—Established 1878   Opposite Central Station
Manager, Thomas Chalmers
Open from 6 A.M. till 11 P.M.

HAMILTON SOLDIERS HOME AND INSTITUTE—Established 1878.
Gilmour's Buildings, Almada Street
Honorary Secretary, Capt. F. F. T. Hobbs
Manager, Private Daniel Madigan, 26th Regt. (Cameronians).
Open from 6 A.M. till 11 P.M.

BURNBANK COFFEE HOUSE AND READING ROOM
Established 1878
Manager, George Moffat
Open from 6 A.M. till 11 P.M.

HAMILTON PENNY SAVINGS BANK—Established 1874.
Sums from One Penny upwards received.
Place of Collection—St. John's Grammar School, Monday Evenings

HAMILTON POST OFFICE SAVINGS BANK.
Open from 9 till 6, Saturdays till 8
Sums from 1s to £30 received

HAMILTON BUILDING & PROPERTY INVESTMENT CO. (Limited),
Established 1876.
Secretary, Wm. Brown; *Treasurer*, J. Cunninghame Kay; *Factor*, David Matthew

SCOTTISH SAVINGS INVESTMENT AND BUILDING SOCIETY
(of Glasgow)—38 Cadzow Street
W. Naismith, *Agent*

STANDARD PROPERTY INVESTMENT COY., Limited (of Edinburgh),
Almada Street
Wm. Brown & Co., *Agents*

HAMILTON BUILDING SOCIETY.
Trustees—J. G. C. Hamilton, Esq. of Dalzell; John Meek, Esq. of Fortisset; A. Grant, Esq., Rose Villa; J. C. Forrest, Esq. of Auchinraith.
Joint Managers, Hugh M'Callum and James Cassels.

QUEENSLAND FREE AND ASSISTED EMIGRATION OFFICE—
38 Cadzow Street
W. Naismith, *Agent*

SOCIETIES, ASSOCIATIONS, &c.

HAMILTON ORPHAN SOCIETY—Established 1809.
President, Rev. T. R. Anderson; *Secretary*, Alex. Taylor; *Treasurer*, John Henderson; *Admitting Committee*, Wm. Naismith and Gavin Cross.

HAMILTON ORPHAN AND CHARITY SCHOOL ASSOCIATION.
(Instituted, 1839.)
President, W. A. Dykes; *Secretary and Treasurer*, Patrick Keith.

YOUNG MEN'S CHRISTIAN ASSOCIATION.
President, W. A. Dykes, The Orchard
Hon. Secretary, Alex. Taylor *Hon. Treasurer*, David Patrick

TONIC SOL-FA CHORAL ASSOCIATION.
Hon.-President, Thomas Fairbairn; *President*, John Henderson
Organist, Herr Schröder; *Conductor*, Lauchlan Taylor
Secretary, J. M. Calder; *Treasurer*, James D. Rankin

SAFFRONHALL MUSICAL ASSOCIATION.
Conductor, William Barrie; *Secretary and Treasurer*, Thomas Naismith

HAMILTON AGRICULTURAL SOCIETY.
President, John Watson, of Earnock   *Vice-President*, John Bell
Treasurer, Abram Torrance

LANARKSHIRE FARMERS' SOCIETY.
President, The Duke of Hamilton
Vice-Pres., Sir T. E. Colebrooke, Bart., of Crawford, M P.
Secretary and Treasurer, Wm. Forrest, Allanton

HAMILTON, BLANTYRE, AND CAMBUSLANG PLOUGHING SOCIETY.
Secretary and Treasurer, L. S. Smellie

HAMILTON HORTICULTURAL SOCIETY.
President, W. A. Dykes. The Orchard; *Treas.*, Thomas Rankin; *Secy.*, William Brown

HAMILTON ORNITHOLOGICAL ASSOCIATION.
President, David Wilson; *Secretary and Treasurer*, W. Millar.

HAMILTON AUXILIARY TO THE NATIONAL BIBLE SOCIETY OF SCOTLAND.
President, Alexander Mitchell
Treasurer, Andrew Cassels   *Secretaries*, Wm. Pollok and T. S. Michie
Repository, W. Naismith, 38 Cadzow Street

HAMILTON COLPORTEUR,
(In connection with Religious Tract and Book Society of Scotland).
Treasurer and Secretary, R. Kirkpatrick

MECHANICS' INSTITUTION—Instituted 1846
Librarian, William Dalziel   Library open on Tuesday nights at Burgh Bldgs.

CURLING CLUBS.

LANARKSHIRE CURLING CLUB—Wm. Forrest, President; Bailie Cassels, Vice-President; Wm. Forrest, Treasurer; Patrick Keith, Secretary.

HAMILTON CURLING CLUB—Samuel F. Simpson, President; John Clark and John Bell, Vice-Presidents; John Hinds, Treasurer; James Waddell, Secretary.

HAMILTON DOUGLAS AND CLYDESDALE SKATING AND CURLING CLUB.—Secy. and Treas., Wm. Forrest, Allanton

FREE MASONS.

PROVINCIAL GRAND LODGE OF THE MIDDLE WARD OF LANARKSHIRE—John Clark Forrest, of Auchinraith, Provincial Grand Master; William M'Murdo, P. G. Secretary, Holytown; Archibald King, P. G. Treasurer, Motherwell. Instituted, 27th September, 1866.

PROVINCIAL GRAND ROYAL ARCH CHAPTER OF THE MIDDLE WARD OF LANARKSHIRE—John Clark Forrest, of Auchinraith, Provincial Grand Superintendent; William M'Murdo, Holytown, Provincial Grand Scribe E; James Cameron, 6 High Patrick Street, Provincial Grand Treasurer. Instituted, 29th April, 1878.

HAMILTON ST. JOHN KILWINNING LODGE OF FREE MASONS, No. 7—James Mackie, 7 Holmes Street, R. W. Master; Thomas Fleming, 80 Cadzow Street, Secretary; J. B. Soutter, Gleniffer Villa, Treasurer (Instituted 1695)

HAMILTON LODGE OF FREE MASONS, No. 233—James Cameron, 6 High Patrick Street, R. W. Master; James Lambie, 1 Ann Street, Secy.; John Dalziel, Townhead Street, Treasurer (Instituted, 5th February, 1810).

HAMILTON ROYAL ARCH CHAPTER, No. 172—John M'Ghie, 13 Hope Street, First Principal; William Rennie, Barracks, Scribe E; Alexander Sheriffs, Newton, Treasurer (Instituted 1877)

FREE GARDENERS.

HAMILTON OLIVE LODGE OF FREE GARDENERS, No. 5 (1827)—James Wright, jun., Castle Street, R.W. Master; John Wright, 22 Church Street, Secretary; Charles Freebairn, Quarry Street, Treasurer

HAMILTON THISTLE LODGE OF FREE GARDENERS, No. 24 (1864)—Adam Murray, Tuphall Road, R.W. Master; Thomas Milligan, Union Street, Secretary; Peter Clark, Quarry Street, Treasurer (Instituted 1827)

HAMILTON VINE LODGE OF FREE GARDENERS—Walter Wheeling, 12 Townhead Street, R. W. Master; Andrew Scott, Portland Place, Secretary; James Wheeling, Duke Street, Treasurer

BURNS CLUBS.

HAMILTON BURNS' CLUB (OLD), Instituted 1869—Alexander Paterson, 10 Brandon Street, President; Robert Binning, Townhead Street, Secretary; James Allan, 18 Low Patrick Street, Treasurer

HAMILTON BURNS' CLUB—Provost Forrest, President; William Pollok, Secretary; J. C. Kay, Treasurer (Instituted 1877)

CO-OPERATIVE SOCIETIES.

HAMILTOM CO-OPERATIVE SOCIETY (Instituted, 1861)—William M'Ghie, Treasurer

HAMILTON INDUSTRIAL CO-OPERATIVE SOCIETY (Established 1862).—Alex. Crawford, Treasurer

CLUBS, SOCIETIES, &c.

FRIENDLY AND FUNERAL SOCIETIES.

HAMILTON FUNERAL SOCIETY (Instituted 1825)—George Paterson, Low Quarry, President; Robert Lambie, Ann Street, Secretary; Robert Scott, Gateside Street, Treasurer; Alex. Crawford, 9 Woodside Walk, Collector

HAMILTON 2D FUNERAL SOCIETY (Instituted 1836)—Thomas Gibson, Church Street, President and Treasurer; John Wright, 22 Church Street, Secretary; Alexander Crawford, 9 Woodside Walk, Collector

ST. MARY'S PERMANENT FRIENDLY FUNERAL SOCIETY, &c.—Thos. Loudon, President; John Rocks, Vice-President; John Tonner, Secretary

HAMILTON YOUNG SOLDIER'S FRIENDLY SOCIETY—David Cross, 91 Quarry Street, President; David Adams, Holmes Street, Secretary; Andrew Barrie, 11 Haddow Street, Treasurer

HAMILTON GENTLE SHEPHERDS' FRIENDLY SOCIETY (Instituted, 27th February, 1818).—John Smith, Preses; A. Hendry, Quarry road, Secretary; Wm. M'Ghie, Treasurer.

BAKERS' FRIENDLY SOCIETY (Instituted 1793).—James Hamilton, 11 Campbell Street, Preses; John Torrance, writer, Cadzow Villa, Secretary and Treasurer; John Watson, baker, Bothwell, and David Bryden, baker, Uddingston, Key-Masters

TRADE SOCIETIES.

HAMILTON GROCERS' ASSISTANT ASSOCIATION—Claud Millar, Brandon Street, President; Thomas M'Ghie, Woodside Walk, Secretary; Thomas Pate Loudon, Miller Street, Treasurer

HAMILTON OPERATIVE JOINERS' SOCIETY—Andrew Summers, President, Hugh Hamilton, Hope Street, Secretary; James Taylor, Hope Street Treasurer

LANARKSHIRE MIDDLE WARD MASTER WRIGHTS MUTUAL ASSOCIATION— Robert Miller, President; James M'Call, Treasurer; Alexander Wilkie, Secretary

CRICKET AND FOOTBALL CLUBS.

YOUNG MEN'S CHRISTIAN ASSOCIATION CRICKET CLUB—Alex. Carmichael, Beckford Street, Captain; Peter B. Wilkie, Orchard Street, Secretary; Thomas Selkirk, Townhead Street, Treasurer

HAMILTON ACADEMICALS ATHLETIC AND FOOTBALL CLUB—Roger Allan, Quarry Place, President; Thomas Miller, Burnbank, Secretary; Gavin Frame, 30 Almada Street, Treasurer

HAMILTON THISTLE CRICKET AND FOOTBALL CLUB (Instituted 1862)—Wm. Findlay, Lamb Street, President; James Lambie, 1 Ann Street, Vice-President; James Lambie, 1 Ann Street, Secretary and Treasurer

MISCELLANEOUS CLUBS, &c.

HAMILTON BOWLING CLUB (Instituted 1841)—Provost Forrest, President; Archibald Taylor, Vice-President; J. B. Soutter, Secretary; James Keith, Treasurer

HAMILTON BILLIARD CLUB (Limited)—Patrick Keith, President; James Matthews, Secretary; James Mackie, Treasurer

ANCIENT ORDER OF FORESTERS, COURT BRANDON No. 5912—John Welsh, Bent Road, Chief Ranger; Robert Cuningham, 67 Quarry Street, Secretary; Hugh Russell, 21 Muir Srteet Treasurer.

INDEPENDENT ORDER OF GOOD TEMPLARS.

Lodges which meet in GOOD TEMPLARS' HALL, HAMILTON.

DISTRICT LODGE (No. 36), Lanark, Middle Ward, South-western. D.D.G.W.C., Gavin Cross, Burgh Buildings ; D.S.J.T., James Hardie, Low-waters ; D.S., A. Sandilands, Nisbet's Buildings.

No. 70—BRITANNIA'S HOPE. Meets every Tuesday Evening at 8.15. D.G.W.C.T., James Young, 1 Quarry Street, Hamilton ; W.C.T., James Fulton, Low Patrick Street. Instituted 1870.

No. 321—CADZOW CASTLE. Meets every Wednesday Evening at 8 15. D.G.W.C.T., Peter Cunningham, Portland Place ; W.C.T., Alexander Cross, Orchard Place. Instituted 1871.

No. 547—VALE OF CLYDE. Monday, at 8.15. D.G.W.C.T., Thomas Irvine, 42 Muir Street ; W.C.T., H. Richardson, Hamilton Barracks. Instituted 1871.

No. 4—BRITANNIA'S HOPE JUVENILE LODGE. Thursday, at 8. Superintendent, Joseph Wilson, 17 Low Patrick Street. Instituted 1870.

MISSION HALL, LOW-WATERS.

No. 220—CADZOW OAKS. Wednesday, at 8.15. D.G.W.C.T., Wm. Mitchell, 13 Wilson Terrace, Cadzow Colliery ; W.C.T., James Hardie, Low-waters. Instituted 1877.

No. 337—CADZOW OAKS JUVENILE LODGE. Wednesday, at 6.30. Superintendent, James Hardie, Low-waters. Instituted 1877.

No. 560—MILITARY LODGE. Meets in SOLDIER'S INSTITUTE, Almada Street. W.C.T., Sergeant Charles Smith. Instituted 1878.

BURNBANK COFFEE HOUSE.

No. 323—UDSTON. Thursday, at 7.30. D.G.W.C.T., Lachlan Taylor, Burnbank ; W.C.T., Andrew Dick, Enfield Place, Burnbank. Instituted 1877.

No. 309—YOUTHS' TREASURE JUVENILE LODGE. Thursday, at 6. Superintendent, John M,Ghee, 76 Main Street, Burnbank. Instituted 1877.

HAMILTON GOOD TEMPLARS' HARMONIC ASSOCIATION.

President, Charles Dick, Woodside Walk, Hamilton ; Minute Secretary, Thomas Cunningham, Low Patrick Street ; Musical Secretary, Henry Morrison, Portland Place ; Financial Secretary, Alex. Cross, Orchard Place ; Treasurer, John Cooper, High Patrick Street. Instituted 1877.

SURGEONS.

Crawford, Christopher, M.D., C.M., Auchenarden, Cadzow Street
Lennox, Walter W., M D, Auchenarden, Cadzow Street
Loudon, James, M D, Linnwood, Union Street
Marshall, John, M.D., Auchingamont
Robertson, R. T. C., M.B., L.R.C.S.E., Bent road
Turner, Robert, M.B., C.M., 46 Almada street

REGISTRAR OF BIRTHS, &c.—Wm. Moffat ; *Assist.*, Thomas Haig Moffat

BANKS AND AGENTS.

Bank of Scotland, J. C. Kay
British Linen Co., Samuel F. Simpson, John Martin, Sub-Agent
Clydesdale, David Patrick
Commercial, Thomas Smith Michie
Royal, T. J. & W. A. Dykes

INSURANCE OFFICES AND AGENTS.

Belfast Fire Co., A. Sandilands
Briton Medical and General Life, Wm. Moffat
Caledonian, E. P. Dykes, D. & J. Cassels, James Mackie, jun., Wm. Moffat, jun., and Robert Turner
City of Glasgow, J. Clark Forrest
County, D. & J. Cassels and James Mackie, jun.
Crown, J. Cunninghame Kay
Edinburgh, John Martin
English and Scotch Law Life, David Patrick
General, John Rae
Guarantee Association of Scotland, James Mackie, jun.
Guardian Fire and Life, J. H. M. Bairnsfather
Imperial Fire, Thomas S. Michie
Indisputable, William Barclay
Insurance Co. of Scotland, D. C. Barr, P. B. Mitchell, and D. N. Cross
Leeds and Yorkshire, Wm. Rankin
Life Association of Scotland, Thomas S. Michie and James Beveridge
Liverpool, London, and Globe. Wm. Pollok, H. M'Callum, and James Beveridge
London and Southwark, J. Kemp, jun
London Provident Life, Jas. Mackie, jun.
London & Provincial Horse, Carriage, and Live Stock Insurance Coy., Jas. D. Clarke, CE, Agent; John Young, M R C V S L, Inspector
Lancashire, George Kemp
Manchester Fire, J. D. Clarke
National Provincial Plate Glass, Wm. Moffat
North British and Mercantile, Keith & Patrick, J. C. Forrest, and J. C. Kay
Northern, Robert S. Christie
Norwich Union, Robert Livingstone and J. D. Clarke
Norwich and London Accident, James Beveridge and Robert Livingstone
National Provident Life, J. H. M. Bairnsfather
Phœnix, R. A. Paton
Provincial, J. G. Peat
Prudential Life, J. M'Brain and Robt. Sharp
Queen, David Patrick
Reliance, George Kemp and William Cassels
Royal, Samuel Ford Simpson
Scottish Equitable, Wm. Brown and A. Macdougall
Scottish Amicable, William Pollok
Scottish Fire, William Moffat and George Turner
Scottish Imperial, David Miller
Scottish Legal Life, James Thomson
Scottish Plate Glass Insurance Coy., James Beveridge
Scottish Provident, W. A. Dykes
Scottish Provincial, James Peebles and John Miller
Scottish Union and National, John Torrance, W. Brown & Co., Robert Archibald, and William Naismith
Staffordshire Fire, Robt. Livingstone and Wm. Cassels
Standard Life, J. B. Soutter
Sun, James Bell
United Kingdom Temp., John Tainsh
West of England, James Mackie, jun.
Westminster, Wm. Brown

NEWSPAPER.

Hamilton Advertiser, Saturday, W. Naismith, publisher

MARKETS.

Third Friday of October—Cattle and Hiring. Third Friday of April—Cattle and Hiring. Weekly Market held on Friday

---

FAST DAYS.

Summer—Thursday before second Sunday of June *Winter*—Thursday before second Sunday of December
Yeomanry Review and Races usually held early in May

FAST-DAYS.

AIRDRIE—Thursday before last Sunday of April and third Sunday of October
BIGGAR—Wednesday before third Sunday of April
CARSTAIRS—Friday before last Sunday of March and August
COATBRIDGE—Thursday before last Sunday of April and October
GLASGOW—Thursday before second Tuesday of April and Thursday before last Tuesday of October
HAMILTON—Thursday before second Sunday of June and December
LANARK—Thursday before third Sunday of April and first Sunday of November
RUTHERGLEN—Same as Glasgow
STONEHOUSE—Wednesday before fourth Sunday of January and June
STRATHAVEN—Friday before last Sunday of June and second Sunday of December
WISHAW—Thursday before third Sunday of July and November

FAIRS, CATTLE MARKETS, &c.

JANUARY

Biggar..........Last Thursday o.s.—Horses and Hiring
Glasgow........Every Wednesday, except first and third   Horses—Cattle every Thursday
Strathaven.....Thursday—General business

FEBRUARY

Carnwath.......Last Friday—Hiring
Douglas........First Wednesday
Lanark.........Last Tuesday—Seeds and Hiring

MARCH

Biggar.........First Tuesday—Seeds and general business
Carluke........Second Thursday
Douglas........Third Friday
Lesmahagow....Second Wednesday—Hiring
Peebles........First Tuesday—Hiring
Strathaven.....First Thursday

APRIL

Biggar.........Last Thursday—Horse, Hiring, &c
Carnwath.......First Wednesday
Hamilton.......Third Friday—Cattle and Hiring
Lanark.........Wednesday before first Monday—Grit Ewes and Hoggs; second Wednesday—Plants
Strathaven.....First Thursday—Cattle, Horsess, and Hiring

MAY

Airdrie........Last Tuesday
Carluke........21st—Cattle
Carnwath.......First Wednesday
Douglas........Friday after Whitsunday—Hiring
Lesmahagow....Wednesday after 11th—General business
Rutherglen.....Friday after 4th—Cows and Horses
Stonehouse.....Last Wednesday—Cows

JUNE

Biggar.........Thursday after 11th—Horses, Cattle and Pigs
Douglas........Second Wednesday o.s.—Shearers
East Kilbride..Friday after 10th
Lanark.........Monday and Wednesday before 12th—rough sheep
Leadhills......Second Friday—Cows
Muirkirk.......Second Friday—Cattle and Sheep
Rutherglen.....Tuesday after 4th
Shotts.........Third Tuesday o.s
Strathaven.....Last Thursday—Cattle

JULY

Biggar..........Third Thursday—Wool Shearers
Carnwath......First Thursday
Crawfordjohn..First Friday
Rutherglen....Friday after 25th
Stonehouse....Third Wednesday—Wool and Cows

AUGUST

Biggar..........Last Thursday—Cattle Show
Carnwath.....Second Wednesday o.s.—Lambs, &c
Chapelton......Tuesday before 12th
Douglas........Second Friday o.s.—Horse and Cattle Show
Lanark..........Wednesday before 12th—Horses; Monday and Tuesday before—Lambs; second Tuesday after—Lamb fair, black-faced crosses, and Cheviot lambs
Lesmahagow....Wednesday after Lanark—Cattle and Sheep
Rutherglen.....Friday after 25th

SEPTEMBER

Biggar..........15th if Thursday, if not, Thursday after—Horses, Cattle, &c
Douglas........First Friday

OCTOBER

Bathgate......Fourth Wednesday—Cattle
Biggar,........Last Thursday o.s.—Horses, Cattle and Hiring
Carluke........31st—Cattle
Carnwath......Friday before 31st
Douglas ....Third Friday—Servants
Hamilton......Third Friday—Cattle and Hiring
Lanark........Thursday after Falkirk Tryst—Cattle and Hiring
Strathaven....Thursday after Lanark Hiring—Cattle and Horses

NOVEMBER

Lanark........Wednesday o.s.—Cattle
Rutherglen....Wednesday before first Friday—Horses; first Friday—Cows; Friday after 25th—Horses and Cows
Shotts.........Last Tuesday o.s
Stonehouse....Last Wednesday—Cows
Strathaven.....First Thursday.

DECEMBER

Lanark.........Last Tuesday—General business
Lesmahagow...First Wednesday (if not 1st of Month) and two following Mondays

---

POPULATION.

Population of Burgh, 1861.......10,686 | Population of Parish, 1861........3,359
  Do.   do., 1871......11,496 | Do.   do., 1871........5,305

Increase in ten years in Burgh, 810, Do. in Parish, 1946

Supposed Population in Burgh and Parish in 1878, 20,000

This Burgh, with Airdrie, Falkirk, Lanark, and Linlithgow, returns one Member to Parliament. Falkirk is the returning Burgh

Municipal and Parliamentary Constituency of Hamilton, 1878..1504

John Ramsay, of Kildalton, M.P. (L)

HAMILTON POST OFFICE.
QUARRY STREET—JAMES BELL, POSTMASTER.
Box Closes For

Glasgow, ...	5.30, 9.50, 11.40, 4.55, 8.25.	
Edinburgh, ...	5.30, 9.50, 11.40, 3.40, 8.25.	
Perth, ...	5.30, 11.40 A.M., 8.25 P.M.	
London, ...	5.25 and 8.25 P.M.	
Wishaw, Blantyre, &c, ...	5.30, 9.50, 11.40, 4.55, 8.25.	
Strathaven, ...	7 A.M., 4.15 P.M.	
Stonehouse, ...	7 A.M., 5.15 P.M.	
Larkhall, ...	7 A.M., 5.15 P.M.	
Motherwell, and all parts of Lanarkshire not included in above, ...	5.30 A.M., 5.25 P.M.	
Pillar Letter-Box Collections . ..	9.15, 10.50 A.M., 3.55, 6.45 P.M.	

Sundays at 8 P.M.
Deliveries—7.15 A.M., and 4.5 and 7.20 P.M.
Telegraph Office Open from 7 A.M. till 9 P.M.
Money Orders and Savings Bank, from 9 A.M. till 6 P.M.

COLONIAL AND FOREIGN MAILS.

AUSTRALIAN COLONIES—Victoria, South Australia, Western Australia, and Tasmania; also, Queensland, New South Wales, and New Zealand, if addressed "*Via* Melbourne," Brindisi Route. Queensland; also, Victoria, New South Wales, and Tasmania, if addressed "*Via* Brisbane," Southampton Route,.................. New South Wales and New Zealand; also, Victoria, South Australia, Queensland, and Tasmania, if addressed "*Via* San Francisco," San Francisco Route,................... Queensland; also, Victoria, New South Wales, and Tasmania, if addressed "*Via* Brisbane, Brindisi Route,..................... Victoria, South Australia, Western Australia, and Tasmania; also, Queensland, New South Wales, and New Zealand, if addressed "*Via* Melbourne, Southampton Route,"
INDIA.—*Via* Southampton, every Wednesday, *Via* Brindisi, every Thursday.
CANADA.—By Canadian Packet, every Thursday, at 4.55 P.M.
UNITED STATES.—Every Tuesday, Thursday, and Saturday, 5.25 P.M.
NATAL.—Every Wednesday.
BUENOS AYRES.—*Via* Southampton, 8th and 23d of each month; by French Packet, 2d and 16th of each month, *Via* Liverpool every Monday.
These Dates and Hours are subject to Monthly Alterations.

LETTER-CARRIERS.

James Bryson, -	29 Muir Street
Thomas Scott, -	32 Brandon Street
James Colquhoun,	13 Ramsay's Buildings
William M'Ghie,	12 Ramsay's Buildings
William Polson, -	3 Ramsay's Buildings
James Aitchison,	27 Low Patrick Street (Chapelton Post)
William Harris, -	10 Ramsay's Buildings (Ferniegair)

OMNIBUS ARRANGEMENTS.

Hamilton to Motherwell, ...	9, †4.45, 6.30.
Motherwell to Hamilton, ...	†4, 7.10, 9.
Motherwell Bridge to Wishaw, ..	9.30, 12.20, 2.10, †5.10, *5.30, 7.
Wishaw to Motherwell Bridge, ..	10.24, 1.5, 4.1.
Hamilton to Wishaw, ...	9, †4.45, 6.30.
Wishaw to Hamilton, ...	†9.20, 6.30, 8.15§

†Saturdays only. *Daily, except Saturdays.

LIST OF VOTERS.—1878-79.

First Ward.

Abercrombie, William, contractor, 40 Almada street
Allan, James, bricklayer, 9 Oriel buildings, Beckford street
Allan, James, joiner, 73 Muir wynd
Allan, William, mason, 2 Fore row
Alston, Robert L., ship-owner, Newfield, Burnbank road
Anderson, Alexander, sinker, Russell's buildings, Burnbank road
Anderson, David, manager, Oakbank, Windmill road
Anderson, Robert, engine-keeper, 81 Almada street
Anderson, T. R., clergyman, Bothwell street
Andrews, Alexander, shoemaker, 39 Muir street
Archibald, Robert, writer, Burnside House
Austine, John, coalmaster, Oak Lodge, Almada street

Baird, George, mason, 95 Muir street
Baird, Malcolm, miner, 75 Almada street
Bairnsfather, John Hugh M'Intosh, solicitor, 29 Almada street
Bald, James, labourer, 35 Muir street
Ballantyne, Thomas, mason, 72 Almada street
Bannatyne, Andw., accountant, Douglas Lodge, Clydesdale street
Barclay, William, writer, Bothwell street
Barlas, John, store-keeper, 8 second block, Society buildings, Beckford street
Barr, Robert, joiner, 4 Almada street
Barrie, George, shoemaker, 14 Barrack street
Baxter, Thomas, flesher, 63 Almada street
Bell, James, postmaster, Springbank House, Windmill road
Benton, James, labourer, 66 Almada street
Binning, Hugh, plumber, 7 Muir street
Bishop, Thos. G., tea merchant, Craven Cottage, Windmill road
Bone, David, gardener, Russell's buildings, Burnbank road
Bonomy, John, junior, mason, 58 Almada street
Bowman, Thomas, manufacturer, Bellevue, Clydesdale street
Breckonridge, William, merchant, 87 Muir street
Brock, Thomas, factor, M'Alpine's buildings, Beckford street
Brown, Alexander, mason, 12 Almada street
Brown, Charles, engine-keeper, 9 Society buildings, Beckford st.
Brown, John, carter, Russell's buildings, Burnbank road
Brown, William, writer, Townfield, Clydesdale street
Brownlie, William, weaver, 87 Almada street

E

LIST OF VOTERS.—FIRST WARD.

Bryson, James, letter-carrier, 29 Muir street
Bryson, Nathaniel, printer, 4 Almada street
Buchan, Alexander G., grocer, 65 Almada street
Buchanan, Peter, wine merchant, Viewfield, Burnbank road
Bulloch, James, engineman, 51 Almada street
Burns, David, joiner, 17 Barrack street

Caird, Alexander, contractor, 1 Oriel buildings, Beckford street
Cairns, Darby, coachman, Buchanan's buildings, Barrack street
Cairns, James, tobacconist, Cairnlea, Clydesdale street
Campbell, Colin, carter, 10 Almada street
Cameron, John, Dunmore cottage, Clydesdale street
Campbell, Thomas, miner, Almada street
Campbell, William, writer, 20 Almada street
Carmichael, Peter, police inspector, 13 Society buildings, Beckford street
Cassels, John, shopman, 21 Almada street
Cassidy, Patrick, miner, 33 Muir street
Chalmers, Richard, labourer, 2 Fore row
Chalmers, Thomas, pitheadman, 21 Muir street
Chalmers, William, beadle, Auchingramont
Chassels, John, woodcutter, 2 Back row, Muir street
Chassels, William, cowfeeder, 97 Almada street
Christie, John, gardener, 2 M'Alpine's buildings, Beckford st.
Christie, John, writer, Orchard place, Bothwell road
Clark, Archibald, joiner, Oriel buildings, Beckford street
Clark, Patrick, labourer, 14 Barrack street
Clarke, Daniel, Linnview, Auchingramont
Clelland, Matthew, miner, 29 Muir street
Clifford, Andrew, miner, 69 Almada street
Cochrane, Alexander, portioner, Bellfield house, M'Ghie street
Combe, Robert, grocer, 50 Cadzow street
Cooper, Allan, weaver, 93 Almada street
Cooper, John, 1 Bothwell road
Craib, Alexander, coachman, Derry lane
Craig, John, labourer, 42 Fore row
Currie, James, smith, 71 Muir wynd

Danaher, Rev. James, Chapel house, Cadzow street
Davidson, Thos., pipe manufacturer, Brandon Villa, Bothwell rd.
Dick, James, carter, 23 Barrack street
Dick, John, carter, Muir street
Dick, William, wood merchant, Rockview Cottage, Low quarry
Dickson, John, mason, 18 Almada street
Dickson, Thomas, smith, 66 Almada street
Dobbie, John, grocer, Purdie's Buildings, Burnbank road
Donighan, James, groom, 1 Saffronhall crescent
Downie, Robert, mason, Portland place
Duncan, Hugh, timber merchant, Bellevue terr., Clydesdale st.
Duncanson, Rev. Peter C., U.P. Manse, Auchingramont

Dykes, Douglas, Auchingramont
Dykes, James A., procurator-fiscal, Alstonville
Dykes, William Alston, writer, The Orchard, Auchingramont

Edgar, Charles, missionary, Beckford street
Edward, Jas., sergeant-major, Buchanan's buildings, Barrack st.
Edwards, George, draper, 21 Almada street
England, James, warder, Buchanan's buildings, Barrack street

Fairley, George, ironmonger, Rosehill Cottage, Almada street
Fairley, Robert, upholsterer, 52 Almada street
Ferguson, Andrew, teacher, Saffronhall crescent
Ferrie, Richard, upholsterer, Muirbrow House, Muir street
Fleming, Alexander, joiner, third block, Society buildings, Beckford street
Fleming, John, grain dealer, Almada street
Forbes, Colin, plasterer, Oriel buildings, Beckford street
Forrest, John Clark, banker, Muir House
Frame, Gavin, carter, 4 Almada street
Frame, John, shopman, Paterson's buildings, Barrack street
Frame, Robert, junior, joiner, Burnbank road
Fraser, Matthew, labourer, 19 Society buildings, Beckford st.
Freer, Robert, grocer, Burnbank road
French, Henry, millwright, 7 M'Ghie street
Frew, James, ironfounder, Burnbank road
Frew, John, ironfounder, Dunrod cottage, Burnbank road
Frew, Robert, ironfounder, Russell's buildings, Burnbank road
Frew, Thomas, ironfounder, 22 Burnbank road

Gafney, Thomas, miner, Paterson's buildings, Barrack street
Gibson, James, weaver, 19 Muir street
Gilchrist, James, mason, 2 M'Ghie street
Gillon, John, sergeant, 27 Barrack street
Gilmour, James, wright, Gilmourhill, Windmill road
Gow, Adam L., clerk, 11 Barrack street
Graham, Robert, blacksmith, 19 Barrack street
Gray, John, upholsterer, 6 Society buildings, Beckford street
Green, Robert, blacksmith, Paterson's buildings, Barrack street
Greenshields, Alexander, joiner, Saffronhall crescent
Griffiths, Robert, mason, 2 Almada street
Hamilton, Abram, labourer, 92 Muir street
Hamilton, Andrew, dairyman, 71 Almada street
Hamilton, Angus, woodcutter, 84 Muir street
Hamilton, Clement M., bricklayer, 21 Almada street
Hamilton, Hugh, carter, 53 Almada street
Hamilton, James, agent, 81 Muir wynd
Hamilton, John, china merchant, 91 Almada street
Hamilton, John Adams, enginekeeper, 11 Beckford street
Hamilton, Rev. Henry Monteith, Muirhall
Hamilton, Robert, bricklayer, 29 Almada street

Harvey, Thomas, mason, 6 Almada street
Hawkins, Charles, miner, 29 Muir street
Hay, Thomas, carter, Saffronhall crescent
Henderson, Charles Greenhall, clergyman, Parsonage, Auchingramont
Henderson, John, merchant, Linnview, Auchingramont road
Henderson, Thomas, Auchingramont
Henderson, Walter, sawyer, 62 Almada street
Hepburn, James, Chantingrove
Hill, Alexander, fireman, 23 Beckford street
Hill, John, shoemaker, 6 Beckford street
Hogg, John Thomas, druggist, 23 Almada street
Howie, John, contractor, 56 Muir street

Inglis, Charles, agent, Bellevue terrace, Clydesdale street

Jackson, Daniel, clergyman, Windsor terrace
Jackson, James, sergeant, Paterson's buildings, Barrack street
Jamieson, Robert, iron dresser, 3 Society buildings, Beckford st.
Jeffrey, Thomas, hill clerk, 8 Beckford street
Jerrit, Frederick Montreal, pensioner, M'Alpine's buildings, Beckford street
Johanson, J. L., timber merchant, Dovre Villa, Clydesdale street
Johnston, John, painter, 11 Muir street
Johnstone, James, contractor, 19 Burnbank road
Johnstone, James, contractor, Beckford street
Johnstone, Robert, tailor, 14 M'Ghie street
Jones, Henry, sergeant, 15 Barrack street

Kay, James Cunningham, writer, Auchingramont
Kelly, Charles, miner, 75 Muir wynd
Kemp, Simon, painter, 73 Muir wynd
Kemp, George, auctioneer, 16 Almada street
Kemp, James, Silverwells
Kenneth, Robert, pattern maker, 26 Almada street
Keogh, Jeremiah, grocer, Paterson's buildings, Barrack street
Kerr, Duncan, miner, 1 Fore row
Kerr, Robert, weaver, 39 Muir street
Kerr, William, mason, 81 Almada street
Kirkpatrick, Roger, cashier, Closeburnville, Auchingramont
King, John, weaver, 29 Muir street

Laird, James, auctioneer, Bourtreehill, Cadzow street
Lang, David, clerk, 11 Barrack street
Lawson, John, mason, 68 Almada street
Leadbetter, James, carter, 8 M'Ghie street
Lees, John, miner, 31 Muir street
Leggate, Alexander, joiner, 56 Almada street
Leggate, Robert, joiner, 56 Almada street
Lennox, Dr Walter Walker, physician, Auchenarden, Cadzow st.

LIST OF VOTERS.—FIRST WARD.

Lewis, Alexander, platelayer, 70 Almada street
Ligertwood, Charles, tailor, 7 Beckford street
Livingstone, Robert, clerk, 18 Saffronhall crescent
Lochhead, James, baker, 8 Muir street
Loudon, James, phys cian, Linnwood, Union street
Lytle, Robert, warehouseman, Herbertfield, Burnbank road

Macindoe, William, weaver, 64 Almada street
Main, Robert, reporter, Purdie's buildings, Burnbank road
Marshall, John S., physician, Auchingramont
Marshall, Robert, contractor, 1 Barrack street
Martin, John, carter, 21 Muir street
Martin, William, mason, 70 Almada street
Mason, James, 68 Muir street
Mathieson, Kenneth, miner, 68 Almada street
Maxwell, David joiner, Douglas cottage, Douglas street.
Maxwell, James, blacksmith, Paterson's buildings, Barrack st.
Maxwell, James, joiner, Rosehill cottage, Almada street
Maxwell, William, Almada street
Maxwell, William, clerk, 99 Almada street
Meek, John, Cadzow bank
Merry, John, weigher, 48 Muir st.
Millar, John, clerk, 25 Almada street
Miller John, weigher, 29 Burnbank road
Mitchell, Adam, weaver, 8 Muir street
Mitchell, John, flesher, M'Alpine's buildings, Beckford street
Moffat William, architect, Auchingramont
Monteith John, carter, 33 Almada street
Moore, William, coachman, 1 Society buildings, Beckford street
Morgan, John, 12 Society buildings, Beckford street
Morgan, James, engineman, M'Alpine's buildings, Beckford st.
Muir, James, sergeant, 41 Muir street
Murray, John, joiner, 18 Muir street
Murray, John, tailor, 8 Beckford street
Myres, David, measurer, M'Ghie street
M'Alpine, Robert, Udston House
M'Cann, Hugh, miner, 60 Muir street
M'Carroll, Patrick, miner, M'Alpine's buildings, Beckford st.
M'Caughie, Thomas, fireman, M'Alpine's buildings, Beckford st.
M'Cauley, Andrew, gasman, 8 Quarry place
M'Cowan, David, shoemaker, 42 Fore row
M'Cready, John, railway porter, 17 Beckford street
M'Crone, James, mason, 41 Muir street
M'Donald, Donald, plasterer, 31 Muir street
M'Hardy, Captain Wallace Bruce, Bothwell street
M'Kay, George, Violetbank, Auchingramont
M'Kay, Peter, police inspector, Society buildings, Beckford st.
M'Kenna, Edward, vandriver, 19 Muir street
M'Kenzie, John, clerk, Foundry House, Burnbank road
M'Kenzie, Arch., blacksmith, Muirbank Cottage, Windmill road

LIST OF VOTERS.—FIRST WARD.

M'Kerrow, William Henry, Zambesi Cottage, Burnbank road
M'Lay, Alexander, oil and grease manufacturer, Auchingramont Cottage
M'Levie, James, miner, 27 Muir street
M'Lintock, Walter, weaver, 35 Muir street
M'Nair, Duncan, grocer, M'Alpine's buildings, Beckford street
M'Naughton, John, spirit retailer, 27 Almada street
M'Neil, Hugh, miner, 14 Barrack street
M'Pherson, John, police inspector, Society buildings, Beckford st.
M'Quade, Anthony, labourer, 35 Muir street
M'Taggart, Godfrey, carriage hirer, 74 Almada street

Naismith, Samuel, tanner, Windmill Cottage, Windmill road
Naismith, James, porter, 91 Almada street
Neilson, David, plumber, 9 Almada street
Neilson William, joiner, Saffronhall crescent

O'Neil, James, shanker, 19 Muir street

Park Joseph, miner, Society buildings, Beckford street
Park, Robert, miner, Society buildings, Beckford street
Paterson, Thomas, Hillside, Auchingramont
Paterson, William, Sheriff-clerk-depute, 119 Almada street
Peat, John Graham, architect, Portland park
Peebles, James, clerk, Crosspark, M'Ghie street
Pollock, James, smith, Wellhall road
Pollock, William, blacksmith, Oriel buildings, Beckford street
Potts, Samuel, joiner, Oriel buildings, Beckford street
Prentice, William, carter, 4 Barrack street
Purdie, John, builder, Burnbank road
Purdie, Alexander, mason, 66 Almada street

Queen, Hugh, marble cutter, 33 Muir street

Rae, John, blacksmith, M'Alpine's buildings, Beckford street
Rankine, William, sergeant, 81½ Almada street
Renfrew, Alexander, Coatshill Cottage, Stonefield, Blantyre
Rennie, Wilson, joiner, 18 Almada street
Reynard, Thomas, blacksmith, Beckford street
Ritchie, George W., colporteur, 61 Almada street
Robb, Alexander, cattle-dealer, 19 Burnbank road
Robb, James, gardener, 12 Almada street
Robb, William, cattle-dealer, Parkview House, Clydesdale street
Robbie, James, confectioner, Windsor terrace, Bothwell street
Robertson, Archibald, slater and plasterer, 21 Barrack street
Robertson, George, hatter, Mayfield Cottage, M'Ghie street
Robertson, James, joiner, 20 Miller street
Robertson, John, mason, 8 Beckford street
Robertson, John, oil merchant, Clydesdale street
Robertson, Robert, plasterer, 8 Almada street

LIST OF VOTERS.—FIRST WARD. 71

Robertson, Thomas, blacksmith, 27 Burnbank road
Robertson, William, woodcutter, 72 Muir street
Rodgers, David, grocer, 25 Almada street
Ross, Andrew, engineman, 6 Beckford street
Ross, Hugh, police inspector, Society buildings, Beckford street
Russell, Gavin, draper, Clydesdale street
Russell, George, teacher, Montreal House, Bothwell road
Russell, Henry, spirit dealer, King's Arms, Muir street
Russell, Hugh, wright, 21 Muir street
Russell, William, grocer, 23 Muir street

Saunders, John, vandriver, Oriel buildings, Beckford street
Schröder, Henry, teacher, Saffronhall place, Muir street
Scott, John L., Thorn Villa, Clydesdale street
Shaw, Anthony, cutter, Saffronhall crescent
Sherry, Thomas, carter, 65 Muir street
Simpson, George, engine-keeper, Society buildings, Beckford st.
Simpson, James C., coalmaster, Fernbank, Bothwell road
Simpson, Robert, miner, 25 Barrack street
Simpson, Samuel Ford, banker, Auchingramont
Smart, Andrew, flesher, 27 Almada street
Smellie, Lawson S., auctioneer, King's Arms, Muir street
Smellie, William, labourer, 25 Muir street
Smith, James, grocer, Auchingramont
Smith, John, fruiterer, Leggate's bdgs., Peacock Cross, Union st.
Smith, Robert, draper, Leven Villa, Auchingramont
Sommerville, Richard, mason, 70 Almada street
Sommerville, Wm., ironmonger, Roseneath Cottage, Almada st.
Soutter, Joseph Brough, solicitor, Gleniffer Villa, M'Ghie street
Spence, Henry, lithographer, 87 Almada street
Spens, Walter C., sheriff-substitute, Bellevue, Clydesdale street
Stark, Alex., engine-driver, M'Alpine's buildings, Beckford st.
Steel, Hugh, commercial traveller, Muirbank House, 30 Muir st.
Steel, James, clerk, 21 Almada street
Steel, James, engineman, Society buildings, Beckford street
Steven, William, mason, 42 Fore row
Stewart, Alexander, manufacturer, Fairfield House, Clydesdale st.
Stewart, John, miner, Russell's buildings, Burnbank road
Stewart, Robert, blacksmith, Beckford street
Strang John, engineman, 25 Beckford street
Stratton, James, inspector, M'Alpine's buildings, Beckford st.
Summers, Andrew, joiner, 41 Muir street
Summers, Robert, confectioner, 5 Bothwell road
Syme, James, carter, Beckford street

Tait, Andrew Jack, bank clerk, 2 Muir street
Tait, John, baker, 4 Muir street
Tarleton, Joseph, woodcutter, Portwell
Taylor, John, tinsmith, M'Alpine's buildings, Beckford street
Taylor, William, Douglas cottage, Douglas street

LIST OF VOTERS.—FIRST WARD.

Tennent, Andrew, miner, 14 Barrack street
Tennent, Thomas, banker, Strathaven
Ternie, James, cellarman, 31 Muir street
Thomas, William, dresser, 62 Almada street
Thomson, Anthony, mason, 24 Almada street
Thomson, John, farrier, Saffronhall crescent
Thorburn, Thomas, confectioner, The Hollies, Burnbank road
Thorburn, Willam, 13 Muir street
Torrance, John, grain dealer, 6 Bothwell road
Torrance, John, writer, Cadzow villa
Torrance, John, shoemaker, Cadzow cottage, Windmill road
Trench, Rev. Thomas, Bellfield House, M'Ghie street
Turnbull, Robert, pensioner, Paterson's buildings, Barrack st.
Turner, George, architect, 14 Almada street
Turner, William, labourer, 19 Burnbank road

Urquhart, John, Auchingramont house, Auchingramont

Walker, D., clergyman, Oakley house, Bothwell Road
Walker, John, joiner, Oriel buildings, Beckford street
Walker, John, wright, 41 Almada street
Wallace, Rev. George, clergyman, F.C. Manse, Union street
Warnock, John, grocer, 58 Almada street
Watson, James, carter, Paterson's buildings, Barrack street
Watson, John, coalmaster, Earnock
Watson, John, joiner, 3 M'Ghie street
Watson John, dairyman, Russell's buildings, Burnbank road
Watson, William, blacksmith, Wellhall road
Watt, Alexander, writer, Almada Hill
Weir, James, labourer, 25 Muir street
Weir, William, blacksmith, Almada street
Welsh, Thomas, bricklayer, Oriel buildings, Beckford street
White, Thomas, vanman, 41 Almada street
Whiteford, Joseph, miner, 14 Barrack street
Wilkins, Charles, sergeant, 70 Almada street
Williamson, William James, engineman, 18 Almada street
Willmore, John, house steward, Saffron Villa, Windmill road
Wilson, Archibald, grocer, 12 Barrack street
Wilson, James, miner, 27 Society buildings, Beckford street
Wishart, Alexander, porter, Clydesdale street
Wright, Thomas, gardener, 81 Almada street

Young, James, spirit merchant, Peacock-cross, Burnbank
Young, Geo., silk manufacturer, Bellevue Cottage, Clydesdale st.
Young, Stephen, cowfeeder, M'Ghie street

Second Ward.

Adams, James, baker, 3 Park road
Adams, James, weaving manufacturer, 23 Lamb street
Adams, John, joiner, 10 Union street
Adams, Thomas, contractor, Orchard street
Allan, Arthur, engineman, 18 Gateside street
Allan, Daniel, engineman, M'Laren's buildings, Portland place
Allan, Robert, builder, Orchard place
Anderson, Alexander, gardener, 4 Tuphall road
Anderson, David, gardener, Whiteford's buildings, Low Quarry
Anderson, John, mason, 5 Tuphall road
Anderson, James, engine-keeper, 14 Gateside street
Anderson, Thomas, mason, 48 Union street
Armour, Robert, pointsman, Allan's buildings, Portland place
Aymers, George, labourer, 24 Brandon street

Baillie, Andrew, labourer, 3½ Quarry road
Baillie, John, grocer and joiner, 28 and 30 Union street
Bain, David, plasterer, 18 Hope street
Baird, Alexander, 33 Chapel street
Baird, Archibald, ironmonger, Hopeton Cottage, Park road
Balance, George, hawker, Lamb street (dead)
Bannatyne, David, mason, 24 Union street
Barr, Duncan C., accountant, Gavinbank Cottage, Park road
Barr, John, joiner, 17 Hope street
Barr, John, shoemaker, 6 Whiteford's buildings, Low Quarry
Barrie, Andrew, saddler, 7 Union street
Barrie, David, flesher, 10 Gateside street
Barrie, William, bank clerk, Wilson's buildings, Low-waters
Bell, Alexander, joiner, M'Laren's buildings, Portland place
Bell, John, 6 Hope street
Bell, John, grain-dealer, 16 and 18 Gateside street
Bell, Peter, 12 Leechlee street
Bell, Peter, carrier, 12 Lamb street
Bell, Walter, potato-merchant, Turner's buildings, Portland pl.
Bell, John, mason, 6 Union street
Beveridge, James, accountant, 9 Union street
Binning, James, quarrier, 23 Orchard street
Bird, Jas., coachbuilder, Tainsh's buildings, Butterburn place
Black, Richard, shoemaker, Allan's buildings, Portland place
Blacklock, James, schoolmaster, Hamilton Academy, Hope st.
Blyth, Alexander, flesher, Tainsh's buildings, Butterburn place
Brackenridge, John, joiner, Chassells' buildings, Portland place
Brown, James, builder, Portland place
Brown, John, painter, 8 Orchard street
Brown, John, joiner, Ellengowan Cottage, Park road
Brown, Thomas, painter, 5 Brandon street
Brown, William, builder, Orchard place
Brownlie, James, bricklayer, 52 Union street

LIST OF VOTERS.—SECOND WARD.

Brownlie, Rennie, baker, Tainsh's buildings, Butterburn place
Brunton, Robert, coachman, 2 Chapel street
Buchanan, James, plasterer, 3 Ann street
Buchanan, James, plasterer, 28 Leechlee street
Buchanan, William, 9½ Union street
Buchanan, William, baker, 14 Quarry road
Burnes, Felix, miner, 34 Leechlee street

Cairns, John, miner, 16 Leechlee street
Campbell, John, collier, 19 Lamb street
Carlyle, John Edminston, clerk, Park road.
Chalmers, David, tinsmith, 18 Low Patrick street
Chalmers, John, shoemaker, 4 Ann street
Chassells, Mirrlees, builder, Portland place
Cherrie, Thomas, saddler, Glengyle Cottage, Portland place
Christie, Charles, clothier, 7 Cadzow buildings
Cinnamond, James, hatter, Orchard place
Coats, John, carrier, 73 Cadzow street
Connelly, Bernard, shoemaker, 13 Leechlee street
Connelly, Cornelius, labourer, 10 Quarry road
Constable, George, grocer, 57 Cadzow street
Copeland, John, joiner, Turner's buildings, Portland place
Corbet John, baker, 21 Low Quarry
Cossar, John, draper, 8 Cadzow buildings
Craig, John, weaver, 17 Union street
Craig, Robert, plasterer, 9 Brandon street
Crichton, James, contractor, Turner's buildings, Portland place
Cross, Gavin, tailor and clothier, Orchard place
Cross, George, tailor, 4 Chapel street
Cross, James, farmer, Nethershields, Chapelton
Cross, John, labourer, 19 Lamb street
Cross, Thomas, grocer, 18 and 20 Union street
Cross, William, tailor, 29 Lamb street
Craw, John, quarrier, Turner's buildings, Portland place
Crow, Alexander, mason, 44 Union street
Cullen, James, miner, 4 Hope street
Cunningham, Peter, shoemaker and house factor, M'Laren's buildings, Portland place
Currie, Alexander, plasterer, 5 Union street

Dalziel, Gavin, bill-poster, 7 Union street
Dalziel, John, shoemaker, 5 Quarry street
Davidson, Robert, mason, 10 Orchard street
Dick, James, wood-merchant, 12 Low Patrick street
Dick, John, flesher, 75 Cadzow street
Dick, Robert W., printer and stationer, 9 Cadzow buildings
Dickson, William, baker, 52 Brandon street
Dixon, Peter Watson, Tuphall
Dobbie, John, blacksmith, 33 Lamb street
Dobbie, William, quarrier, 5 Tuphall road

LIST OF VOTERS.—SECOND WARD. 75

Doherty, William, spirit-dealer, County Restaurant, Almada st.
Doyle, James, draper, Chassells' buildings, Portland place
Drummond, William, miller, Tainsh's buildings, Burnside street
Duncan, Andrew, porter, 31 Orchard street
Dunlop, Robert, writer, Ardenlea, Park road
Dunn, James, miner, 1 Park road
Dunn, William, Park road

Eglinton, William, quarrier, 20 Hope street
Evans, John, coachbuilder, Butterburn place
Ewing, Archibald, plasterer, 30 Quarry road
Ewing, John, meter-examiner, Gas Works

Fairbairn, Daniel, engineman, 13 Orchard street
Fairbairn, Thomas, artist, 10 Union street
Falconer, Alexander, labourer, 44 Brandon street
Ferguson, David, tailor, 17 Cadzow street
Ferguson, George, printer, 13 Orchard street
Ferguson, James, blacksmith, 27 Orchard street
Ferguson, John, tailor, 26 Brandon street
Ferguson, John, collier, Lamb street
Ferguson, John, weaver, 14 Gateside street
Findlay, James, mason and dairyman, 21 Lamb street
Findlay, John, plasterer, 32 Brandon street
Fisher, John, grocer, 26 Brandon street
Fleming, Gavin, spirit-retailer, 34 Gateside street
Fleming, James, cattle-dealer, 28 Gateside street
Forbes, Andrew, horse-keeper, 34 Brandon street
Forrest, Daniel, collier, 9 Lamb street
Forrest, James, tailor, 7 Union street
Forrest, William, farmer, Allanton
Fortune, George, joiner, Turner's buildings, Portland place
Frame, David, baker, Tainsh's buildings, Butterburn place
Frame, John, carter, 22 Union street
Frame, John, cowfeeder, 44 Low quarry
Frame, John, joiner, 48 Union street
Frame, John, weaver, 50 Union street
Frame, Robert, cowfeeder, 10 Lamb street
Fraser, John, slater, 17 Leechlee street
Fulton, John, van-driver, 28 Quarry road
Funston, Thomas, miner, 27 Quarry road

Gibson, James, currier, 13 Union street
Gibson, John, leather merchant, 23 Union street
Gibson, Thomas, baker, 3 Church street
Gilchrist, John, flesher, Turner's buildings, Portland place
Gilchrist, William, carter, 1 Quarry road
Gillon, James, currier, 40 Union street
Gilmour, William, portioner, Hepziebah Lodge, Park road
Gourlay, Colin, shanker, 8 Lamb street

LIST OF VOTERS.—SECOND WARD.

Gowans, Hugh, mason, Ferniegair
Gowans, William, mason, 12 Gateside street
Grant, Alexander, Rose Villa, Brandon street

Hamilton, Andrew, saddler, 55 Cadzow street
Hamilton, Daniel, superintendent of markets, Park road
Hamilton, Hugh, joiner, 15 Hope street
Hamilton, James, flesher, 22 Brandon street
Hamilton, James, grocer, 24 Brandon street
Hamilton, James, watchmaker, 6 Ann street
Hamilton, James, wright, 10 Union street
Hamilton, John, lace-agent, 23 Lamb street
Hamilton, John, quarrier, 16 Gateside street
Hampton, John, baker, 7 Tuphall road
Hardy, John, labourer, 32 Chapel street
Harris, William, quarrier, 22 Leechlee street
Hart, James, tailor, 29 Orchard street
Hawkins, Alexander, vanman, 14 Chapel street
Hawkins, Robert, miner, 14 Chapel street
Hamilton, James, joiner, 3 Park road
Hamilton, John, mason, Allan's buildings, Portland place
Hamilton, John, joiner, Brown's buildings, Quarry road
Heard, Archibald, mason, Brown's buildings, Quarry road
Henderson, John, builder, Portland place
Henry, Andrew, clerk, 6 Quarry road
Henry, William, grocer, 2 Union street
Higgans, Hugh, dairyman, 26 Brandon street
Higgins, James, engineer, Park road
Holman, William, baker, 28 Quarry road
Hood, John, pointsman, 60 Union street
Horn, John, labourer, 27 Quarry road
Houston, William, miner, Hope street (left)

Jack, Arthur, plasterer, 10 Lamb street
Jones, Charles, shoemaker, 2 and 4 Park road
Johnstone, Alexander, joiner, Whiteford's buildings, Low Qry.
Johnstone, Andrew, 14 Orchard street
Johnstone, Andrew, pointsman, 4 Hope street
Johnstone, George, vanman, Whiteford's buildings, Low Quarry

Kay, Andrew, plasterer, 13 Hope street
Kay, George, baker, 25 Lamb street
Kemp, Charles, painter, 28 Chapel street
Keith, Patrick, writer, Clydesdale Bank, Cadzow street
Kellar, Alexander, Bent cottage
Kelly, Edward, beadle, 52 Union street
Kerr, James, portioner, 48 Union street
Kinnon, Thomas, causewayer, 24 Gateside street
Kirkland, Robert, labourer, 12 Leechlee street
Kirkland, Robert, weigher, 6 Lamb street

LIST OF VOTERS.—SECOND WARD. 77

Kirkpatrick, Robert, station-master, Templehall, Gateside street
Kirkwood, Thomas, blacksmith, M'Laren's buildings, Portland place

Laidlaw, Archibald, accountant, Brown & Henderson's buildings, Portland place
Lambie, Robert, shoemaker, 1 Ann street
Leggate, Arthur, portioner, Strathaven
Leggate, James, carter, 21 Leechlee street
Leishman, John, inspector, Brown & Henderson's buildings, Portland place
Lewars, Robert, miner, 5 Leechlee street
Lightbody, Thomas, engineer, Turner's buildings, Portland pl.
Lindsay, Archibald, baker, 12 and 14 Union street
Lindsay, Donald, pitheadman, 13 Lamb street
Lindsay, John, mason, 10 Chapel street
Lindsay, John, porter, 24 Quarry road
Lindsay, William, miner, Burnside
Lightbody, Robert, baker, 6 Ann street
Little, James, quarrier, 4 Hope street
Lochore, William, quarrier, Robertson's buildings, Portland pl.

Mackay, Alexander, joiner, Turner's buildings, Portland place
Mair, Archibald, joiner, Robertson's buildings, Portland place
Martin, John, banker, Lochside cottage, Bent road
Martin, John, road surfaceman, 29 Orchard street
Mathieson, Daniel, miner, 10 Quarry road
Mathieson, Thomas, carter, 27 Quarry road
Maxwell, David, cork-cutter, 24 Campbell street
Meickle, Robert, flesher, 22 Campbell street
Meickle, Robert, junior, flesher, Spalding's buildings, Chapel st.
Menzies, Thomas, painter, Turner's buildings, Portland place
Menzies, Walter, green grocer, Allan's buildings, Portland place
Miller, Robert, coachbuilder, 14 Orchard street
Miller, Robert, miner, 36 Quarry road
Miller, Thomas, blacksmith, 46 Union street
Miller, William, cooper, 16½ Campbell street
Miller, William, carter, 17 Orchard street
Miller, William, joiner, 40 Brandon street
Milligan, Thomas, miner, 15 Union street
Mitchell, James, missionary, 13 Union street
Mitchell, Peter B., Islay Cottage, Bent road
Mitchell, William, plumber, 28 Chapel street
More, Alexander, weaver, 42 Brandon street
Morrison, Henry, slater, Chassells' buildings, Portland place
Morton, John, storekeeper, M'Laren's buildings, Portland place
Mowbray, John, portioner, Brandon Cottage, Orchard street
Muir, Robert, joiner and haberdasher, M'Laren's buildings, Portland place
Murphy, James, causewayer, 12 Chapel street

LIST OF VOTERS.—SECOND WARD.

Murray, Adam, miner, 3 Tuphall road
Murray, Francis, jun., Bellridden cottage, Park road
M'Beath, Robert, miner, M'Laren's buildings, Portland place
M'Brain, James, insurance agent, Park road
M'Call, James, joiner, 6 Ann street
M'Cowan, James, shoemaker, 22 Campbell street
M'Creadie, William, wright, 30 Chapel street
M'Culloch, William, shoemaker, 28 Chapel street
M'Dermid, Charles, watchman, 21 Quarry road
M'Dermot, William, labourer, 10 Quarry road
M'Donald, Alexander, Foreman joiner, 6 Tuphall road
M'Geechan, John, tailor, Chassells' buildings, Portland place
M'Ghie, Gavin, baker, Taylor's buildings, Chapel street
M'Ghie, Thomas, joiner, 13 Union street
M'Gourlick, John, miner, 16 Lamb street
M'Gregor, John, quarrier, 9 Tuphall road
M'Guiness, Joseph, miner, 8 Leechlee street
M'Ginnis, Michael, carter, 9 Leechlee street
M'Kinnes, James, gardener, 14 Hope street
M'Kay, Alexander, constable, 11 Union street
M'Kay, John, constable, 3 Cadzow buildings, Cadzow street
M'Kay, Lewis, clerk, Brandon Cottage, Orchard Street
M'Laughlan, John, labourer, Leechlee street
M'Lauchlan, William, labourer, 18 Leechlee street
M'Lellan, Robert, labourer, 32 Quarry road
M'Clements, John, spirit-dealer, 20 Brandon street
M'Master, John, shopman, 9 Brandon street
M'Murray, Alexander, blacksmith, 15 Orchard street
M'Naughton, Wm., grain-merchant, Douglas Gdns., Uddingston
M'Neil, Thomas, miner, Tainsh's buildings, Butterburn place
M'Phie, John, labourer, 29 Orchard street

Naismith, William, printer, The Priory, Townhead street
Nicol, Andrew, spirit-merchant, 2 Lamb street
Nicol, William, cowfeeder, 13 Brandon street
Nicol, William, screeman, 56 Union street
North, Andrew, miner, Robertson's buildings, Portland place
Nugent, George, quarrier, 15 Leechlee street

Parker, Absalom, draper, 12 Brandon street
Paterson, Gavin, calenderer, Lochside House, Bent road
Paterson, John, painter, 6 Hope street
Paterson, John, quarrier, 14 Quarry road
Paterson, Thomas, grocer, 49 Low Quarry
Paterson, William, builder, Park road
Patrick, William, labourer, 25 Leechlee street
Penman, George, grocer, 39 Quarry road
Penman, Matthew, mason, Turner's buildings, Portland place
Pollok, William, writer, Park road
Potter, John, warder, 13 Union street

Prentice, James, baker, 2 Orchard street
Prentice, John, pit manager, Robertson's bdgs., Portland place

Rae, John, tinsmith, 2 Brandon street
Ramsay, Robert, pitheadman, 32 Gateside street
Ramsay, Thomas, miner, 9 Tuphall road
Ramsay, William, miner, 23 Orchard street
Reid, Peter F., news-agent, &c., M'Laren's bdgs., Portland place
Rennie, William, 50 Union street
Robertson, James, tailor, 13 Lamb street
Robertson, Robert Thim Craig, M.D., Bent road
Robertson, William, joiner, Barleath cottage, Gateside street
Ronald, Alexander, constable, 3 Cadzow bdgs., Cadzow street
Rose, David, manufacturer of export clothing, Park road
Ross, James, miner, 7 Leechlee street
Rowat, George, gardener, 29 Campbell street
Roy, Robert, pitheadman, 11 Quarry road
Russell, George, weaver, 48 Union street
Russell, James, quarrier, 26 Leechlee street
Russell, Thomas, quarrier, 18 Campbell street
Russell, George, tailor, 41 Quarry road

Scott, Andrew, draper, 41 and 43 Low quarry
Scott, John, contractor, 2 Parklea, Park road
Scott, Robert, painter, Robertson's buildings, Woodside walk
Scott, Robert, twister, 26 Gateside street
Scott, Thomas, postman, 32 Brandon street
Scott, Thomas, draper, 41 and 43 Low quarry
Shearer, John Mackie, weaver, 44 Brandon street
Shearer, Robert, broker, 12 Lamb street
Sime, Robert, miner, 6 Lamb street
Simpson, Alexander, engineman, 3 Union street
Simpson, James, carting contractor, 11 Hope street
Simpson, Thomas, engineman, 1 Hope street
Sinclair, Andrew, plumber, M'Laren's buildings, Portland place
Siseman, John, dairyman, Chassells' buildings, Portland place
Small, Edward, pawnbroker, 9 Castle street
Smellie, William, cowfeeder, 12 Hope street
Smith, Alexander, inspector of poor, 11 Brandon street
Smith, John, grocer, 9 Orchard street
Smith, Malcolm, mason, 11 Hope street
Spalding, William, labourer, 8 Lamb street
Steel, James, carting contractor, 10 Tuphall road
Steel, John, drysalter, Bothwell
Steven, George, carter, 7 Orchard street
Steven, William, 24 Leechlee street
Stevenson, Thomas, rope-spinner, 1 Ann street
Stewart, Andw., grocer, Brown & Henderson's bdgs., Portland pl.
Stewart, Andrew, mason, 21 Orchard street
Stewart, William, church-officer, 1 Chapel street

LIST OF VOTERS.—SECOND WARD.

Stewart, William, constable, 16 Hope street
Stewart, William, gardener, 8 Union street
Stirling, John, junior, Fairburn cottage, Park road
Strachan, David, farmer, Laighstone Hall
Strang, Robert, portioner, 35 Quarry street
Sturge, Hiram, 28 Chapel street
Summers, Mark, pitheadman, Turner's buildings, Portland place
Swan, William L., game-dealer, Allanbank
Symington, Andrew, greengrocer, Cadzow bdgs., Cadzow street

Tainsh, John, senior, confectioner, Quarryhall
Taylor, Archibald, plumber, 18 Chapel street
Taylor, James, joiner, 5 Hope street
Taylor, Matthew, weaver, 16 Lamb street
Taylor, Robert, plasterer, 44 Union street
Tennent, James, cattle-dealer, &c., 17 Brandon street
Thomson, James, insurance agent, 5 Union street
Todd, John, weaver, 11 Leechlee street
Todd, William, weaver, 11 Leechlee street
Totan, James, vanman, Tainsh's buildings, Burnside
Turner, Archibald, joiner, 3 Brandon street
Turner, James, mason, Turner's buildings, Portland place
Turner, Robert, mason, Turner's buildings, Portland place

Wallace, George, surfaceman, 20 Quarry road
Wallace, John, labourer, 10 Quarry road
Walker, George, porter, 31 Orchard street
Walker, James, engineer, Threshalea, Portland place
Walker, William, Tainsh's buildings, Butterburn place
Wardrope, John, grocer, Main street, Wishaw
Wardrobe, John, labourer, 16 Lamb street
Warnock, William, tailor, 20 Hope street
Watson, James, carter, Whiteford's row, Low Quarry
Watson, James, labourer, 4 Chapel street
Watson, John, shoemaker, 3 Tuphall road
Weir, Alexander, grocer, Chassells' buildings, Portland place
Weir, Thomas W., grocer, Portland place
Wheelan, James, weaver, 12 Quarry road
White, William, brassfounder, 22 Chapel street
Whiteford, Adam, flesher, 50 Quarry street
Whiteford, Andrew, labourer, 54 Brandon street
Whitehouse, Henry, weaver, 12 Quarry road
Wilkie, Alexander, joiner, Orchard place
Wilkie, James, joiner, 12 Orchard street
Wilson, Andrew, 6 Orchard street
Wilson, George, labourer, Lamb street
Wilson, John, pitheadman, Portland place
Wilson, Robert, printer, 4 Ann street
Wiseman, James, watchmaker, 4 Hope terrace
Wightman, John, sawyer, Whiteford's row, Low Quarry

Young, John, smith, 24 Chapel street
Young, John, junior, V.S., 24 Chapel street
Yuill, James, baker, Robertson's buildings, Portland place

Third Ward.

Adams, David, mason, 23 Holmes street
Adams, James, joiner, 23 Holmes street
Adams, John, schoolmaster, Clydesdale street
Aitchison, David, 19 Low Patrick street
Aitchieson, Henry, weaver, 27 Low Patrick street
Allan, Andrew, painter, 29 Low Patrick street
Allan, James, confectioner, 7 Duke street
Alston, Thomas, grocer, 90 Townhead street
Anderson, Daniel M'A., agent, 1 Holmes street
Anderson, James, agent, 1 Holmes street
Anderson, James, coachman, 4 St. John's lane

Baillie, Alexander, gardener, Silvertonhill
Bain, John Fleming, musicseller, 38 Townhead street
Baird, Thomas, portioner, Udston Mains
Ballantyne, James, mason, 35 Portland place
Ballantyne, John, Woodlands gate
Ballantyne, John, baker, 9 Duke street
Ballantyne, William, blacksmith, 26 Portland place
Barr, John, lathsplitter, 17 High Patrick street
Barrie, Andrew, tanner, 11 Haddow street
Barrowman, James, fireman, 3 Low Patrick street
Bell, James, late carrier, 76 Townhead street
Bell, James, miner, 5 Portland place
Bell, William, fruit merchant, Royal buildings, Duke street
Beveridge, James, pit engineer, 2½ Low Patrick street
Black, David, merchant, Portland place
Blaney, Dennis, miner, 11 Low Patrick street
Brannagan, Robert, miner, 12 Low Patrick street
Brakenridge, David, Portland park
Brodie, Robert, grocer, 3 Low Patrick street
Brown, James, goods porter, 28 James street
Brown, William, painter, 29 Gateside street
Brownlie, Gavin, miner, 23 James street
Brownlie, James, miner, 7 Baillie's causeway
Brunton, Thomas, plasterer, Lawrie place, Baillie's causeway
Brydon, Thomas, goods porter, 1 St. John's lane
Buchanan, Andrew, manufacturer, 21 Low Patrick street
Buchanan, James, 19 Low Patrick street

Cairnon, Andrew, labourer, 39 Gateside street

F

LIST OF VOTERS.—THIRD WARD.

Cameron, Duncan, lace agent, 6 Holmes street
Campbell, John, baker, 14 Townhead street
Campbell, John, joiner, 29 Gateside street
Campbell, John, pitheadman, 25 Portland place
Canfield, Thomas, agent, London street, Larkhall
Carruthers, Dougal, joiner, 1 Holmes street
Cassels, Andrew, merchant, Gowanlee Cottage, Park road
Cassels, John, merchant, Auchingramont
Cassels, William, junior, clerk, Silverray, Portland park
Chalmers, Thomas, shoemaker, 29 Duke street
Clark, George, miner, 9 Portland place
Clark, James D., engineer, Sommerville place, Quarry street
Clark, John, blacksmith, 53 Quarry street
Clark, Peter, miner, 14 Low Patrick street
Clark, Peter, grocer, 61 Quarry street
Clelland, James, grazier, Portland cottage, Portland place
Cochrane, Nathaniel, shoemaker, Sommerville place, Quarry st.
Colquhoun, William, weaver, 13 Ramsay's buildings
Cooper, Richard, weaving agent, 26 High Patrick street
Cornes, Henry, quarryman, 19 Portland place
Cornock, James, shoemaker, 40 High Patrick street
Corns, Thomas, quarryman, Gateside street
Cowan, Hope, goods porter, 6 John street
Cowan, William, confectioner, Mackie's buildings, Quarry st.
Craig, David, enginekeeper, 17 High Patrick street
Craig, James, labourer, 33 High Patrick street
Craig, James, weaver, 9 Ramsay's buildings
Crawford, Alexander, weaving agent, 9 Woodside walk
Crawford, James, commercial traveller, 9 Woodside walk
Crawford, James, carter, 7 Duke street
Crawford, John, clerk, Robin's buildings, Portland park
Cross, David, spirit-retailer, 89 Quarry street
Cross, Robert, labourer, 6 Portland place
Cross, William, tailor, 18 Townhead street
Cullen, James S., superintendent of police, 77 Quarry street
Cunningham, James, painter, 28 High Patrick street
Cunninghame, John, shoemaker, 13 Low Patrick street
Cunningham, Robert, corkcutter, Sommerville place
Cunninghame, William, corkcutter, 6 Low Patrick street
Cunninghame, William, goods clerk, 7 John street
Currie, William, wright, 8 Woodside walk
Cuther, Jacob, miner, 4 Portland place
Cuther, John, miner, 5 Portland place

Dallas, David, currier, 7 Portland place
Dalziel, William, town-officer, 58 Townhead street
Dick, Charles, mason, 2 Woodside walk
Dick, Thomas, flesher, 12 Duke street
Dickson, William, goods porter, 13 James street
Donald, David, weaver, 21 High Patrick street

LIST OF VOTERS.—THIRD WARD.

Donald, Robert, portioner, Portland park
Doyle, Hugh, broker, 42 Townhead street
Drysdale, David, mason, 2 Portland place
Duncan, William, grocer, Nisbet's buildings
Dykes, John Joseph, Woodside cottage

Ferguson, Thomas, porter, Laurie place, Duke street
Ferrie, Christopher, quarryman, 19 Gateside street
Finlay, William, pointsman, 12 John street
Fisher, James, joiner, Portland park
Fisher, John, cooper, 23 Gateside street
Fisher, John, joiner, Portland park
Fisher, Thomas, joiner, Portland park
Fleming, William, joiner, 13 Holmes street
Fletcher, William, grocer, Portland park
Forrest, Alexander, smith, 23 Portland park
Forrest, James, weaver, 14 Low Patrick street
Forrest, Samuel, joiner, 34 Portland place
Forsyth, Alexander, miner, 9 Holmes street
Frame, William, grocer, 21 Duke street
Frame, William, post-runner, 5 St John's lane
Fraser, Andrew, plasterer, 11 Holmes street
Fulton, James, painter, 6 Low Patrick street
Fulton, Robert, slater, 1 Haddow street

Gall, George W., engineer, 5 St. John's lane
Gardiner, John, cowfeeder, 12 Miller street
Gardiner, William, carter, Miller street (dead)
Gardiner, William, gardener, 20 High Patrick street
Gardiner, William, gardener, 25 Low Patrick Street
Gardner, Henry, tobacconist, Marybank place, Quarry street
Gibson, John, mason, 6 Duke street
Gilchrist, Archibald, grocer, Sommerville place, Quarry street
Glass, James, beamer, 14 Low Patrick street
Glenny, Thomas, blacksmith, 21 High Patrick street
Graham, William, labourer, 3 Haddow street
Granger, James, lace-manufacturer, 13 John street

Haddow, James, mason, Beechwood Cottage, Portland place
Haley, James, draper, Marybank place, quarry street
Hamilton, Alexander, mason, 11 Woodside walk

Hamilton, Andrew, sinker, 2 Duke street
Hamilton, James F., grocer, 2 Townhead street
Hamilton, John, greengrocer, 31 Duke street
Hamilton, John, tailor and clothier, 32 Townhead street
Hamilton, Joseph, dealer, 14 Baillie's causeway
Hamilton, Thomas, miner, 2 Duke street
Hamilton, Thomas, clerk, Portland park
Hamilton, Thomas, compositor, 6 High Patrick street

Hamilton, William, grocer, 28 Townhead street
Hamilton, William, law clerk, 6 St. John's lane
Hamilton, William, teacher, Portland park
Hanline, James, grocer, Robin's buildings, Portland park
Hanna, David, miner, 18 Miller street
Harcus, Sinclair, joiner, Robertson's buildings, Woodside walk
Hargrave, Joseph, clerk, Hawthorn villa, Portland park
Harris, George, senior, pitheadman, High Patrick street
Harris, George, junior, 40 High Patrick street
Harris, William, postman, 10 Ramsay's buildings
Haughie, Hugh, hawker, 56 Townhead street
Hay, Robert, flesher, Garvald villa, Portland park
Henderson, James, weaver, 3 Woodside walk
Henderson, John, mason, 18 Holmes street
Henry, David, quarrier, 15 Portland place
Hewitt, Thomas, gardener, 35 Gateside street
Holmes, James, farmer, Cornsilloch, Dalserf, Carluke
Hunter, James, Royal Hotel, Quarry street
Hunter, James, miner, 9 Gateside street

Inglis, Alexander, joiner, 9 Nisbet's buildings, Baillie's causeway
Irvine, John, miner, 13½ High Patrick street

Jack, Andrew H., tailor, 9 Nisbet's buildings, Baillie's causeway
Jackson, Daniel, cowfeeder, 16 James street
Johnstone, William, borer, 9 Portland place

Kay, George, miner, 9 Portland place
Keefe, Michael, coachman, Royal buildings, 12 Duke street
Kemp, John, painter, 75 Quarry street
Kemp, John, painter, 76 Townhead street
Kemp, Simon, painter, Mackie's buildings, Quarry street
Kerr, Robert, joiner, 11 Miller street
Kilpatrick, David, Portland place
Kilpatrick, John, hammersmith, 4 Low Patrick street
Kirk, David F., printer, Brevier cottage, Portland park
Kirkland, James, grocer, Windmillhill, Motherwell

Lang, Alexander, 3 Portland park
Lawrie, John, quarrier, 16 John street
Lawson, Thomas, mason, 12 John street
Lightbody, Thomas, 38 High Patrick street
Loudon, John, grocer, 8 Low Patrick street

Mackie, James, collector, 5 Holmes street
Mackie, James, junior, accountant, Royal buildings, Duke st.
Mackie, Robert, gardener and church officer, 17 Miller street
Mackie, William, saddler, Royal buildings, Duke street
Martin, Alexander, carter, 37 Low Patrick street
Martin, James, weaver, 11 Nisbet's buildings, Baillie's causeway

Martin, Thomas, merchant, 9 High Patrick street
Mason, James, grocer, Portland park
Mather, James A., Spencerside, Townhead street
Maxwell, John, labourer, 26 Portland place
Miller, David, writer, 1 Quarry street
Miller, Robert, junior, saddler, 40 Townhead street
Miller, Thomas, labourer, 15 High Patrick street
Miller, William, grocer, 11 John street
Mitchell, William, plumber, 22 Quarry street
Mochrie, Robert, grocer, 79 and 81 Quarry street
More, James, Commercial buildings, Townhead street
Muir, Alexander, pie baker, 11 Quarry street
Murphy, Patrick, labourer, 58 Townhead street

M'Cabe, John, teacher, Brevier cottage, Portland park
M'Cormick, Charles, carter, 21 Low Patrick street
M'Donald, Donald, platelayer, 8 John street
M'Donald, John, 11 James street
M'Dougall, Robert, miner, 13 High Patrick street
M'Farlane, Rev. John T., Spencerfield
M'Ghie, William, postman, 11 Ramsay's buildings
M'Ghie, William, slater, 4 Woodside walk
M'Gregor, Daniel, labourer, 26 Portland place
M'Gregor, John, weaver, 5 Haddow street
M'Guire, Patrick, miner, 1 Woodside walk
M'Intosh, Richard, druggist, 43 Cadzow street
M'Intyre, James, weaver, 15 High Patrick street
M'Kee, Samuel, joiner, 31 Portland place
M'Kendrick, William, miner, 13 High Patrick street
M'Kendrick, William, jun., miner, 13 High Patrick street
M'Lintock, William, china merchant, 15 Gateside street
M'Munn, John, woodcutter, 9 James street
M'Naught, Peter, carter, 39 Gateside street
M'Naughton, James, collier, 17 Holmes street
M'Nay, Joseph, station-master, Mackie's buildings
M'Pherson, John, miner, 16 Portland place
M'Queen, Henry, labourer, 7 Gateside street
M'Ready, James, mason, 8 Woodside walk
M'Walter, David, guard, 13 James street

Naismith, James, Justice of the peace clerk, 25 James street
Naismith, James, miner, 12 Low Patrick street
Naismith, William, weaver, 5 Portland place
Napier, Daniel, 15 Low Patrick street
Neilson, George, labourer, 6 High Patrick street
Neilson, George, policeman, 16 Low Patrick street
Nicol, James, green-grocer, 27 Duke street
Nicol, John, spirit merchant, 27 and 29 Gateside street
Nimmo, David, draper, 19 Duke street
North, John, clerk, Taylor's buildings, Chapel street

LIST OF VOTERS.—THIRD WARD.

O'Donald, John, miner, 28 James street
Orr, Thomas, engineman, 6 High Patrick street
Orr, William, toy shop, Lawrie place, Duke street

Park, William, tailor, 10 Miller street
Paterson, James, quarrymaster, Duke street
Paterson, James, spirit merchant, Lilybank, Wellhall road
Paterson, John tinsmith, Sommerville place, Quarry street
Paterson, William, blacksmith, 36 Townhead street
Patrick, David, writer, Woodview, Burnbank
Pettigrew, John, Craighead lodge, by Hamilton
Polson, William, letter-carrier, 3 Ramsay's buildings
Prentice, Robert, joiner, 23 High Patrick street
Prentice, Robert, labourer, 13 High Patrick street
Prentice, William, 3 Low Patrick street

Rennie, James, tailor, 33 Gateside street
Riddle, John, mason, 17 Portland place
Robb, Allan, baker, 23 Duke street,
Robertson, Archibald, Robertson's buildings, Woodside walk
Robertson, William, 1 Holmes street
Robertson, William, joiner, Barleath Cottage, Gateside street
Ross, William, pitheadman, 17 Holmes street
Rowatt, John, fireman, 18 Low Patrick street
Russell, Andrew, tailor, 29 Duke street
Russell, John, Woodside house
Russell, Thomas, shoemaker, 12 James street

Sandilands, Andrew, sheriff-officer, 17 Nisbet's buildings, Baillie's Causeway
Sandridge, Thomas, miner, 39 Gateside street
Scott, Alexander, joiner, 7 Haddow Street,
Scott, James, clerk, 12 Ramsay's buildings
Scott, James, mason, 29 Duke street
Scott, Robert, storekeeper, Lawrie place, Baillie's causeway
Selkirk, Thomas, wood merchant, 78 Townhead street
Selkirk, William, joiner, 7 Haddow street
Sharpe, James, jun., blacksmith, 43 Townhead street
Shepherd, James, quarrier, 39 Gateside street
Simpson, James, flesher, 9 Duke street
Sinclair, George, commission agent, Park cottage, John street
Small, Leonard, joiner, 4 Baillie's causeway
Small, Patrick, pawnbroker, 9 Castle street
Smart, James, enginekeeper, Lawrie place, Duke street
Smellie, James, road surfaceman, 28 Portland place
Smith, James B., merchant, Mackie's buildings, Quarry street
Smith, John, hostler, 92 Townhead street
Smith, John, weaver, 29 Duke street
Smith, William, sen., agent, 5 Miller street
Square, John, coachbuilder, 19 Holmes street

Steel, Robert, weaver, 29 Low Patrick street
Steel, William, agent, 2 St. John's lane
Steven, George, house factor, 44 Townhead street
Steven, John, mason, 15 High Patrick street
Stevenson, John, ropespinner, 77 Townhead street
Summers, John, mason, 17 Holmes street
Summers, John, pitheadman, 7 Portland place
Summers, Robert, mason, 22 Portland place

Tainsh, John, junior, 3 Holmes street
Taylor, Alexander, slater (adjoining ropework) Baillie's causeway
Templeton, Archibald, grocer, Sommerville place, Quarry street
Tevan, John, porter, 23 James street
Thomson, David, pitheadman, 33 High Patrick street
Thomson, David, grocer, 41 Gateside street
Thomson, George, shoemaker, 2 Duke street
Thomson, James, coachwright, 8 Duke street
Thomson, William, pit joiner, 31 High Patrick street
Thomson, William, carter, 18 Miller street
Twaddle, James, pointsman, 6 John street

Waddell, William, baker, 9 Holmes street
Walker, James, engineer, Threshalea Cottage, Portland place
Wallace, William, carriage hirer, 1 John street
Wardrop, David, carriage hirer, 1 Townhead street
Watson, Robert, 77 Quarry street
Wheeling, James, Duke street
Wheeling, Walter, cloth manufacturer, and spirit merchant, 12 Holmes street
Whiskers, William, miner, 9 James street
Whiteford, James, labourer, 36 High Patrick street
Wilkie, William, painter, Kingston cottage, Woodside walk
Wilkison, John, joiner, 13 Gateside street
Wilson, David, baker, 50 Townhead street
Wilson David, miner, 18 Portland place
Wilson, Francis, wright and grocer, 25 Portland place
Wilson, James, weaver and grocer, 26 High Patrick street
Wilson, John, farmer, Blackbog
Wilson, John, weaver, 6 John street
Wilson, John Alexander, grocer, 36 Townhead street
Wilson, Thomas, plasterer, 33 Gateside street
Wood, William, schoolmaster, Clydesdale College
Wright, John, bootcloser, 5 Haddow street

Young, David, miner, 9 Baillie's causeway
Young, James, porter, 10 John street
Young, James, sheriff-officer, 1 Quarry street
Young, Thomas, bar-officer, 9 Holmes street
Young, William, enginekeeper, 7 Haddow street

FOURTH WARD.

Adams, John, chimney-sweeper, 21 Church street
Aitchieson, Adam, chemist, 6 Quarry place
Aiton, John, smith, 16 Quarry street
Aiton, William, baker, 9 Chapel street
Allan, William, merchant, 28 Cadzow street
Allan, William, presser, 8 Quarry place
Arnott, Andrew, upholsterer, 9 Chapel street

Banner, Bernard, miner, Wide close, 37 Church street
Barrie, John, miner, 3 Young street
Begg, Alexander, grocer, 6 Back-o'-barns, and 38 Church street
Bell, Thomas S., draper, 31 Cadzow street
Binning, James, broker, 49 Castle street
Binning, Robert, bookbinder, 45 Townhead street
Brerton, Thomas, 13 New wynd
Brown, John, spirit dealer, 55 Townhead street
Brown, Robert, tinsmith, 1 Quarry street
Brown, William, plumber, 6 Quarry place
Brown, William, tinsmith, 36 Castle street
Brownlie, William, grocer, Grammar school square
Bruce, James, Castle street
Bruce, James, fruiterer, 35 Cadzow street
Bruce, John, spirit merchant, Postgate
Bulloch, William, spirit retailer, 25 Campbell street
Burns, Robert, labourer, 23 Campbell street
Burns, Thomas, gasman, 9 Chapel street

Cairns, John, portioner, 5 Church street
Cairncross, Alexander, florist, 23 Cadzow street
Cairncross, James, florist, 23 Cadzow street
Cameron, James, lathsplitter, 69 Townhead street
Cameron, John, eating-house keeper, 47 Townhead street
Cameron, William, grocer, Brown's buildings, Quarry street
Campbell, Ananias, poultry merchant, 43 Campbell street
Campbell, William, plumber, 3 Chapel street
Cassels, William, spirit merchant, 37 Castle street
Cassells, Thomas B., tailor, 46 Quarry street
Cassidy, William, labourer, 2 Young street
Cathcart, Charles, miner, 16 Young street
Chalmers, William, spirit dealer, 4 Quarry street
Chassels, John, clothier, Brown's buildings, Quarry street
Clarkson, John, fruiterer, 4 Quarry place
Collins, Bernard, labourer, 13 Grammar school square
Connor, John, labourer, 46 Church street
Cooper, Peter, sergeant, Burgh police, 4 Quarry place
Cooper, Thomas, 1 Bothwell road
Conway, Peter, carter, 13 Postgate
Corbet, Robert, shoemaker, 51 Townhead street

Corrigan, Daniel, miner, 9 Young street
Cosgrove, Thomas, coachtrimmer, 5 Campbell street
Cowper, William, clothier, 82 Cadzow street
Crawford, Joseph, coachbuilder, 19 Church street
Cross, Alexander, weaver, 41 Townhead street
Cruickshanks, Francis, draper, 3 Cadzow street
Currie, James, plasterer, 4 Quarry place
Currie, William, gardener, 2 Edinburgh road
Cunningham, Alexander, chimney-sweeper, 24 Church street

Dalziel, John, joiner, Crawford's buildings, Townhead street
Dalziel, William, labourer, 51 Townhead street
Davidson, James, contractor, 41 Campbell street
Dick, John, tobacconist, 6 Quarry street
Dick, Robert, flesher, 27 Cadzow street
Dick, Robert, junior, flesher, 20 Cadzow street
Docherty, Thomas, broker, 53 Castle street
Dodds, Michael, miner, 68 Castle street
Donnelly, Patrick, hawker, 36 Church street
Donnelly, William, labourer, 7 Sheilinghill
Douglas, Robert, shopman, 8 Quarry place
Doyle, Hugh, broker, 42 Townhead street
Dunlop, James, merchant, 28 Cadzow street
Durrenan, John, 17 New wynd

Ewart, James, pitman, 4 Quarry place

Ferguson, Allan, miner, 9 Campbell street
Ferguson, David, tailor, 17 Cadzow street
Ferguson, James, inland revenue officer, Wddiefield, Baillie's causeway
Findlay, Robert, coachman, 6 Quarry place
Finlayson, Alexander, grocer, 63 Townhead street
Finlayson, Matthew, carrier, 21 Chapel street
Fleming, Thomas, draper, 7 Townhead street
Fletcher, George, grocer, Turner's buildings, Portland place
Forrest, Charles, tailor, 25 Church street
Forrest, Henry, tailor, 29 Campbell street
Forrest, William, tailor, 6 Church street
Forsyth, James, spirit merchant, 4 Church street
Fotheringham, William, miner, 1 Blackswell
Frame, Robert, grocer, 10 Castle street
Fraser, Alexander, tailor, 11 Townhead street
Freebairn, Charles, rope-spinner, 34 Quarry street

Gardiner, James Waterston, cooper, 2 Castle street
Grindall, William, coachbuilder, 19 Church street

Hamilton, Andrew, Castlehill crescent
Hamilton, James, auctioneer, 11 Campbell street

LIST OF VOTERS.—FOURTH WARD.

Hamilton, James, weaver, 51 Townhead street
Harris, John, postman, 13 Church street
Hawkins, James, miner, 9 Campbell street
Henderson, Alexander, grocer, Wharrie house, 44 Muir street
Hendry, David, tobacconist, 42 Cadzow street
Henshilwood, James, labourer, 7 Chapel street
Hillan, Hugh, restaurant, 16 and 18 Quarry street
Hinds, John, grocer, 31 Church street
Hood, James, spirit retailer, 1 Castle street
Hunter, Edward, spirit retailer, 36 Quarry street
Hunter, Matthew, police constable, 8 Hope street

Inglis, Rev. John, Manse, Blackswell

Kane, Dennis, hawker, 34 Church street
Keith, James, grocer, Marionfield, Castlehill crescent
Keith, Henry, Huttonbank, Townhead street
Kelly, James, broker, 59 Castle street
Kemp, Thomas, mason, 2 Young street
Kennan, Michael, 9 Grammar school square
King, William, Motherwell

Leonard, Peter, miner, Castle street
Lightbody, John, baker, 58 Cadzow street
Lynch, Peter, miner, 1 Postgate

Mackie, John, hedger, 25 Church street
Mackie, John, cowfeeder, 49 Townhead street
Mackill, Robert C., druggist, 56 Cadzow street
Malone, Martin, labourer, 10 Grammar school square
Marr, William C., tailor, 8 Castle street
Mason, John, baker, 48 Church street
Mather, William, Townhead house, Townhead street
May, Michael, blacksmith, 5 Sheilinghill
Michie, Thomas S., banker (Commercial Bank), Cadzow st.
Miller, Robert, joiner, 11 Sheilinghill
Minto, Thomas, hotel keeper (Douglas and Clydesdale Hotel), Townhead street
Morrison, Alexander, ironworker, 18 Church street
Murdoch, John, miner, 60 Townhead street
Murphy, Patrick, labourer, 17 Back-o'-Barns
Murray, Henry, restaurant keeper, Brown's buildings, Quarry place, Quarry street

M'Auly, John, baker, 13 Church street
M'Beth, Robert, miner, 41 Townhead street
M'Call, Archibald, joiner, 13 Church street
M'Cusker, Bernard, labourer, 10 Grammar school square
M'Evoy, James, commission agent, 25 Castle street
M'Fail, John, miner, 4 Quarry place

LIST OF VOTERS.—FOURTH WARD.

M'Farlane, Robert, weaver, 11 Young street
M'Geechan, Charles, tailor, 17 Townhead street
M'Ghie, Richard, miner, 58 Townhead street
M'Ginlay, Charles, spirit dealer, 33 Castle street
M'Gown, John, labourer, 13 Young street
M'Guire, James, labourer, Wide close, 37 Church street
M'Guire, Charles, miner, 16 Young street
M'Guire, Owen, labourer, 4 Sheilinghill
M'Guire, William, miner, Wide close, 37 Church street
M'Intosh, Charles, New Wynd
M'Laren, John, painter, &c., 26 Castle street and 7 Cadzow st.
M'Nish, Joseph, barber, 20 Quarry street
M'Phail, Matthew, currier, 49 Townhead street
M'Taggart, William, labourer, 2 Sheilinghill
M'Queen, Norman, dentist, 33 Cadzow street

Naismith, John, miner, 9 Young street
Naismith, John, tanner, Windmill cottage, Windmill
Naismith, Gavin, tinsmith, 21 Cadzow street
Nicol, James, broker, 47 Castle street

O'Hara, Martin, labourer, 10 Grammar school square
O'Neil, Edward, labourer, 51 Castle street

Paterson, George, master of works, 1 Edinburgh Road
Paterson, James, spirit dealer, 8 Young street
Paterson, James, draper, 33 Townhead street
Paterson, Thomas, waggon builder, 10 Church street
Paton, Hugh, miner, 28 Church street
Paton, Robert A., ironmonger, 36 Cadzow street
Pettigrew, William, weaver, 33 Church street
Pomphrey, John, carriage hirer, Quarry street
Prentice, John, contractor, 52 Quarry street

Ramsay, Thomas, 41 Church street
Rankin, James, 14 Castle street
Rankin, John, 12 Castle street
Rankin, Thomas, nursery and seedsman, 12 Castle street
Reilly, James, labourer, 19 Young street
Reilly, Thomas, Campbell street
Reilly, Michael, miner, 43 Castle street
Robertson, William, boot closer, 12 Young street
Robin, Robert, Castlehill
Rocks, John, broker, 57 Castle street
Rogers, George, grocer and spirit merchant, 29 Chapel street
Ross, Charles, painter, 81 Townhead street
Ross, David, miner, 9 Campbell street
Ross, William, baker, 66 Cadzow street
Rowan, John, shoemaker, Cadzow street (dead)
Russell, Archibald, coalmaster, Wishaw House

Russell, John, potato dealer, 30 Portland place

Sands, John, rag-dealer, 70 Castle street
Sands, John, hawker, Castle street
Scott, Adam, stationer, 44 Quarry street
Scott, James, gardener, 11 Church street
Scott, John, cowfeeder, 49 Townhead street
Sharpe, James, veterinary surgeon, 43 Townhead street
Shearer, Robert, late innkeeper, Spence's buildings, Quarry st.
Small, Joseph, pawnbroker, 9 to 17 Castle street
Smart, James, coalmaster, Angus lodge
Smith, Alexander, postman, 2 Quarry place
Smith, Henry, carter, 6 Church street
Smith, Robert, grocer, Castlehill crescent
Smith, Robert A., Castlehill crescent
Sommerville, James, cooper, 12 Quarry street
Spalding, Colin, hotelkeeper, Commercial Hotel, Townhead st.
Spence, James, fruiterer, 4 Cadzow street, and 42 Quarry street
Steel, John, grocer, Church street
Stevenson, John, rope-spinner, 77 Townhead street
Stewart, Andrew, rope-spinner, 3 Blackswell
Stewart, David, lath-splitter, 71 Townhead street
Stewart, John, druggist, 18 Cadzow street
Stirling, Charles, coachbuilder, 5 Bothwell road
Stirling, John, senior, coachbuilder, 3 Campbell street
Stobo, Archibald, labourer, 25 Church street
Struthers, Andrew, cattle dealer, 2 Quarry place
Swan, Alexander, enginekeeper, 33 Chapel street

Taylor, Alexander, mineral factor, Staneacre
Taylor, Alexander, plasterer, 6 Quarry place
Taylor, Lachlan, plumber, Craigview, Burnbank road
Templeton, Robert, coachman, 6 Quarry place
Thomson, Noble, carter, 16 Church street
Thomson, Robert, draper, 13 Cadzow street
Torrance, Thomas, shoemaker, 70 Cadzow street
Toner, John, broker, 35 Castle street

Waddell, James, innkeeper, County Hotel, 22 Cadzow street
Warren, John, spirit dealer, 10 Campbell street
Watson, John, china merchant, 44 Church street
Welsh, John, fishmonger, 21 Castle street
White, Alexander, baker, 2 Campbell street
Willans, Richard, cab driver, 11 Chapel street
Willoughby, William, labourer, 6 Young street
Wilkinson, Robert, grocer, 31 Castle street
Wilson, David, fodder dealer, 8 Church street
Wilson Henry, hairdresser, 12 Cadzow street
Wilson, John, slater, 29 Campbell street
Wright, James, joiner, 23 Church street

Wright, James H., bookseller, 37 Cadzow street
Wright, John, joiner, 22 Church street
Wright, Joseph, baker, 33 Church street
Wylie, John, grocer, Garnocklea, Auchingramont

Young, John, blacksmith, 6 Church street
Young, Thomas, restaurant, 60 Quarry street
Yuille, Alexander D., shopman, 11 Campbell street

Extended Burgh.

Aitken, John, miner, Gladstone street, Burnbank
Alexander, Robert, blacksmith, Low-waters
Allan, George, Burnbank terrace, Burnbank
Allan, Robert, shoemaker, Glasgow road
Andrews, Robert, miner, Whitehill road
Arbuckle, William, Gladstone street, Burnbank
Arbuckle, William, engineman, Ann street, Burnbank

Ballantyne, James, labourer, Wellhall bridge
Bannatyne, Andrew, quarryman, Low-waters
Barrie, James, Ann street, Burnbank
Barrie, William, clerk, Low-waters
Beggs, Robert, miner, Low-waters
Berry, William, miner, Maryfield place, Low-waters
Bertram, William, farmer, Greenfield
Birrell, William, miner, Gladstone street, Burnbank
Blair, Alexander, miner, Whitehill road
Blyth, Archibald, manager, Bent colliery
Brown, David, dealer, Greenfield place
Brown, Michael, Gladstone street, Burnbank
Brown, William, miner, Bent road
Brownlie, Claud, cowfeeder, Low-waters
Brownlie, James, thatcher, Low-waters
Brownlie, William, miner, Low-waters
Bruce, John, miner, Burnbank terrace, Burnbank

Campbell, Charles, Burnbank
Campbell, Samuel H., grocer, Glasgow road (dead)
Carr, Andrew, carter, Glasgow road
Cassells, William, spirit merchant, Low-waters
Clifton, James, labourer, Greenfield
Cockburn, John, Low-waters
Coffey, Joseph, Glasgow road
Cook, Robert, Gladstone street, Burnbank
Cook, William, miner, Whitehill road

LIST OF VOTERS.—EXTENDED BURGH.

Cooper, Alexander, labourer, Greenfield
Corbett, Matthew, Burnbank
Crozier, John, labourer, Low-waters
Cowan, John, quarrier, Low-waters
Craig, Alexander, farmer, Udston
Craig, James, Ann street, Burnbank
Craig, John, miner, Low-waters
Craig, John, farmer, Udston
Craig, William, farmer, Udston
Crichton, Lawson, miner, Whitehill road
Cullen, Walter, Burnbank
Cullen, Walter, miner, Glasgow road
Cuthbertson, Robert, miner, Low-waters
Cuthbertson, Thomas, miner, Low-waters

Dalgliesh, Henry, Hilton Bank, Wellhall road
Dalziel, John, Gladstone street, Burnbank
Davidson, Thomas, Glasgow road
Delaney, John, Ann street, Burnbank
Devine, Robert, miner, Whitehill road
Dick, David, carter, Low-waters
Dickson, George, Burnbank terrace
Docherty, Bernard, miner, Robertson's buildings, Low-waters
Docherty, John, miner, Gladstone street, Burnbank
Docherty, Thomas, miner, Burnbank
Dogan, William, miner, Robertson's buildings, Low-waters
Donald, William, plumber, Greenfield place
Donnachy, John, Glasgow road
Downie, John, drainer, Robertson's buildings, Low-waters
Dyet, James, miner, Greenfield road
Dyet, Robert, miner, Greenfield road

Eadie, William, miner, Greenfield road

Fairley, John, smith, Low-waters
Fairley, John, junior, smith, Low-waters (dead)
Farrell, James, Gladstone street, Burnbank
Fegan, John, shoemaker, High Blantyre road
Finlayson, John, Glasgow road
Fox, Felix, labourer, Gladstone street, Burnbank

Gault, James, bricklayer, Bent road
Geddes, Thomas, junior, spirit-dealer, Eddlewood buildings, Low-waters
Gibson, Peter, miner, Whitehill road
Gibson, William, spirit-dealer, Low-waters
Gilchrist, James, Burnbank terrace
Gillespie, James, Glasgow road
Gillespie, Robert, Glasgow road
Gonogal, John, High Blantyre road

LIST OF VOTERS.—EXTENDED BURGH.

Goodwin, John, carter, High Blantyre road
Gordon, Robert, moulder, Bent road
Gowans, Alexander, builder, Gowans' buildings, Low-waters
Gowans, Walter, joiner, Low-waters
Graham, William, grocer, Low-waters
Gray, Robert, miner, Gladstone street, Burnbank
Gunn, John, miner, John street, Greenfield

Hall, John, miner, Greenfield road
Halliday, John, Gladstone street
Halliday, Martin, platelayer, Greenfield place
Hamilton, George, Adjutant, Burnbank House
Hamilton, James, mason, Bent road
Hamilton, William, joiner, Bent road
Hamilton, William, miner, Gladstone street, Burnbank
Hamilton, William, Robertson's buildings, Low-waters
Harley, William, flesher, Fairley's buildings, Low-waters
Hastie, James, manager, Greenfield
Heatherington, William, blacksmith, Whitehill road
Hogg, Robert, greengrocer, Low-waters

Irvine, Joseph, miner, Low-waters

Jackson, George, Burnbank terrace
Jeffrey, Thomas, Ann street, Burnbank
Johnstone, Archibald, Windsor street, Burnbank
Johnstone, James, miner, Glasgow road
Johnstone, John, labourer, Maryfield place, Low-waters

Kelly, Edward, pitheadman, Whitehill road
Kergan, William, china merchant, Glasgow road
Keswick, William, sinker, Whitehill road
Kilpatrick, James, Gladstone street, Burnbank
King, Robert, joiner, Burnbank terrace.
Kirkpatrick, Alexander, of Allanshaw
Kyle, James, tailor, Gowans' buildings, Low-waters

Laird, James, Gladstone street, Burnbank
Lang, John, Glasgow road
Lang, John, enginekeeper, Burnbank terrace
Leggate, John, miner, Greenfield
Lindsay, James C., shoemaker, Barnfield cottage, Low-waters

Mackie, John, hedger, Low-waters
Marshall, Peter, miner, Whitehill road
Marshall, William, labourer, Burnbank terrace
Miller, Alexander, joiner, Victoria place, Burnbank
Miller, Matthew, miner, Whitehill road
Mitchell, Alexander, Ardenclutha
Mitchell, John, Glasgow road

LIST OF VOTERS.—EXTENDED BURGH.

Moffat, John, joiner, Bent road
Moore, James, Gladstone street, Burnbank
Morrison, David, Gladstone street, Burnbank
Morton, Alexander, bricklayer, John street, Greenfield
Muir, Thomas, Gladstone street, Burnbank
Muir, Thomas, miner, Gladstone street, Burnbank
Murdoch, James, shanker, Robertson's buildings, Low-waters.
Murphy, Edward, miner, Low-waters
Murphy, Thomas, miner, Low-waters
Murray, William, High Blantyre road
M'Alpine, Robert, builder, Udston
M'Alpine, William, bricklayer, Burnbank terrace
M'Arthur, Roderick, miner, Burnbank terrace
M'Cafferty, John, miner, Whitehill road
M'Cartney, Hugh, surfaceman, Low-waters
M'Cormick, William, baker, Glasgow road
M'Donald, Alexander, M.P., Wellhall
M'Donald, Robert, miner, Whitehill road
M'Fadyane, Hugh, Gladstone street, Burnbank
M'Graw, John, miner, Low-waters
M'Kenna, Patrick, John street, Greenfield
M,Killop, John, Windsor street, Burnbank
M'Kinlay, J. High Blantyre road
M'Leish, John, Glasgow road
M'Lure, Robert, pensioner, Whitehill road
M'Neil, Neil, miner, Windsor street, Burnbank
M'Neill, Archibald, Glasgow road
M'Neill, Robert, Glasgow road
M'Phail, Daniel, miner, Burnbank terrace
M'Pherson, Neil, miner, Ann street, Burnbank
M'Skimming, James, quarryman, Low-waters (left)
M'Taggart, Thomas, Ann street, Burnbank

Naismith, John, leather-merchant, Maryfield cottage, Low-wtrs.
Naismith, John, miner, John street, Greenfield
Naismith, Thomas, miner, Burnbank terrace

O'Hare, John, sinker, Whitehill road
O'Neill, James, grocer, Greenfield place

Park, Dugald, Glasgow road
Park, George, bricklayer, Windsor street, Burnbank
Paterson, James, Wellhall road
Paterson, James, labourer, Bent road
Paterson, Rev. T. M. B., Greenbank, Wellhall road
Paterson, Robert, cooper, Low-waters
Peacock, James, Ann street, Burnbank
Pinkerton, Robert, quarryman, Gowans' buildings, **Low-waters**
Purdie, J. builder, quarry, Greenfield
Purdie, W., builder, quarry, Greenfield

LIST OF VOTERS.—EXTENDED BURGH.

Rae, Allan, miner, Low-waters
Ramsay, James, miner, Whitehill road
Rankin, John, joiner, Bent road
Rankin, Robert, Gladstone street, Burnbank
Rankin, Thomas, nurseryman, Allanshaw
Renwick, John, weaver, Low-waters
Reynard, Henry, gardener, Burnbank
Robertson, George, joiner, Burnbank
Robertson, John, builder, Burnbank
Robinson, Robert, Burnbank terrace
Russell, James, engine-keeper, Bent road
Russell, James, miner, Burnbank
Russell, John, miner, Low-waters

Scobbie, John, Gladstone street, Burnbank
Scott, John, Greenfield
Scott, Joseph, miner, Burnbank
Smith, John, blacksmith, Burnbank terrace
Sorbie, Thomas, miner, Maryfield place, Low-waters
Spiers, William, labourer, Gladstone street, Burnbank
Steel, John G., grocer, Gowan's buildings, Low-waters
Stevenson David, blacksmith, Glasgow road
Stewart, Charles, joiner, Glasgow road
Struther, James, manufacturer, Chantinghall
Summers, William, miner, Gladstone street, Burnbank

Taylor, Lachlan, brassfounder, Greenfield
Thomas, William, Glasgow road
Tonner, Michael, miner, John street, Greenfield

Waddell, George, miner, Greenfield
Walker, Hugh, shanker, Robertson's buildings, Low-waters
Wallace, John, miner, Gladstone street, Burnbank
Warnock, James, farmer, Auchingramont
Warnock, John, farmer, Auchingramont
Watt, David, Glasgow road
Watt, Robert, bricklayer, Burnbank terrace
Weir, John labourer, Greenfield place
Welsh, John, gardener, Bent road
Westwater Andrew, merchant, Greenfield place
Whitehouse, Henry, weaver, Low-wters
Whitehouse, John, quarryman, Maryfield place, Low-waters
Wilson, Duncan, spirit dealer, Low-waters
Wilson, George, miner, Whitehill road
Wilson, James, wright, Low-waters
Wilson, John, grocer, Bent road
Wiseman, Donald, mason, Gowan's buildings, Low-waters
Woodward, Thomas, merchant, Victoria place, Burnbank.
Wotherspoon, Thomas, farmer, Hillhouse

G

GENERAL DIRECTORY.

HIGH AND LOW BLANTYRE.

Adam, C. & W., joiners, High Blantyre
Adams, Thomas, grocer and provision merchant, Stonefield
Adamson, Lawrence W., Rosebank cottage, Blantyre
Agnew, Mrs, fruiterer, Larkfield, High Blantyre
Aitkenhead, John, grocer, Hunthill
Aitkenhead, J. & R., builders, Hunthill, High Blantyre
Alexander, James, shoemaker, High Blantyre
Anderson, Alexander, Wheatlandhead farm, High Blantyre
Anderson, J., haircutter, Hart's buildings, Stonefield
Anderson, John, grocer, Stonefield
Anderson, William, cement works, Calderside, High Blantyre

Bannatyne, Colonel, Millheugh, High Blantyre
Bannatyne, Mrs, Millheugh, High Blantyre
Barr, James, baker, High Blantyre
Barr, James, draper, High Blantyre
Barron, Thomas, grocer, M'Alpine's buildings, Stonefield
Begg & Son, H., blacksmiths, High Blantyre
Beveridge, Robert, grocer, Stanley place, Stonefield
Black, Henry, greengrocer, Springwell, Blantyre
Blackley, William, baker and spirit merchant, Causeystane, High Blantyre
Blackwood, James, Greencroft, High Blantyre
Blantyre Bowling Club—Green, Stonefield road
Brown, Brothers, Messrs, painters and decorators, M'Alpine's buildings, Stonefield
Brown, Mrs Dr, Elderbush cottage, High Blantyre
Brown, James, saddler, Auchinraith, High Blantyre
Brown, T. J., Springfield cottage, Stonefield, Low Blantyre
Brown & Son, Archibald, ironmongers, Stonefield
Bruce, James, spirit merchant, Larkfield, High Blantyre
Bryson, John, Low Blantyre Store
Buchanan, John, grocer and spirit merchant, Woodburn place, Stonefield
Buchanan, John, grocer, Stonefield road
Burnett, Andrew, contractor, Craigmuir colliery, **High Blantyre**
Burns, Mrs, dairy, Larkfield, High Blantyre

Cameron, Duncan, flesher, Woodburn place, and spirit merchant, Glasgow road, Stonefield
Campbell, Matthew, nurseryman, Auchinraith, High Blantyre
Chambers, William, joiner and builder, Springwell. House—The Flat, Motherwell
Clark, Charles, carter, Avon buildings, Stonefield
Clark, Mrs, grocer, Larkfield, High Blantyre
Clark, R. A., confectioner, Commercial place, Stonefield road
Clark, Walter, of Crossbasket, High Blantyre
Clelland, George, Greenblairs farm, High Blantyre
Clelland, T. & E., grocers, Auchinraith, High Blantyre.
Coats, John, Blantyre farm, High Blantyre
Coats, John, spirit merchant, Stonefield
Cochrane, J. R., Calder Glen
Cochrane, J. & R., Birdsfield brick works, High Blantyre
Cook, William, Janefield Cottage, High Blantyre
Cook, William, wine and spirit merchant, Stonefield
Craig, Albert, grocer, Springwell place
Craig, Allan, wine and spirit merchant, High Blantyre
Craig, Archibald, Birdsfield farm, High Blantyre
Craig, James, grocer, Stonefield road
Craig, James, haircutter, M'Alpine's buildings, Stonefield
Craig, John, Bellsfield farm, High Blantyre
Currie, Alexander, stationer, Gardiner's place, High Blantyre

Dalgleish & Kerr, weaving factory, Low Blantyre
Davidson, Robert, Auchinraith saw mills, Blantyre
Deans, Gavin, baker, Stonefield
Dickson, John, lime merchant, Newfield, High Blantyre
Dickson, Robert, Broomhouse farm, High Blantyre
Dixon (Limited), W. S., Blantyre collieries; manager—James Watson, Side cottage; cashier—Neil Douglas, Side cottage
Dobbie, John, tailor, M'Alpine's buildings, Stonefield
Douglas, Neil, cashier, Side cottage, High Blantyre
Downie, Dr, Park villa, Apothecary Hall, Stonefield
Downie, William, grocer and spirit merchant, Kirkton, High Blantyre
Duncan, James, baker, Woodburn place, Stonefield
Dunlop, W. T., grocer, Kirkton, High Blantyre
Dunlop & Co., Colin, Craigmuir colliery, High Blantyre
Dunlop & Co., James, Park colliery, High Blantyre

Fegan, Hugh, pawnbroker, Grimson's buildings, Stonefield
Ferguson, Brown, Haughhead farm, High Blantyre
Fern, Mrs, grocer, Larkfield, High Blantyre
Fisher, David, manager, gas-works, Stonefield road
Fleming, John, draper and grocer, Auchinraith, High Blantyre
Ford, George, spirit merchant, Springwell buildings, Stonefield
Forrest, Alex., spirit merchant, Hart's buildings, Stonefield
Forrest, C. & A., contractors, Larkfield, High Blantyre

Fowler, Peter, draper, Gardiner's place, High Blantyre
Frame, Thomas, Blantyre Park Farm
Frame, William, carter, Grimson's buildings, Stonefield
Frawley, Rev. Thomas, Roman Catholic Chapel
Fullarton, Robert, Cemetery keeper, High Blantyre

Galbraith, Isabella, fruiterer and confectioner, High Blantyre
Gardner, Andrew, spirit merchant, Auchinraith, High Blantyre
Gardiner, John, Newmains Cottage, High Blantyre
Gardiner, Robert, ironmonger, High Blantyre
Geddes, Thomas, junr., grocer, M'Alpine's buildings, Stonefield
Getty, Walter, saddler, Stanley place, Stonefield
Gilmour, Andrew, grocer and spirit merchant, Stonefield
Gow, Mrs, Holmston
Graham, Andrew, dairy, Stanley place, Stonefield
Grant, Dr., Apothecary hall, Gardiner's place, house—Springfield Cottage, High Blantyre
Grant, Dr, surgery, Grimson's buildings, Stonefield
Gray, John, greengrocer, Springwell buildings, Blantyre
Gray, Robert, merchant, Stonefield

Hamilton, Daniel, grocer, Springwell place, Blantyre
Hamilton, James, Blantyre works Farm
Hamilton, James, Newhouse farm, High Blantyre
Harris, George, registrar and postmaster, High Blantyre
Hart, Thomas, tobacconist, Hart's buildings, Stonefield
Hart, William, ironmonger, plumber and gasfitter, Hart's buildings, Stonefield
Harvey, William, spirit merchant, Springwell buildings, Stonefield.
Hastie, David, contractor, Stonefield Farm
Hastie, John, ironmonger, Gardiner's place, High Blantyre
Hay, John George, Post Office, Low Blantyre
Hay, John, farmer, Auchintibber, High Blantyre
Hazeals, James, plumber and gasfitter, High Blantyre
Henderson, Robert, clothier, Stonefield
Hendrie, John, grocer and shoemaker, Hendrie place, High Blantyre
Hepburn, William, shoemaker, Commercial place, Stonefield rd.
Hill, James, tailor and clothier, Turner's buildings, Stonefield
Hogg, J. & G., Stonefield Medical Hall, Avon buildings, Stonefield
Houston & Co., C. N., drapers, Stonefield
Howie, John, dairy, Grimson's buildings, Stonefield
Hunter, Smart, spirit merchant, Auchintibber

Jackson, Alexander, Barnhill farm, High Blantyre
Jackson, Mrs, Old place, High Blantyre
Jackson, Mrs, Rosebank Cottage, Low Blantyre
Jackson, James, of Bardykes, Low Blantyre

Jackson, John, Blantyre farm, High Blantyre
Jackson, John, Stonefield store
Jackson, Thomas, Blantyre Park farm, High Blantyre
Jackson, William, of Blantyre park, High Blantyre
Jamieson, Andrew, engineer, Stonefield
Jenkins, Samuel, tailor, Auchinraith, High Blantyre
Jures, Matthew, greengrocer, M'Alpine's buildings, Stonefield

Kerr, Robert, Woodhouse
Kirkpatrick, Andrew, stationmaster, Caledonian Railway Station

Laing, Alexander, fruiterer, Stonefield road
Laird, Alexander, colliery manager, Side cottage, H. Blantyre
Laird, Charles, grocer, Auchintibber, High Blantyre
Lang, John S., house factor, and insurance agent, Springwell buildings, Stonefield
Lee, Alexander, grocer, Hunthill, High Blantyre
Lees & Co., boot and shoemakers, Broompark place, and Gilmour's place, Stonefield. Factory—Maybole
Little, John, fruiterer, Stonefield road
Loudon & Co., J., grocers and provision merchants, Larkfield, High Blantyre

Marshall, William, grocer, Commercial place, Stonefield road
Maxwell, John, shoemaker, Auchinraith, High Blantyre
Merry & Cuninghame, Auchinraith Collieries. William Wilson, manager; John Stewart, cashier
Michie, A. G., stationmaster, C.R. Station, High Blantyre
Miller, Alexander, Blantyre saw mills, Stonefield
Minigle, Thomas, grocer, Causeystane, High Blantyre
Minto, R. S., watchmaker and jeweller, Stonefield road
Mitchell, Isabella, news-agent, Stonefield road
Mitchell & Forrest, joiners, Stonefield
Monaghan, James R., saleroom, Larkfield, High Blantyre
Monteith & Co., Henry, dye works.—John Strathearn, manager. John Laing, cashier
Moore, J. W., of Greenhall, High Blantyre
Morris, Mrs M., dairy, M'Alpine's buildings, Stonefield
Muir, Hugh, flesher, Commercial place, Stonefield road
Muir, James, Broompark farm, High Blantyre
Muir, Robert, draper and clother, High Blantyre
Muirhead & M'Lean, Misses, dressmakers, Springwell buildings, Stonefield
Murdoch, Mrs Robert, Haughhead farm, High Blantyre
M'Alpine, Robert, Stonefield brick works
M'Arthur, J., railway inspector, School lane, High Blantyre
M'Caffrie, John, wine and spirit merchant, Springwell place Blantyre
M'Call, Alexander, ironmonger, Turner's buildings, Stonefield
M'Callum, Hugh, Agent of Clydesdale Bank, Blantyre

M'Callum, Robert, grocer, High Blantyre
M'Clusky, John, pawnbroker, Woodburn place, Stonefield
M'Cormick, James, West Neuk, High Blantyre
M'Donald, Patrick, sale rooms, Hart's buildings, Stonefield
M'Donald, Rev. Robert, Free Church Manse, Low Blantyre
M'Dougall, W. C., F.C. missionary, Burnbank
M'Gregor, John, of Neilson, Shaw, and M'Gregor, Glasgow, Hyde Park, High Blantyre
M'Guire, Angus, grocer, Gardiner's Place, High Blantyre
M'Harg, James, Orchardhead Cottage, High Blantyre
M'Intyre, Miss, spirit merchant, Auchinraith, High Blantyre
M'Kendrick, Allan, carter, Hart's buildings, Stonefield
M'Kerrow, Hugh, grocer, Auchintibber, High Blantyre
M'Kinnon, Charles, Boweshill
M'Lelland, James, blacksmith, Auchinraith, High Blantyre
M'Murray, John, Barnhill Tavern, Barnhill, High Blantyre
M'Nair, William, spirit merchant, Kirkton, High Blantyre
M'Naughton, David, spirit merchant, Stanley place, Stonefield
M'Neill, Nigel, F.C. missionary, Stonefield
M'Tyre, Alexander, Craigknowe Farm
M'William, Alexander, Craigmuir farm, High Blantyre
M'William, Thomas, Greenhall farm, High Blantyre

Naismith, James, of Coatshill, Low Blantyre
Naismith, John, grocer, Auchinraith, High Blantyre
Ness, John, The School-house, Low Blantyre
Nimmo, John, grocer and draper, Nimmo's buildings, Stonefield
Nisbet, William, sale room, Hart's buildings, Stonefield
Oliver, R. W., draper, Grimson's buildings, Blantyre

Pairman, Alexander, grocer, Low Blantyre
Pate, Alexander Stewart, grocer, Springfield, High Blantyre
Paterson, James, Blantyre House
Penman, W. & L., funeral undertakers and carriage hirers Causeystane, High Blantyre
Pettigrew, William, Priory Villa, Low Blantyre
Pollock, Robert, contractor, Glebe cottage, High Blantyre
Prentice, W. A., watchmaker and jeweller, Auchinraith, High Blantyre

Rae, Robert, sale room, Nimmo's buildings, Stonefield
Rae, William, grocer, Stonefield road
Reid, James, Blantyre Lodge, Low Blantyre
Reid, William, Calderside farm, High Blantyre
Renfrew, Alexander, Coatshill Cottage, Stonefield, Low Blantyre
Renfrew, Alexander, Shott farm, High Blantyre
Riddock, Alexander, missionary, United Presbyterian Church, Glasgow road
Roberts, William, spirit merchant, Glasgow road, Low Blantyre
Robertson, David, Coatshill Farm

Robertson, Peter, grocer, Springwell place, Blantyre
Robertson, Robert, joiner and builder, Larkfield, High Blantyre

Scott, Mrs, Basket farm, High Blantyre
Scott, Mrs, Blantyre farm, High Blantyre
Scott, John, of Boathouse
Scott, Thomas, Priestfield Farm, High Blantyre
Scott, William, grocer, Stonefield
Scott, William, stationer, Grimson's buildings, Stonefield
Shanks, James (of Arthur & Co., Glasgow), Greengairs Cottage
Shaw, Robert, of Thornhill, Low Blantyre
Sillar, William, Inspector of poor and sanitary Inspector, High Blantyre
Smart, Alexander, Brownlee House, Low Blantyre
Smellie, Mrs, spirit merchant, High Blantyre
Smith, John, sale room, M'Alpine's buildings, Stonefield
Smith & Miller, drapers, Stonefield road
Somerville, William, Blantyre oil works, Stonefield
Sprott, Robert, boot and shoemaker, Springwell bdgs., Stonefield
Sprowl, Mrs, Brownlee House, Low Blantyre
Sprowl, John, boot and shoemaker, High Blantyre
Steel, William, Woodburn Cottage, Low Blantyre
Steven, Robert, market gardener, Low Blantyre
Stewart, Robert, slater and plasterer, Auchinraith, H. Blantyre
Strachan, John, shoemaker, High Blantyre
Struthers, James, shoemaker, High Blantyre
Struthers, J. B., spirit merchant, High Blantyre
Struthers, Mrs, carter, Auchinraith, High Blantyre
Struthers & M'Hutchison, grocers and spirit merchants, Stonefield

Taylor, David H., spirit merchant, Auchentibber, H. Blantyre
Taylor, J., boot and shoemaker, Stonefield road
Templeton, John, blacksmith, Barnhill, High Blantyre
Templeton, William P., blacksmith, High Blantyre
Thomson, John, flesher, Gardiner's place, High Blantyre
Todd, John, baker, Commercial buildings, Stonefield road
Topping, R. M., Brownlee cottage, Glasgow road, Blantyre
Topping & Co., R. M., ironfounders, Stonefield Foundry

Walker, James, joiner, Glasgow road, Blantyre
Warnock, David, joiner, Springfield, High Blantyre
Warnock, Hugh, Laichlyock farm, High Blantyre
Warnock & Walker, joiners, High Blantyre
Watson, Arthur, grocer, Commercial place, Stonefield road
Watson, James, colliery manager, Side cottage, H. Blantyre
Watson, Jane, grocer, High Blantyre
Weir, John, Blantyre park, High Blantyre
Weir, Mrs, Braehead, High Blantyre
Wheelan, James, baker, Larkfield, High Blantyre
Williamson, Thomas, Priestfield Farm, High Blantyre

Wilson, Hugh, grocer and grain merchant, Auchinraith, High Blantyre
Wilson, Robert, plasterer, Causeyshot, High Blantyre
Wright, Rev. Stewart, E.C., The Manse, High Blantyre
Wylie, J. & A., fleshers, Stonefield
Wyllie, Rev. William, pastor, Evangelical Union Church

Young, Alexander, spirit merchant, Cross Keys, Larkfield, High Blantyre
Young, Mungo, Larkfield store, High Blantyre
Young, James, Lodgehill farm, High Blantyre

CHURCHES AND CLERGY.

Established Church, ... Rev. Stewart Wright
Established Church Mission Hall, Stonefield Road,
Free Church, ... Rev. Robert Macdonald
United Presbyterian Church, Glasgow road, .. Mr Riddock, missionary
Evangelical Union Church, ... Rev. William Wyllie
Roman Catholic Church, ... Rev. Thomas Frawley

SCHOOLS AND TEACHERS.

High Blantyre Public School.—Head Master, David Dunlop; Mistress, Miss Aitken
Low Blantyre Public School.—Head Master, John Noss. Mistress, Mrs Margaret Murdoch

SOCIETIES.

FREE MASONS.—Lodge Kilwinning, No. 577. Lodge-Room, J. B. Struthers' Hall.
FREE MASONS.—Lodge Kilwinning, No. 599. Lodge-Room, John Coats' Hall, Stonefield
MECHANICS.—Lodge Vale of Clyde. Lodge-Room, Blackley's Hall

INDEPENDENT ORDER OF GOOD TEMPLARS.

No. 606—BLANTYRE'S HOPE. Instituted 1871. Meets in SCHOOL-ROOM on Saturdays at 8 o'clock. D.G.W.C.T., George Don, Newlands; W.C.T., John Muir, Blantyre Works.
No. 759.—BLANTYRE PRIORY. Instituted 1872. Meets in MASONIC HALL, on Mondays, at 8.15. D.G.W.C.T., Jas. Smith, Auchintibber; W.C.T.; James Paterson, Calderwood Castle Lodge
No. 367.—CRUSADERS. Instituted 1877. Meets in STONEFIELD HALL, on Thursdays, at 8.30. D.G.W.C.T., R. Kirkland, Auchinraith; W.C.T., David Fisher, Manager, Gas Works
No. 135.—JUVENILE OLIVE BRANCH LODGE. Meets in STRUTHERS' HALL, on Mondays, at 7 o'clock. Superintendent, Jas. Smith, Auchintibber.

BANK.—CLYDESDALE—Hugh M'Callum, agent.

BOTHWELL.

Adams, William, Ashley cottage
Aitchison, Mrs, Bothwell bridge
Aitken, Miss, dressmaker, Main street
Alderson, Mrs, Myrtlebank
Anderson, Mrs, Caledonia cottage
Andrew, A. R., M.A., H.M. Inspector of Schools
Apothecary Hall, Dr Goff
Auld, John, Laighlands farm

Bain, J. F., professor of music, 1 Silverwells crescent
Bain, Miss, Ladies' Seminary, Merrylea
Baird, James, Bothwell haugh
Bald, W. R., Fallside house
Barrie, Andrew, Longdales farm
Beardmore, Isaac, Symington lodge
Beatson, G. B., Devar villa
Boyle, James, Belle villa
Brannigan, John, shoemaker, Silverwells place

Cairnduff, J. W. Whitelaw's loan
Caldwell, M., Post office, Main street
Colman, J. J., Caledonia cottage
Colquhoun, Miss, Anchorage cottage
Crawford, Mrs, spirit merchant, Main street
Crichton, William, fruiterer, Main street
Cunninghame, Mrs, Woodhead

Deas, Alexander, stationmaster, Glasgow, Bothwell, Hamilton & Coatbridge Railway Company
Dickson, George, Thornbank
Dickson, jun., George, flesher, Main street
Dobbie, Miss, dressmaker, Main street
Dolan, John, carriage-hirer, Main street
Don, Alexander, Kelvin cottage
Donald, John, St. Andrew's cottage
Donald, W. J. A., Whitelaw cottage
Downie, Mrs, clothier, Main street
Drake, W. R., inspector of poor, Apsley house
Duff, Alexander, Roxburgh cottage
Dunglass, Lord, Bothwell castle
Dunlop, Miss, Victoria cottage
Dunn, Mrs, Balmoral cottage
Dunn, John, Fairfield lodge

Easton, J. F., Viewfield

Edgar, John, stationmaster, Caledonian Railway Company

Fairless, Dr., Private Institution for the Insane, Kirklands
Fleming, Alexander, Raith farm
Fleming, George, ironmonger, Main street
Forrester, David, Hunthill lodge
Freebairn, Andrew, Main street

Galloway, James, Mount Pleasant
Galloway John, Heathbank
Gilchrist, James, Bothwell Park farm
Gray, Robert, Field house
Greig, Mrs, Hawthorn cottage
Guthrie, Mrs, Silverwells crescent
Goff, Dr., The Lindens
Gow, Misses, Silverwells cottage

Hamilton, John, Mayfield
Harvie, Miss, milliner, Silverwells place
Henderson, William, Fern cottage
Hennedy, David, Whitehall
Hewitt, Gavin, joiner, Main street
Hill, Mrs, Mount Pleasant
Hinshaw, Robert, Powburn Dean
Horn, Robert, master Bothwell Public School

Inglis, R. A., Roxburgh villa

Jack, William, The Crescent
Johnston, Thomas, Clyde brae
Johnstone, Thomas, manager William Baird & Company's Bothwell Castle Pit

Kennedy, David, Oriel villa
Knox, James, grocer and spirit merchant, Main street

Lang, Mrs, Whitehall
Lee, Mrs, news-agent and fruiterer, Main street
Long, John, Old Hall house
Loudon, Thomas, Douglas Arms Inn
Lyon, Gabriel, Mount Blue

Mann, James, Fairfield house
Marshall, William Fernhill
Miller, David, Bridge house
Miller, Mrs, Bridge house
Milne, Mrs, The Rowans
Moody, Miss, Strathclyde
Moody, Robert, Benview
Morrison, John, Blane house

Morton, G., Athole villa
Murray, George, grocer and wine merchant, Main street
Murray, Mrs, news-agent
M'Allister, Archibald, Merlewood
M'Bride, Mrs, Clyde hotel.—*See advt.*
M'Callum, Miss, Strathview
M'Corquodale, E., Argyle villa
M'Creath, George, Lavern house
M'Crie, John, Millside house
M'Dougall, Mrs, fish merchant, Main street
M'Eachran, Neil, Glen Eden
M'Ilroy, William, contractor, Longdales
M'Ilvride, A. B., Craigielea
M'Kenzie, Duncan, shoemaker, Main street
M'Nab, William, agent, Clydesdale Bank

Napier, James, Maryfield
Nelson, Hugh, Ashley park

Pairman, Alexander, grocer, Bellevue
Paton, J., confectioner, Main street
Patrick, Matthew, grocer, Main street
Pirie, David, Backsweethope farm
Potter, John A., Dunclutha
Pringle, A. L., Silverwells villa
Pringle, John, Westwood
Purdie, James, china merchant, Main street

Reid, Miss, Forelaw house
Rintoul, Peter, Bothwell bank
Robertson, John, Bothwell park
Russell, Miss, Silverwell house

Scott, J. G., Fairyknowe
Scott, J. & A., smiths, Main street
Shaw, Miss, Old Hall house
Shearer, Gavin, grocer and wine merchant, Agra Bank
Smith, Francis, Fairmount
Smith, John, Anchorage cottage
Sommerville, Mrs, Greenbank
Steel, Gavin, Hillpark
Steel, James, Manaar
Steel, John, Sweethope
Steven, John, flesher, Main street
Stevenson, John, Hillside
Stiell, D., Woodfield
Stirling, Hugh, painter, Main street
Strathearn, John, Wood Dean

Todd, John, baker, Bellevue

Torrance, D. W., Viewfield
Trotter, Robert, Kirkfield
Tyndall, Mrs, Bank buildings

Watson, William, The Academy
Watson, Mrs, draper, Main street
Watson, James, Viewbank
Watson, John, baker, Bellevue
Watt, James, Rosepark
White, John, tobacconist, Main street
Wilson, Charles, Glen Elg
Wink, James, Fairleigh
Wood, Mrs, Roxburgh villa
Wood, Willam, tailor and clothier, Forelaw house

Young, Mrs, Castlebank
Yuill, John, The Crescent

CHURCHES AND CLERGY.

Established Church, ... Rev. John Pagan, The Manse
Free Church, ... Rev. Andrew Doak, F.C. Manse
United Presbyterian Church, ... Rev. A. L. Dick, Wooddean Manse

SCHOOLS AND TEACHERS.

Bothwell Public School.—Master, Robert Horn; Mistress, Miss Munro
Franciscan Convent, Elmwood

SOCIETIES.

FREE GARDENERS.—Lodge "Hawthorn," No. 1. Lodge-room, Douglas Arms Hall
BURNS CLUB—William M'Nab, secretary
BAND OF HOPE—Wm. W. Bain, supt.; W. B. Alexander, treasurer
YOUNG MEN'S CHRISTIAN ASSOCIATION—Place of meeting, Mission Hall, Main Street
YOUNG MEN'S MUTUAL IMPROVEMENT ASSOCIATION—Place of meeting, Mission Hall
CURLING CLUB—George Fleming, secretary
MUSICAL ASSOCIATION—Hugh M'Nab, conductor
BOWLING CLUB—.—— Stevenson, secretary; J. Rogerson, treasurer
BOTHWELL AND UDDINGSTON AGRICULTURAL SOCIETY—Andrew W. Kirkwood, Beltan Cottage, secretary
HORTICULTURAL SOCIETY—Robert Horn, secretary
PUBLIC LIBRARY.—Place of Meeting, Mission Hall. Robert Horn, librarian; Robert Inglis, treasurer

INDEPENDENT ORDER OF GOOD TEMPLARS.

No. 883—HOPE OF BOTHWELL. Instituted 1873. Meets in MISSION HALL on Mondays at 8 o'clock. D.G.W.C.T, W. W. Bain, 1 Silverwells Crescent; W.C.T., Wm. Ashfield, Hamilton Barracks.

BANKS, &c.

CLYDESDALE BANK—William M'Nab, agent
PENNY BANK—Wm. W. Bain, cashier; W. B Alexander, accountant
ROYAL INSURANCE Co.—Gavin Shearer, agent

BOTHWELL POST OFFICE—Postmistress, Margaret Caldwell
Registrar of Births, Marriages, and Deaths—William M'Nab
Population in 1871—Village, 1,209; Parish, 19,292

UDDINGSTON.

Addie, James, Thorniewood house
Addie, John, Viewpark
Alexander, Mrs, Laurel hill
Alexander, James, carter, Old mill road
Alexander, James, flesher, Old mill road
Alexander, Richard, Roseneath, Douglas gardens
Anderson, James, carter, Old mill road
Anderson, James, nurseryman, Meadowbank
Anderson, John, Myrtle cottage, Powburn road
Anderson, Miller, Birkenshaw farm
Andrews, M. M., watchmaker, Bellshill road
Auchinvole, David, Lilybank house, agent for Bank of Scotland

Baillie, Wm., Holmwood house
Baird, M. B., Charleville
Baird, John, spirit merchant, Main street
Baird, William, builder, Croftbank cottage
Barber, Matthew, Greenholm
Barr, John, news-agent, Towie place
Barr, Wm., Douglas gardens
Bell, Miss, Newton cottage
Bell, Thomas, Brownhill villa
Bennie, Mrs, Claremont house
Bennie, William, Southfield villa
Bog, James, Mossbank cottage
Boyd, Henry, Agelea, Douglas gardens
Boyes, Edward, Burnpark
Braidwood, John, Victoria cottage
Brand, John Clyde house
Brown, David, Kamesburgh terrace
Brown, George, Medical hall, Glasgow road
Brown, Robert, Edina house, Gardenside
Brownlee, James, Gresham
Bruce, Robert, teacher
Bruce, William, Clifton cottage
Bryce, A. S., Birkenshaw,
Bryden, James, baker, Glasgow road
Burdon, Mrs, Springbank

Cameron, Allan, plumber, Hotel buildings
Campbell, Wm., Old mill road
Clark, Alexander, carter, Bankfoot
Clark, George, Crosshill villa
Clark, Mrs, Hawthorn cottage
Clark, Wm., Briarfield

Coats, Charles, Dunglass villa, Douglas gardens
Co-operative Store, Old mill road
Craig, James, Sunnyside villa
Crawford, Dr William, Linncluden house
Crawford, Hugh, blacksmith, Old mill road
Cullen, Rev. James, Albert cottage
Cullen, William, family grocer, Loanhead
Cullen, William, Kamesburgh terrace

Davidson, Robert, Bonnington villa
Dewar, Mrs, Loanhead cottage
Diamond, John, grocer, Bellshill road
Dick, Walter, Salem villa, Douglas gardens
Don, William, Woodlea
Donald, James, tobacconist and billiard rooms, Main street
Douglas, Robert, boot and shoemaker, Wellbank buildings
Douglas, Robert, letter-carrier, Eglinton's land, Old Glasgow rd.
Drummond, Adam, Doonbank villa, Gardenside

Fairbairn, John, Royal hotel
Fairley, Mrs, grocer, Main street
Ferguson, John, Ashton villa, Douglas gardens
Fisher, Mrs Robert, Prospect bank
Fisher, Peter, Murrayfield villa
Fleming, Mrs, Mineralbank villa
Ford, Andrew, dairyman, Old mill road
Forrest, James, grocer, Main street
Forrester, James, Carolside

Gardner, Andrew, Burnbank house
Gibson, Robert, Lindens house
Gilchrist, James, nurseryman and seedsman, Main street
Gilchrist, William, ironmonger, Main street
Goldie, Hugh, Gowanlea cottage
Goldie and Co., Hugh, ironfounders
Gordon, Miss, Croft cottage
Gourlay, Thomas, Jane villa, Douglas gardens
Gray, George, Bankhead
Gray, John, Glenara, Gardenside
Gray, John, Mayfield house
Gray, John, of John Gray and Co., Prospect house
Gray, John, Springwell
Gray, Robert, Clyde bank, Powburn road
Gray and Co., John, Uddingston Iron works
Grieve, John, Thistle cottage, Powburn road

Hamilton, David, Annfield lodge
Hamilton, W. M,, Kamesburgh terrace
Hamilton, Samuel, Albion cottage
Hamilton, Duncan, Fernlea

Halket, Thomas, architect, Margaret villa
Harley, William, Coney bank
Hayman, Thomas, Netherton house, Douglas gardens
Hendman, Donald, Croftbank villa
Hendrie, John, Maryville colliery
Herbertson, John, Meadowbank house
Hood, Robert, Alliwal villa
Hornal, James, blacksmith, Bellshill road
Howe, William, Fern dean
Howieson, John, builder, Abington house
Hughes, Peter, Clyde view
Hyslop, Lawrence, manager, Gas Works

Inglis, Alexr., Pomona villa
Inglis, John, Crofthill place

Jack, James, Mains cottage
Jack, John, Birkenshaw, cottage
Johnston, Miss, young gentlemen's boarding school, Carlton House School, Glasgow road, and young ladies' boarding school, Carlton house, Douglas gardens
Johnston, Thomas, Gardenside
Johnstone, J. K., Castlecroft

Keith, Duncan, Blyth Holm
Kenneth, J. S., Hawthorn bank, Douglas gardens
King, William, Woodbine house
Kirkhope, George, Bothwell Castle farm
Kyle, William, Millar bank

Laidlaw, Samuel, Kingston villa, Douglas gardens
Lang, Mrs, Sherwood
Latta, Thomas, grocer and spirit merchant, Magdala place
Leslie, William, Annsfield villa
Liddel, John, carriage hirer, Royal hotel
Liddel and Son, Gavin, grocers, Aberdour place
Lindsay, Mrs, Gowanbrae
Lindsay, James, saddler, Hotel buildings
Littlejohn, James, Claremont house
Logan, William, Loudonbrae
Lorimer, John, Bothwell Castle farm
Lowe, J. H., Oakbank cottage
Lusk, James, Ferneybank

Marshall, A., spirit merchant
Marshall, Alex., Clydeview house
Marshall, T., broker, Towie place
Marshall and Thomson, plumbers, Dechmont view
Mason, John, Dalzione, Douglas gardens
Mathieson, Mrs, fruiterer, Main street

Meikle, James, Roslea, Douglas gardens
Millar, Alexander, Greenrigg cottage
Miller, Miss, Clydeview house
Miller, James, Henrietta villa, Douglas gardens
Miller, Wm., Springwell place
Mitchell, David, Parkview
Mitchell, Mrs, Mount pleasant
Mitchell, Robert, Armadale villa
Morris, William, Bourtreehill, Douglas gardens
Morton, James, Comely bank
Morton, John, tailor and clothier, Main street
Morton, Richard, slater, Hotel buildings
Morton, William, carter, Bellshill road
Morton, William, grocer, Bellshill road
Murray Adam, Hotel buildings
Murray, George, ironmonger, Hotel buildings
Murray, John, Mount pleasant
M'Allister, Mrs, Maryfield house
M'Alpine, William, Rockby lodge, Douglas gardens
M'Callum, Mrs, Mount Pleasant
M'Callum, James, grocer, flesher, and draper, Bellshill road
M'Callum and Co., drapers, Main street
M'Coll, John, family grocer, Main street
M'Crae, James, Crofthead dairy
M'Dougally, John, fish merchant, Main street
M'Eachran, J. J., Bothwell villa, Douglas gardens
M'Farlane, Thomas, Rosebank cottage
M'Ilroy E., contractor, Alliwal villa
M'Indoe, J., boot and shoemaker, Springwell place
M'Intyre, Archibald, Thornlee, Douglas gardens
M'Kechnie, Donald, Croftbank farm
M'Kenzie, James, railway refreshment bar, Glasgow road
M'Kerrow, Miss, Bothwell Castle farm
M'Laren, John, painter, Hotel buildings
M'Lean, Thomas, Birkhill, Gardenside
M'Leish, Daniel, clothier and postmaster, Hotel buildings
M'Leod, Mrs, news agent, Bellshill road
M'Lurkin, Wm. G., Muriel cottage
M'Nab, Mrs, Kildonian villa
M'Naughton, Alexander, Glenlyon house
M'Naughton, William, Stramore, Douglas gardens
M'Nee, William, Merion villa, Douglas gardens
M'Neil, James, 4 Clutha place

Neil, Samuel, Pembroke cottage
Neil, William, upholsterer, Springwell place
Neville, James, stationer, Main street
Nisbet and Son, T., china and provision merchants, Bellshill rd.

Park, J. H. M., Gowary villa

Paterson, John, Thornlea cottage
Paterson, John, flesher, Main street
Paul, Alexander, Dairy cottage
Pearson, Mrs, Clarence lodge, Douglas gardens
Pollock, Mrs, Gardenside villa
Pollock, James, Elvin cottage
Pollock, John, dairyman, Easter farm
Poynter, John E., Clyde Neuk
Preston, James, Hollymount, Birkenshaw

Rain, William, tailor and clothier, Bellshill road
Rankin, John, Craigielea
Reid, Miss, Springwell place
Reid, Mrs, Thistle bank
Rennie, Joseph, Allan villa
Rennie, Thomas, Birkenshaw
Renton, Robert, La Belle villa, Douglas gardens
Richmond, James A., family grocer, Main street
Riley, James, North Cotehouse
Ripon, George, Hollygate lodge
Robertson, Daniel, boot and shoemaker, Hotel buildings
Robertson, Miss, Blair lea, Douglas gardens
Robertson, Mrs, Galamuir
Robertson, John, Claremonte house
Robertson, William, Loancroft
Rome, W. L., Balvaird house
Rowat, Alexander, Primrose bank
Rutherford, James, Horton villa

Sclanders, David, Annesley, Douglas gardens
Scott, Andrew, Birkenshaw house
Scott, Mrs, Croftbank
Scott, James, Loanhead house
Scott, John, Springfield house
Scott, Robert, fruit merchant, Totham cottage
Scott, S. E., Craigievar, Douglas gardens
Scott, William, Marr lodge
Semple, Peter, draper, Old mill road
Shand, Thomas, family grocer, Main street
Shands, William, plasterer, Sydney place
Shanks, Robert, Glenbank
Sharp, W. and A., joiners and cabinetmakers, Wellbank bdgs.
Shaw, Gavin, Earlston villa
Shaw, J., greengrocer, Croftbank street
Shearer, Mrs, Porterswell House
Short, Alexander, spirit merchant, Towie place
Simpson John, draper, Hotel buildings
Simpson, John, Springfield
Smellie, Andrew, spirit merchant, Old mill road
Smith, Andrew, Corland cottage

H

Smith, A. H., Glen Elg
Smith, Henry, Springpark
Smith, Mrs, Park villa
Smith, James, H.M. Inspector of schools, Douglas Gardens
Smith, John, toll-keeper, Powburn toll
Smith, Robert, Daisy bank
Smith, Thomas, Bothwell Castle farm
Somerville, John, Towie cottage
Sommerville, John, draper and clothier, Main street
Steel, William, Annfield cottage
Steel, William, grocer, Harmony cottage
Stevenson, Robert, carter, Thornlea cottage
Stewart, John, Elie bank
Stobo, Eliza, dressmaker and milliner, Hotel buildings

Tant, John Yellowlees, physician and surgeon, Winton place, Garden side
Thom, J. and R., contractors, Croftbank place
Thomson, James Newall, Bellvue cottage, Powburn road
Thomson, John, Kamesburgh terrace
Thomson, R. C., Helenslea
Thomson, R. R. B., Oakwood

Waddell, Wm., grocer, fruiterer, and spirit merchant, Bellshill rd.
Walker, George, Bon Accord lodge, Douglas gardens
Walker, Thomas, Apothecary hall, Murray place
Walker, Wilson, Croft view
Wallace, George, furnishings, Bellshill road
Wallace, Robert, plasterer, Hathornbank
Watson, John, butcher, Hotel buildings
Watson, Mrs, Douglas cottage, Douglas gardens
Watson, William, baker and restaurant, Main street
Weddal, Mrs, Park villa
White, James, flesher, Bellshill road
White, Matthew, Holm farm
White, William H., Clydeview
Wilkie, Lieut.-General, Knowehead
Wilson, James, family grocer, Dechmont view
Wilson, Mrs, Holmpark
Wilson, Mrs, Leabank cottage, Gardenside
Wilson, William, hairdresser and tobacconist, Bellshill road
Wilson, W. H., Williesden, Powburn road
Wood, John, Castle croft
Wright, William, Springfield cottage, Douglas gardens

Young, James, contractor, Douglas gardens
Young, James, Greenhead cottage
Young, Miss, Uddingston educational institute
Young, Mrs, Laurel bank
Yuill, Alexander, baker, Bellshill road

CHURCHES AND CLERGY.

Established Church, ... Rev. John Mackintosh, The Manse, Gardenside
Free Church, ... Rev. Ivie M'Lachlan, Ellen Gowan, Douglas Gardens
United Presbyterian Church, ... Rev. John M'Luckie, The Manse, Douglas Gardens
Evangelical Union Church,.. .. .. Rev. Dr. Bowman, Lorne Cottage

SCHOOLS AND TEACHERS.

Carlton House School (for the board and education of young ladies)—Lady Principal, Miss Johnston
Educational Institute (day and boarding), Rosemount—Lady Principal, Miss Young; head-master, John Campbell
Free Church School—Master, James Smith; Mistress, Miss Cunningham
Subscription School—Master, Robert Bruce; Mistress, Miss Gordon

SOCIETIES.

AGRICULTURAL SOCIETY.—Secy., Andrew Kirkwood; Treas., J. Russell
BOWLING CLUB.—Secy. and Treas., Robert Bruce
FREE GARDENERS.—R.W.M., Andrew Boyd; Treas., John Williamson.
FREE MASONS.—Lodge "St. Bride," No. 579. Lodge-room, Latta's Hall, Glasgow road—R.W.M., John Baird, Bellshill; Secy., Thos. Short, Townhead, Bellshill
GOOD TEMPLARS LODGE—Secy., Matthew Finlayson; Treas., Jas. M'Bride
HORTICULTURAL SOCIETY.—Secy., Jas. Neville; Treas., Wm. Millan
UNION HALL.—President, John Howieson; Secy., John Sommervile; Treas., Thos. Shand
YOUNG MEN'S MUTUAL IMPROVEMENT ASSOCIATION.—Secy., David Auchinvole, jun.; Treas., James Rowatt

BANKS AND INSURANCE AGENT.

Bank of Scotland—David Auchinvole, agent
Penny Savings Bank.—Secy., Wm, Millar; Treas., R. W. Thompson
Crown Insurance Coy.—David Auchinvole, agent

RAILWAY STATIONS.

Caledonian—Stationmaster, Thomas Ballantyne
Glasgow, Bothwell, Hamilton, and Coatbridge—Stationmaster, Thos. Brass

POST OFFICE.—Postmaster, Daniel M'Leish

Letters arrive from Glasgow and all parts at 7.10 a.m. and 5 p.m.; and from Motherwell and all parts, at 8.20 a.m.
Letters despatched to Glasgow and the North, at 9.30 a.m. and 2.15 a.m.; and to Motherwell and the South at 8.10 a.m.

Population in 1871—1997
Registrar of Births, Marriages, and Deaths—William M'Nab, Bothwell

MOTHERWELL.

Addie, Gavin, coalmaster, Braidhurst
Algie, Alexander, grocer, Merry street
Allan, Gavin, boot and shoemaker, Brandon street
Allan, Gavin, grocer, Merry street
Alston, James, boot and shoemaker, 90 Merry street
Alston and Lowe, plumbers, etc., Oakfield place, Brandon st.
Anderson, Brothers, American beef store, Royal buildings, Brandon street
Anderson, William, commercial traveller, Brandon place, Brandon street
Anderson, J. and H. V., drapers, Brandon street
Armstrong, George, superintendent of Prudential insurance company, Crosshill cottage, Brandon street

Baillie, Thomas, cabinet-maker and funeral undertaker, Brandon street
Baillie, William, spirit merchant, Railway tavern
Barr, John, potato merchant, Watson street
Beers, and Co., W. H., mercantile stationers, 11 Muir street
Begg, G. B., civil and mining engineer, Brandon street
Black, James, draper, Kings' buildings, Muir street
Blair, Robert, spirit merchant, Muir street
Bonallo, W. C., Dalziel farm
Bowie, W. and J. dyers, Muir street
Boyd, Mary, confectioner, Allan Terrace, Merry street
Braid, C., draper, and grocer
Broad, Josiah, boot and shoemaker, 44 Merry street
Brown, Mrs John, apothecary hall, Merry street
Brown, William, North Motherwell farm
Brownlie, Charles, flesher, Windmillhill
Bryce, J. tailor, Brandon street
Buchanan, Robert, grocer, Merry street
Buchanan, Robert, grocer and spirit merchant, Muir street
Bullock, Walter, baker, Windmillhill
Burgess, Mrs, dressmaker, 112 Windmillhill
Burns, Alexander, clothier, Merry street

Callan, T., grocer, Merry street
Cameron, David, grocer, Victoria place, Muir st. and 22 Milton street

Campbell, ——, Woodruff cottage, Windmillhill
Chambers, William, woodmerchant and builder, Dalziel Saw Mills, Park street ; house—Glenview
Christie, James W., draper, King's buildings, Muir street
Cinnamond, James, hatter, 15 Muir street
Clark, R. and K., tobacconists and hairdressers, Brandon street
Close, Henry, cabinetmaker and funeral-undertaker, Merry st.
Clow, James, painter and paper-hanger, Victoria pl., Muir st.
Colville, David, Dalziel Iron Works
Colville, John, of Dalziel iron works, Hawthorn cottage
Consumers Tea Co., 23 Muir street
Co-operative store, Milton street
Cowan James, Brandon place
Cowan, R. R., pawnbroker, Park street and Hope street
Cowan, Thomas, baker, Muir street
Cowan, William, pawnbroker, Hamilton street
Cringan, Robert, cabinetmaker, Muir street
Cromar, Mrs, The Flat
Cromar and Co., A. G., Polytechnic Warehouse, Muir street
Cullen James, baker, Brandon street
Cunninghame, James, plumber and tinsmith, Merry street
Currie, William B., family grocer, Brandon street

Dalziel Co operative store, Merry street
Darling, William, baker, Oakfield place, Brandon street
Davidson, Mrs, Dalziel Arms Hotel, Brandon street
Davidson, John, fruiterer and confectioner, Victoria place, Muir street
Davidson, John, grocer, 76 Merry street
Dick, John, grocer, North Motherwell
Dickson, George, confectioner, Watson street
Dickson, John, dairy, Windmillhill
Donald, James, spirit merchant, Melville drive
Donald, Robert, spade and shovel maker, Holm forge
Donaldson, Robert, slater, Brandon place
Douglas, James, draper, Merry street
Downie, William, boot and shoemaker, Brandon street
Duncan, Thomas, draper, Muir street
Dunsmore, Peter, Black Bull Inn, Merry st., and County Hotel, Muir street

Easton, George, slater and plasterer, Windmillhill
Edwards, Joseph, grocer, Merry street

Fairley, J. D. writer, Muir street
Ferguson, Mrs, spirit merchant, Muir street
Fisher, Thomas, hatter, Commercial buildings, Brandon street
Fletcher, Alex., grocer, Windmillhill
Forrest, Dr John, Calderview, Merry street
Forrest, Robert, tailor, Muir street

Forsyth, Mrs Thomas, grocer, Hope street
Forsyth, John, grocer and provision merchant, Muir street
Foulis, Robert C., grocer, Brandon street
Frame, Mrs, confectioner, Brandon street
Frame, Mrs, confectioner, Watson street
Fraser, Alex., grocer, Muir street, house—Forrest cottage
Fullarton, John, tobacconist, Murray place, Merry street

Galloway, John, stationer and printer, Merry street
Gibb and Crawford, tailors and clothiers, Brandon street
Gibson, Robert, billiard rooms, Oakfield place, Brandon street
Gillespie, John, joiner and cartwright, Brandon street
Gilmour, Benjamin, grocer, flesher, and baker, Merry street, and flesher, Milton street. House, Rosebank cottage, Merry st.
Girdwood, J. and R., bakers, Muir street
Glasgow Iron Co., Motherwell iron works, (malleable), Thomas Morton, manager
Gold, Janet, tobacconist, Brandon street
Goodwin, Matthew D., North park, Hamilton road
Goodwin, John, Clydeview, Hamilton road
Goodwin and Co., James, ironfounders, Motherwell Foundry
Gordon, Alex., spirit merchant, corner of Watson street
Gourlay, Mrs, fruiterer, Merry street
Gray, James, stationer, Brandon street
Gray, Wm., painter and glazier, Avondale place, Brandon st.
Gray, John, Maybole boot and shoe warehouse, Royal hotel buildings
Grieve, John, crane and engine works, Park street. House, Calderview cottage, Merry street
Guy, Mrs, greengrocer, Brandon street

Halliday, George, sculptor, Brandon street
Hamilton, Alexander, draper, Muir street
Hamilton, James, baker, Merry street
Hamilton, John, Cullen cottage, Windmillhill
Hamilton, J. B., photograper, Brandon street
Hamilton, J. G. C., Dalziel house
Hamilton, Mrs, confectioner, Windmillhill
Hamilton, Mrs D., Brandon hotel, the cross
Hamilton, Thomas, watchmaker and jeweller, Brandon street
Hamilton, William, High Motherwell farm
Hay, Robert, flesher, Muir street
Hay, Robert, Maryfield place
Hislop, Thomas, draper, Merry street
Horn, John, contractor, Brandon street
Horton, Fred, grocer, Commercial buildings, Park street
Hunter, Mrs G., furnishings, Bowes land, Merry street

Industrial Co-operative store, Melville drive

Jack, Robert, agent, bank of Scotland
Johnston, David, Caledonian weighs, Lesmahagow junction; house—Hope street
Johnston, James, draper, 1 Park street
Johnstone, Robert, Ellen bank
Johnstone, Thomas, tailor and clothier, 88 Merry street

Kemp, Alex., painter and paperhanger, Merry street
Kerr, Miss, furnishings, Merry street
King, James, baker, 12 Muir street
King, James, builder, Brandon street; quarries—Knowtop
King, James, King's Arms, Milton street
King, Thomas, builder, Windmill house
King, Walter G., family grocer, Muir street
King, William, Motherwell house
King and Co., Thomas, builders; quarries—Bellside
Kirkland, Dr, Windmillhill
Kirkland, James grocer and spirit merchant, Windmillhill

Lang, Mrs, Low Motherwell farm
Lang, James, grocer and dairyman, Merry street
Lang, Robert, Royal Oak Tavern, Merry street
Lawson, John, grocer, Merry street
Liddle, John, Thornieshot farm
Liddle, Thomas, Brandon place
Lindsay, John, stationer, Victoria place, Muir street
Lindsay, William, cabinetmaker, etc., Cross stone
Lochhead, Robert, confectioner, Brandon street
Loudon, Robert L., confectioner, Avondale place, Brandon st.
Loudon, Thomas, china and fruit merchant, Merry street
Loudon, Thomas, confectioner, Brandon street
Loudon, Thomas, saddler, Royal Hotel buildings, Brandon st.
Ludlan, John, Eagle inn, North Motherwell

Mains, Wm., bookseller and stationer, Brandon street
Marchbank, Samuel, confectioner, Brandon street
Marshall, Mrs, Airbles farm
Marshall, John, family grocer, Muir street
Martin, James, druggist, Brandon street
Meickle, John, printer and stationer, the Cross, Merry street
Merry and Cunninghame, North Motherwell colliery
Miles, Andrew, cooper, Brandon street
Miller, Archibald, Hamilton Street Saw Mills
Miller, Mrs, greengrocer, Oakfield place, Brandon street
Miller, James, spirit merchant, Windmillhill
Miller, John, baker, Windmillhill
Miller, John, blacksmith, Knowetop
Miller, John, contractor, Park street
Miller, John, grocer, Brandon street
Miller, Robert, boot and shoemaker, Clyde street

Milligan, John, draper, Oakfield place, Brandon street
Mitchell, Charles, flesher, Brandon street
Mitchell, James, Parkhead farm
Mitchell, Robert, Braidhurst farm
Moffat, Dr Alex. T., Brandon place, Brandon street
Motherwell co-operative store, Caledonian place, N. Motherwell
Motherwell, iron works co-operative society, 74 and 78 Milton street, Robert Woodside, manager
Morrison, Mrs, confectioner, Brandon street
Morrison, Mrs, confectioner, Hamilton street
Morton, M'Killop, and Co., iron forgers, Motherwell forge
Muir, John, teacher of dancing, Merry street
Muir, Robert L., ironmonger, Brandon street
Muir and Girdwood, joiners, Brandon street
Murray, Alex., family grocer, Murray place, Merry street
Murray, James, flesher, Windmillhill
Murray, Neilson, tailor and clothier, victoria place, Muir street,

M'Andrew and Co., J., Dalziel colliery
M'Callum, James, architect and civil engineer, collector of poor rates, Muir street
M'Callum, Thomas, district loco' superintendent, Caledonian Railway, Parkneuk
M'Callum, William, china and fruit merchant, Victoria place Muir street
M'Donald, James, ironmonger, Brandon street
M'Donald, Jane, dressmaker and milliner, 70 Merry street
M'Ewan, Hugh, spirit merchant, Oakfield Place, Brandon street
M'Innes, Mrs, Russell's buildings, Park street
M'Iver, Norman, tobacconist and hairdresser, Clyde street
M'Kay, Donald, grocer, King's buildings, Brandon street
M'Kendrick, James, saddler, Muir street
M'Killop and Co., blacksmiths, Merry street
M'Neil, Neil, greengrocer, Windmillhill
M'Phail, D. C., accountant, Brandon street
M'Queen, A., writer, Brandon street
M'Skimming, John, tobacconist, Brandon street

Napier, John, draper, Brandon street
Nelson, John, draper, Avondale place, Brandon street
Nimmo, John, grocer, 110 Windmillhill

Orr, Joseph, grocer, Cross-stone

Park, Robert, builder, Brandon street
Paterson, John, fruiterer, 80 Merry street
Paterson, Miss A., dairy, Watson street
Paterson, William, greengrocer, Oakfield place, Brandon street
Paterson & Co., drapers, Brandon street
Penman, Alexander shoemaker, Merry street

Pennicuick, Thomas, Motherwell Inn, Cross
Pettigrew, Robert, brickmaker, Braidhurst
Pettigrew, Thomas, confectioner, Muir street
Pollock Walter, flesher, Oakfield place, Brandon street
Pullar, William, Cullen cottage, Windmillhill
Purdon, John, tobacconist and hairdresser, Victoria place, Muir street
Purdon, Robert, dairy, Victoria place, Muir street

Quinton, R. W., architect and measurer, Brandon street, house—Orchard view

Rae, John, teller, Bank of Scotland—house, Cartcraigs
Ralston, James, draper, Merry street
Ralston and Co., boiler composition manufacturers, Park street
Reid, Andrew, grocer, Muir street
Reid, James, grocer, Royal hotel buildings, Brandon street
Reid, James, grocer, North Motherwell
Reid, John, inspector, mineral department, Caledonian Railway, Hope street
Reid, Miss, Merry street
Reid, Robert, inspector, Caledonian Railway, Muir street
Riddock, Robert, boot and shoemaker, Cross-stone
Robertson, Alexander M'K., postmaster, Brandon street
Robertson, John, joiner, Leslie street
Robertson, John, stationer, Brandon street
Ross, George, boot and shoemaker, Victoria place, Muir street
Ross, Malcolm, architect and measurer Melville drive
Russell, James, Crosshill house, Brandon street
Russell, James, sen., boiler maker, Park street
Russell, John, cabinetmaker and upholsterer, Brandon street
Russell, Miss M., greengrocer, Avondale place, Brandon street
Russell, William, grocer, Merry street
Russell & Co., George, engineers, Park street

Saunders, Mrs Thomas, spirit merchant, Muir street
Scoular, J. and A., fleshers, Victoria place, Muir street
Scott, James, flesher, Brandon street
Scott, James A., spirit merchant, Muir street
Scott, John, Adolphus cottage, Windmillhill
Scott, John, Royal Hotel, Brandon street
Shields, Edward, contractor, Windmillhill
Shirlaw, George, Clyde street
Smellie, William, Corsington farm
Smith, Archibald R., bolt, nut, screw, and washer manufacturer, Albert works—house, Ladywell
Smith, J., milliner and draper, Merry street
Smith, James, clothier, Oakfield place, Brandon street
Smith, John, cabinet-maker, Knowetop
Smith and Co., J., Motherwell bolt works

Sneddon, George, teacher, architect, measurer, and registrar, Merry street
Sneddon, James, confectioner, Cross-stone
Somerhill, Isaac, Maryfield place
Somerhill, James, Rosebank cottage, Merry street
Somerhill, W. H., Maryfield place
Speirs, Archibald, spirit merchant, the Cross
Steel, George, boot and shoemaker, Muir street
Steel, John, grocer and spirit merchant, Knowetop store
Stewart, James, accountant and house factor, Commercial buildings, Brandon street
Stewart, James, draper, Merry street
Stewart, James, medical hall, Merry street
Stewart, W. B., boot and shoemaker, King's buildings, Muir st.
Stratton, William, solicitor, Merry street, house—Morayfield
Strong, Mrs H., grocer, Cross-stone
Summers, Oliver, spirit merchant, Muir street
Sweeney, Agnes, spirit merchant, Milton street
Sweeney, John, spirit merchant, Avondale place, Brandon st.

Taylor, Lachlan, plumber and gasfitter, Brandon street
Taylor, Robert, blacksmith, Hamilton street
Taylor, William, china merchant, Brandon street
Thomson, Dr. S., Jerviston house
Thomson, John, Glasgow carrier, The Loch
Thomson, Mrs John, tobacconist, fruiterer, and stationer, Muir st.
Thomson, Thomas, saw mills, park street
Toner, Thomas, fruiterer, Milton street
Topping, John, Hamilton place

Waddell, George, wood merchant, The Loch cottage
Waddell, John, spirit merchant, Windmillhill
Waddell, William, builder, Calderview cottage, Merry street
Walker, John, restaurant, Brandon street
Wallace, Hugh, carriage hirer, Motherwell Inn stables, The Cross
Wallace, James, pattern-maker, Windmillhill
Wallace, William, carriage hirer and funeral undertaker, Brandon Hotel stables, The Cross
Watson, John, coal master, Motherwell collieries, residing at Earnock, Hamilton
Watson, John, vinegar works, Park street
Watson, John, jun., brickmaker
Watson, Mrs, young ladies' school, Braeside Seminary
Watson, Thomas, Hamilton place
Watson, Thomas, store, Avondale place, Brandon street
Watson, Thomas, Watsonville cottage
Watson, William, wine and spirit merchant, corner of Park st.
Waugh, William, manager, Braeside cottage
Weir, Mrs, Volunteer Inn, Merry street
Welsh, John, watchmaker and jeweller, Clyde street

Whamond, Alexander, teacher, session-clerk, &c., Dalziel School-house
Whitelaw, Thomas, manager, Park street
Williams & Co., John, Camp colliery
Wilson, Dr., Rosshill
Wilson, James, spirit merchant, Commercial buildings, Brandon street
Wilson, James, spirit merchant, Cross Keys, Hamilton street
Wood, David W., draper and jeweller, Woodlea place, Brandon street

Young, James, ironmonger, Merry street
Young, John, flesher, Merry street

POLICE COMMISSIONERS.

Chief Magistrate, William Waddell. Bailies, Thos. Watson and John Lawson. Thomas Morton, William Chambers, Archibald Millar, Alexander Fraser, John Miller, M. D. Goodwin
Clerk, William Stratton. Collector of Burgh Rates, James M'Callum, Muir Street. Sanitary Inspector, James Kirkland, Knowetop

DALZIEL PAROCHIAL BOARD.

Chairman, J. G. C. Hamilton; Inspector, James Stewart; Medical Officer, Dr Thomson; Assistant Medical Officer, Dr Moffat; Collector, Robert Jack, Bank of Scotland; Registrar, George Sneddon

CHURCHES AND CLERGY.

Dalziel Parish Church, Windmillhill, ... Rev. Thomas Hislop
Established Church, Merry Street, ... Rev. David Scott, M.A., B.D.
Free Church, Muir Street, ... Rev. David Ogilvy, M.A.
United Presbyterian Church, Brandon Street, Rev. James Dunlop, M.A.
Evangelical Union Church, Brandon Street,.. Rev. David Greenhill
Primitive Methodist Chapel, Milton Street, .. Rev. James Bastow
Roman Catholic Chapel, Park street, ... Rev. Dr. Glancy
Plymouth Brethren, Roman Road Hall, Merry Street

SCHOOLS AND TEACHERS.

Hamilton Street—Master, Wm. A. Cavet; Mistress, Janet Gibb; Certificated Assistants, Wm. Marshall and James Downie
Dalziel Street—Master, George Sneddon
Muir Street—Master, H. C. Hinds
Windmillhill Street—Master, Alexander Whamond; Mistress, Annie Galt
Glasgow Iron Works. Milton Street—Master, John Stalker
Roman Catholic, Park Street—Mistress, Rose Ann Trainer
Braeside Seminary (Young Ladies)—Mrs Watson

SOCIETIES, ASSOCIATIONS, COMPANIES, &c.

MOTHERWELL WORKMEN'S YEARLY FRIENDLY SOCIETY.—President, John Fullarton ; Treas., Wm. M'Ghie ; Secy., John Bryson

MOTHERWELL CHORAL ASSOCIATION—Conductor, John Marshall ; President, H. S. Kennedy ; Secy., John Meickle ; Treas., James Simpson

MOTHERWELL IRON WORKS CHORAL UNION—Conductor, Thomas Morton

DALZIEL HOSPITAL, Airbles Road

DALZIEL POORHOUSE—Governor, Wm. M'Andrew ; Matron, Mrs M'Andrew

DALZIEL BUILDING SOCIETY.—Manager, Archibald Laidlaw

GAS LIGHT COY.—Manager, John Fullarton ; Secy., J. D. Fairley

MUSIC HALL COY. (Limited)—Chairman, Wm. Barclay, Hamilton ; Secy. and Treas., James Stewart, accountant

VOLUNTEER ARMOURY—Old Tyrolese Cottage, Brandon Street

AUCTION MART, Hamilton Street—J. Shirlaw & Son, auctioneers.

READING ROOMS, Commercial Buildings, Brandon Street—Pres., William Chambers ; Vice-Pres., Wm. A. Cavet ; Treas., Robert C. Foulis ; Secy., G. B. Begg

POST OFFICE, TELEGRAPH, MONEY ORDER, AND SAVINGS BANK, Brandon Street—Alexander M'K. Robertson, Postmaster

BANK.

BANK OF SCOTLAND—Robert Jack, Agent

FREEMASONS.

ST. JOHN'S DALZIEL, No. 406.—R.W.M., John King, ; Secretary, D. M'Phail

LIVINGSTONE ST. ANDREWS, No. 573.—R.W.M., Andrew Donaldson, Merry Street ; Secretary, Wm. Henderson, Windmillhill

INDEPENDENT ORDER OF GOOD TEMPLARS.

UPPERWARD OF LANARKSHIRE DISTRICT LODGE—D.D.G.W.C.T., Thomas Fisher, Brandon Street

Lodges which meet in Old School-Room, Milton Street.

CALEDONIAN THISTLE LODGE, No. 231.—John Brown, W.C.T.

"NIL DESPERANDUM" LODGE, No. 427—Daniel Rankin, W.C.T.

HOPE OF MOTHERWELL JUVENILE LODGE—Thos. Fisher, Superintendent

Lodge which meets in Free Gardeners' Hall, Hamilton Street.

ONWARD STAR LODGE, No. 174—William M'Kelvin, W.C.T.

RAILWAY STATIONS.

Caledonian—Hamilton Road Bridge Station—Wm, M'Ghie, stationmaster

    Do.   Brandon Street Station—James Watson, stationmaster

LARKHALL.

Alexander, Andrew, flesher, Union street and Wellgate street
Allan, Matthew, Church street
Allison, William, Sunnyside farm
Anderson, James, registrar and inspector of poor, 34 Union street

Baird, Mrs David, draper, Raploch street
Barnhill, James, spirit merchant, Raploch street
Barr, Douglas B., ironmonger, Raploch street
Barr, Peter, Machan-hill house
Barr, William, Machan-hill house
Barr & Sons, William, Over-Dalserf and Longlee Collieries
Bell, James, gardener, Muir street
Bell, John, Struther farm
Bell, John, Swinhill farm
Bell, Mrs, Truro cottage, Muir Street
Beaton, Annie, fruiterer and confectioner, the Cross
Beveridge, Alexander, spirit merchant, Wellgate street
Birkenshaw Coal Co., Birkenshaw
Boyd & Co., builders, Broomhill quarry
Brooks, George, tobacconist, London street
Brown, Andrew, grocer, M'Neil street
Brown, Hugh, grocer, Church street
Brown, James, Royal Oak tavern, Raploch street
Brown, John, grocer and flesher, Wellgate street
Brown, Thomas, Skellyton farm
Brown, William, tailor and clothier, Church street
Bruce, Robert, Bruce Arms Inn, Drygate street
Bryce, James, London hotel, London street
Buchanan, Robert, spirit merchant, Union street
Burns, John, Commercial inn, Union street
Burns, William, printer and stationer, Raploch street
Burns & Co., John C., joiners, Church street

Campbell, Alexander, Machan mill
Canfield, Richard, grocer, Raploch street
Canfield, Thomas, draper, London street
Chalmers, Alexander, boot and shoemaker, 32 Union street
Clark, William, weaving agent, Church street
Clelland, Alexander, Beatton's gate
Clements, John, spirit merchant, Church street
Close, Patrick, spirit merchant, Union street
Cochrane & Co., Cornsilloch colliery

Cockburn, John, blacksmith, Church street
Cooper, Mrs John, spirit merchant, Church street
Cooper, Robert G., Braehead house
Cooper, John, slater and plasterer, Raploch street
Cowan, John, spirit merchant, Wellgate street
Cross, William H., Janefield cottage
Crow, John, joiner, M'Neil street

Davidson, William, Durham villa, Church street
Dick, David M'A., clothier, Union street
Dobbie, James, carter, Muir street
Douglas, John, licensed grocer, Drygate street
Downs, James, weaving-agent and sanitary inspector, Raploch st.
Drew, Lawrence, farmer, Merryton farm
Duncan, Thomas, Glenview

Eadie, Mrs E., spirit merchant, the Cross
Eadie, Mrs W., baker, Raploch street
Eadie, Robert, grocer and fruiterer, Raploch street—house, Rose cottage
Easton, Mrs M., Larkhall tavern, London street

Ferguson, Walter, Hawthorn cottage, Muir street
Fleming, Mrs, spirit merchant, Glengowan
Forbes, Mrs, Rose cottage, Muir street
Frame, Alexander, Glenview
Frame, David, builder, Glenview
Frame, James, Glenview
Frame, Robert, joiner, Raploch street—house, Shawfield cottage
Frame, William, grocer, Millheugh
Frame & Co., watchmakers, jewellers, and drapers, the Cross
Frew & Co., James, coalmasters, Raploch colliery, and iron-founders, Vulcan foundry, Muir street

Galloway, William, draper, Raploch street
Gilchrist, Alexander, draper, Raploch street
Gilchrist, Robert, tailor, clothier, and postmaster, Union street
Glasgow Iron Coy., Fairholm colliery

Haddow, James, spirit merchant Raploch street
Hall, Mrs, confectioner, Union street
Hamilton, Andrew, Birkenshaw farm
Hamilton, Andrew, grocer, 1 Wellgate street
Hamilton, Captain MacNeill, of Raploch and Broomhill
Hamilton, Gavin, Broomhill farm
Hamilton, J., fruiterer and confectioner, Church street
Hamilton, Lieut.-Colonel James Stevenson, Fairholm
Hamilton, M'Culloch, & Co., Bog and Home Farm Collieries
Hamilton, William, Kittymuir farm
Henderson, John, East Machan

Henderson, Walter, hairdresser and perfumer, Raploch street
Hepburn, Thomas, builder, Church street
Hyslop, Simon, weaving agent, Union Street

Kennedy, R. S. & Co., brassfounders, plumbers, &c., Macneill street, house—54 Union street
Kirkland, William, Bowmanflat farm
Kirkwood, William, Clydeview house

Lang, Alex., watchmaker and jeweller, the Cross
Lang, Archibald, carter, Raploch street
Lees & Co., Maybole boot and shoe makers, Raploch street
Lindsay, John, spirit merchant, London street
Lohoar, Andrew, spirit merchant, Roslin place
Lohoar, George, High Merryton farm
Lohoar, John, boot and shoemaker, Raploch street
Lohoar, Wm., Merryton cottage
Loudon, Mrs, grocer, Wellgate street

Mackie, John, baker, M'Neil street
Mackie, Thomas, baker, M'Neil street
Mason, James, cooper, Union street
Mason, James, cooper, Wellgate street
Mason, Stephen, Machan house
Mathieson, Robert, Glenavon hotel, Charing cross
Meiklejohn, Wm., watchmaker, Glenview
Merryton Coal Coy., Merryton Colliery
Millar, Alex. L., baker, Union street
Millar, James, boot and shoemaker, Union street
Miller, D. C., Avonbank Bleach Works, Millheugh, house—Avonbank
Millar, John, draper, Charing cross
Miller, James, baker, London street
Miller, William, Apothecary hall, Raploch street
Miller & Rodger, Swinhill Collieries
Mitchell, George, Merryton Braes
Moffat, Mrs James, grocer, Raploch street
Montgomery, John, builder, John street
Morgan, Mrs, spirit merchant, Millheugh
Morrison, James, family grocer, Raploch street
Morrison, John, joiner, Raploch street
Morrison, Robert, grocer, Raploch street
Murray, James, boot and shoemaker, Raploch street
Murray, James, Portland place
Muir, John, Muir street
Muir, William, draper, Raploch street
M'Culloch, Allan, grocer and spirit merchant, Meadowhill store, Muir street
M'Dade, Alexander, grocer, M'Neil street
M'Gill, Francis A., hatter, Wellgate street

M'Kenzie, Dr, Annfield cottage
M'Kenzie, Stewart, Black Bull Inn, Hamilton street
M'Knight, John, Violet bank
M'Lean, John, Millbank, East Machan
M'Leod, William, tailor and clothier, Raploch street
M'Meekin, Wm., blacksmith, the Cross
M'Naughton and Co., David, Broomhill colliery
M'Naughton, David, Appletree cottage, Machan

Newlands, Archd., spirit merchant, Raploch street
Nisbet, Mrs, draper, Hamilton street

Paterson, John, grocer, Wellgate street
Paterson, Robert, grocer, Union street
Paterson, Wm., grocer, Millheugh
Purves, Mrs M., spirit merchant, Masons' Arms, Charing Cros

Ramsay, Andrew, flesher, London street
Reid, George, spirit merchant, London street
Reid, John, draper, Raploch street
Reid, Wm., flesher, Raploch street
Ritchie, Thomas, ironmonger and seedsman, Union street
Ross, John, pawnbroker, Raploch street
Russell, James, grocer, the Cross
Russell, Thomas, spirit merchant, Millheugh

Scanlan, John, spirit merchant, Raploch street
Scott, Mrs J., grocer and spirit merchant, Raploch street
Scott, Mrs J., spirit merchant, Devon Arms, The Pleasance
Shearer, Wm., plasterer, Raploch street
Sheridan, Samuel, Victoria hotel, Raploch street
Sibbald, Wm., Royal hotel, Raploch street
Sinclair, John, tailor, 1 Union street
Smellie, Mrs Gavin, grocer, London street
Smith, George, painter and hairdresser, Wellgate street
Spalding, George, grocer and spirit merchant, Wellgate
Spalding, Thomas, grocer, Wellgate and Raploch streets
Spencer, Andrew, Millburn and Auldton collieries
Spiers, Robert, spirit merchant, Raploch street
Steel, Andrew, grocer, Wellgate
Steel, Wm., Glasgow carrier, Wellgate street
Stewart, Charles, tinsmith and gasfitter, Church street
Stewart, Dr Charles, Mansfield cottage, Church street
Summerlee Iron Coy., Dykehead colliery

Tennant, A. & J., boot and shoe makers, Wellgate street
Thomson, Wm., boot and shoe maker, Church street
Thomson, Thomas, baker, Raploch street
Thorburn, Dr R. T., Bank buildings, Union street
Turner, Dr, 13 Wellgate street

Tyson, Thomas, confectioner, London street

Walker, Matthew, manager, Swinhill collieries, Machan cottage
Walker, Mrs, grocer, Wellgate street
Walker, Simon, flesher, Raploch street
Walker, William, flesher, Wellgate street
Walkinshaw, John, boot and shoe maker, Wellgate street
Watson, Gavin, wood merchant, Wellgate street
Watson, James, wood merchant, Wellgate street
Watson, Robert, joiner, East Machan
Watson, Wm., blacksmith, Church street
Watson, Wm., grocer, Union street
Watson & Walker, grocers and spirit merchants, Raploch st.
Watt, John, draper, Argyle house, Union street
Watt, William, farmer, West Machan
White, John, grocer, Wellgate street
White, William, stationer, the cross
Williamson, James, West Highlees farm
Wilson, Andrew, fruiterer and confectioner, Wellgate street
Wilson, James, draper, Raploch street
Wilson, James, saddler, Raploch street
Wilson, John, Raploch hotel, the cross
Wilson, Wm., joiner, 91 Union street
Wilson, John, Highlees farm
Wilson, Dr, Raploch street
Winning, John, grocer, M'Neil street

CHURCHES AND CLERGY.

Established Church, Church Street, ... Rev. John Crichton
Free Church, Union Street, ... Rev. William Findlay
United Presbyterian Church, Wellgate Street, .. Rev. John Shearar
Evangelical Union Church, Muir Street, ... Rev Robert Brown
Roman Catholic Church, ... Rev. Paul R. Pies

DALSERF SCHOOL BOARD.

Rev. W. P. Rorison (Chairman), Andrew Spencer, William Sim, Thomas Brown, William Templeton.

LARKHALL SCHOOL BOARD.

William Kirkwood (Chairman), Rev. William Findlay, Rev. John Crichton, Rev. John Shearar, Alexander Frame, John Kirkland, R. G. Cooper, Thomas Duncan, clerk.

SCHOOLS AND TEACHERS.

Glengowan—Master, Alex. M'Knight; Mistress, Miss Jack
Academy—Master, James Brown; Mistress, Euphemia M'Donald; Music Teacher, Jane Smith.
Muir Street—Master, John A. Beattie; Mistress, Janet Galt.
Roman Catholic, St. Mary's—Mistress, Margaret M'Killop.

DALSERF PAROCHIAL BOARD.

Chairman, Rev. W. P. Rorison; Medical Officer, Dr M'Kenzie; Inspector James Anderson; Collector, John Macfie, Union Bank of Scotland Stonehouse.

SOCIETIES.

BOWLING CLUB.—Green—Raploch Street. President, D. C. Miller; Vice-President, Thomas Duncan; Treas., James Barr; Secy., John A. Beattie.

DALSERF CURLING CLUB.—President, David Frame; Treasurer, James Boyd; Secretary, James Frame.

DALSERF FARMERS' SOCIETY.—Wm. Watt, President; Treasurer and Secretary, Thomas Watson

FREE GARDENERS.—"Thistle Lodge," No. 13. Alex. Gold, R.W.M.; James Hamilton, treasurer; James Grieve, secretary.

FREE MASONS.—"St. Thomas," No. 306. John Nicol, R.W.M.; James Purves, treasurer; John Corbett, secretary.

FREE MASONS.—"Clydesdale" Lodge, No. 551.—Daniel Wright, R.W.M.; James Bryce, Treasurer; James Stewart, Secretary

FREE MINERS.—"Alexander Lodge." Treasurer, M. Gilmour; Secretary, John Potter.

FUNERAL SOCIETY.—Treasurer, Thomas Scott; Secretary, James Downs.

GOOD TEMPLARS.—"Morning Star Lodge," No. 188. William Henderson, D.G.W.C.T.; John Henderson ,W.C.T.; Archibald Barr, Treasurer; D. M'Naughton, Secretary. Meets in Union Hall on Mondays at 8 P.M.

MUTUAL IMPROVEMENT ASSOCIATION—President, John Montgomery; Vice-President, Wm. Burns; Treasurer, John Winning; Secretary, Robert Struthers

ORNITHOLOGICAL SOCIETY.—President, Wm. M'Leod; Treasurer, John White; Secretary, Wm. Burns.

PUBLIC LIBRARY.—45 Union Street. Open Wednesday nights. President, John Corbett; Treasurer, John Ross; Secretary, Robert Struthers; Librarian, Robert Lightbody.

TONIC SOL-FA ASSOCIATION.—Conductor, John Walkinshaw; Treasurer and Secretary, Thomas Walkinshaw.

VICTUALLING SOCIETY.—Stores—Charing Cross and Wellgate Street. John Kirkland, treasurer; J. C. Burns, secretary.

YOUNG MEN'S CHRISTIAN ASSOCIATION.—Hon. President, James Stewart; President, Wm. Kirkland; Vice-President, Wm. Henderson; Treasurer, Edward Currie; Secretary, D. B. Barr.

UNION BANK OF SCOTLAND, Church Street. Agent, William Forrest. Accountant, William Cunninghame.

GAS COMPANY.—Works—Raploch Street. President, James Anderson; Treasurer, David Scott; Manager and Secretary, John Muter.

CALEDONIAN RAILWAY STATION.—Stationmaster, Archd. Beaton.

HANDBOOK

OF

HAMILTON.

CONTENTS.

	PAGE.
LEGENDARY,	8
DAVID I. AT CADZOW,	9
CIVIL AND RELIGIOUS STRUGGLES,	10
NOTABLE EVENTS,	12
ANTIQUITIES,	13
THE NOBLE FAMILY OF HAMILTON,	16
HAMILTON PALACE:—	
INTERIOR EQUIPMENTS,	7
GREAT HALL,	31
GRAND STAIRCASE,	32
TAPESTRY ROOMS,	32
GALLERY AND OLD STATEROOMS,	33
THE BECKFORD LIBRARY,	33
DUCHESS' PRIVATE APARTMENTS,	34
THE CHARTER ROOM,	35
MISCELLANEOUS,	35
QUEEN MARY AT THE PALACE,	36
OTHER ROYAL VISITORS,	37
VISIT OF THE PRINCE OF WALES,	37
THE MAUSOLEUM,	42
CHATELHERAULT,	46
THE OAKS AND ABORIGINAL BREED OF CATTLE,	47
THE TOWN OF HAMILTON:—	
ECCLESIASTICAL HISTORY,	56
TWO DISTINGUISHED ROMAN CATHOLIC RECTORS,	57
REFORMATION ASSOCIATIONS—THE ATTITUDE OF THE HAMILTONS—JOHN KNOX,	58
CHURCH DISCIPLINE 200 YEARS AGO,	59
PREACHING AT THE GREAT DUKE,	61
PRESENT ECCLESIASTICAL CONDITION,	61
MARTYRS OF THE COVENANT,	64
EDUCATIONAL,	67
MUNICIPAL,	70
BURGH REVENUE,	73

CONTENTS (Continued).

	PAGE.
CHARITIES,	76
PUBLIC BUILDINGS—THE TOWN HALL,	78
THE OLD TOLBOOTH,	78
THE COUNTY BUILDINGS,	79
THE PRISON,	82
MILITARY,	83
POOR-HOUSE AND HOSPITAL,	84
RAILWAYS,	84
RETROSPECTIVE,	85
THE COUNCIL AND THE FERRY FOLKS,	87
POSTGATE OR POSKITE,	88
THE UNREFORMED TOWN COUNCIL,	88
CONVIVIALIA,	89
THE COUNCIL AND PRINCE CHARLIE,	90
A TROUBLESOME JAILOR,	91
MAKING PROGRESS,	92
TREATMENT OF SOCIAL PROBLEMS,	93
MERCANTILE AFFAIRS,	95
FIRES,	98
A TIME OF SCARCITY,	99
HOUSE RENTS,	100
A PIOUS BELLMAN,	100
CHARITY SCHOOLS A CENTURY AGO,	101
TRANSITION,	102

THE COAL INDUSTRY:—

EARLY MINING OPERATIONS,	105
RECENT OPERATIONS AT QUARTER,	106
OVERCOMING THE "ACCIDENT,"	107
THE COAL IN THE TOWN'S LANDS,	109
CADZOW AND OTHER COLLIERIES,	116
MEMORABLE ACCIDENTS,	119

QUARTER:—

MINERALS,	122
POPULATION,	123
ALLOW'S HILL,	124
DARNGABER CASTLE,	124
PLOTCOCK,	125
EDDLEWOOD,	125
IRON WORKS,	128
SOCIETIES, &C.,	128

HANDBOOK.

WE purpose to sketch the early history, notable events and associations, and present condition and prospects of Hamilton and vicinage. The ancient designation of the parish was Cadzow, the etymology of which is uncertain; and the present name was assumed by virtue of a charter, of date 3d July, 1445, granted by James II. of Scotland to James, first Lord Hamilton. In the hoary ruins which crown the precipitous banks of Avon, the leading street of the town, and numerous familiar objects, the ancient name still finds preservation. The parish of Hamilton from north to south is six miles in length, and of nearly equal breadth from east to west, the extent in square miles being 22·25, and in acres 14,240. The northern boundary is formed by the parish of Bothwell; on the east are Dalziel, Cambusnethan, Dalserf, and Stonehouse; on the south and south-west the parish of Glassford; and on the west Blantyre. The district is rich in mineral wealth and natural beauty. The Clyde and Avon water its broad smiling plains, whose fertility and advanced cultivation have long made the locality in reality as well as in name—the orchard of Scotland; while, as the cradle of a powerful race, which exerted a momentous influence on national events, and as the occasional theatre of great occurrences, history has accorded to it in the past a prominent place. For the future, the eminence to be attained will be industrial and commercial, the opening up of its coal field, destined to be second in importance to none in Scotland, having changed, and being likely in a way scarcely possible to realise still further to change, the character of the district.

LEGENDARY.

The ancient kingdom of Strathclyde embraced Lanarkshire within its bounds. After the withdrawal of the Roman power, it is certain that the inhabitants, the Romanised Britains, if they had ever been Christianised, lapsed into heathenism. The received local apostle was St Kentigern, otherwise known as St Mungo, a contemporary of Columba, and regarding three of whose renowned miracles the armorial bearings of the city of Glasgow are a perpetuation. Kentigern had a controversy with a Strathclyde King Morken, and in a sort of despair left to do duty among the Southern Britains in Wales. There afterwards, however, occupied the throne of Strathclyde, Rederech, a pious monarch, eager to restore the gospel to his benighted subjects, and at his desire Kentigern returned. Rederech had his castle at Cadzow, near Barncluith Burn, where Castlehill House now stands. Of him it is related that he had invited a stranger to hunt with him at Cadzow, who, during the intervals of the chase, made himself so agreeable to the fair Queen that she gave him a ring she had received from her husband, and otherwise showed a degree of favour to him, which, on its discovery, enraged Rederech. In a fit of furious jealousy he possessed himself of the ring while the knight was sleeping, threw it into the river, and then, sending for the Queen, asked her for it, and threatened death if it was not produced. The trembling lady sent to the stranger for the ring, but, of course, it was not forthcoming, and, as a last resource, a message was sent to Glasgow to St Mungo, imploring his assistance. The good man was sorry for the Queen, and sent one of his servants to fish, and on opening the mouth of the first fish caught, the ring was found. St Mungo sent it to the Queen, she hastened with it to the King, and her life was spared. This legend is taken from the Breviary of Aberdeen and other sources, and a representation of it forms the reverse of Bishop Wishart of Glasgow's seal in the 13th century. Strathclyde had less renown from its political history than as the theatre of the triumphs of St Kentigern, and it is through him that Rederech comes out of the utter darkness political into the doubtful light of ecclesiastical history.

DAVID I. AT CADZOW.

To step at once from the uncertain footing of the sixth to the increasingly strengthening ground of the twelfth and thirteenth centuries, we find the old Scottish kings in 1153 and 1289 holding their courts at Cadzow, which continued to be royal property till after the Battle of Bannockburn. David I., of saintly memory, before coming to the Throne, by his brother Edgar's dying request, was created Lord of Cumbria, in which district Cadzow was included. He found this portion of his heritage in a miserable state, and sought to ameliorate the condition of his people by the establishment of civil laws and the restoration of ecclesiastical jurisdiction. He granted the Church of Cadzow as an endowment to the newly-founded Cathedral of Glasgow; and, uniting a taste for gardening and love of sport with religious fervour, many of the oaks at Cadzow are believed to have been planted by the kingly hand, and here he hunted

> "The mightiest of all the beasts of chase
> That roam in woody Caledon!"

From here, also, Royal charters were dated: *Apud Castrum de Cadichow*—at our Castle of Cadzow.

CIVIL AND RELIGIOUS STRUGGLES.

The events of which the district was subsequently the scene are well known in Scottish history. In November, 1650, Cromwell sent General Lambert and Commissary-General Whalley to Hamilton, with five regiments of cavalry, to overawe the west country Covenanters or to bring them over to his own terms. They were attacked by Colonel Kerr with 1500 horsemen from Ayrshire. The Covenanters succeeded in securing a number of the horses; but Lambert having rallied his forces, overtook the "spoil-encumbered foe" two miles west of Hamilton, killed Colonel Kerr and about 100 of his troops, and took many prisoners.

On Sunday, 1st June, 1679, Captain Graham (afterwards Viscount Dundee) on his way to the field of Drumclog, seized, near Hamilton, John King, a field preacher, and seventeen other people, whom he bound in pairs, and drove before him towards Loudon Hill. Mr King, who was probably in disguise, is described by Crighton as a "bra muckle carl with a white hat and a great bob of ribbons on the back o't." The Covenanters after their success at Drumclog, deeming it unlawful to fight on the Sabbath except in self-defence, returned to the field of action, where they offered up thanks to the Almighty for the victory they had gained; after which they took some refreshment in Strathaven, and marched to Hamilton in the evening. Next day (June 2) flushed with victory, they resolved to make an attack on Glasgow. One division of them, commanded by Mr Hamilton, attempted to penetrate by Gallowgate, and another party entered by the High Street. But Lord Ross had so completely barricaded the streets, and made such a resistance that the Covenanters were soon compelled to retire, with the loss of Walter Paterson of Carbarns, and five of their party killed and several wounded. After their repulse at Glasgow they rallied on Tollcross Muir, and returned to Hamilton. The more moderate party (June 20) drew up a paper which afterwards obtained the name of the "Hamilton declaration." The purport of it was to forbear all angry disputes and mutual recriminations for the present, to disclaim any intention to overturn the Government, civil or ecclesiastical, and to refer all matters of importance to a free Parliament and a lawfully chosen General Assembly. This proposal was, of course, rejected by the violent party. Their guard was attacked in the night-time at Hamilton Ford, and one of their number (James Cleland) killed. On Saturday, 21st June, the royal army, under the Duke of Monmouth, about 500 strong, reached Bothwell Muir within two miles of the Covenanters' camp. On the morning of Sunday 22d June, the Covenanters, amounting to about 4000 men, were posted between the Clyde and the town of Hamilton, on the brow of the brae near Bothwell Bridge. Rathillet, Hall, and Turnbull, with three troops under their command, and one piece of brass ordnance, guarded the important pass. The result of this most unfortunate rencounter is well known. The Covenanters were put to flight. They fled with great loss chiefly in the direction of Glassford and Strathaven. Gordon of Earlston had reached the parish of Hamilton with a party of Galloway men, when they met their discomfited brethren at Allowshill, near Quarter, where Gordon was met and killed. A great number of the Covenanters found shelter in Hamilton woods, and the amiable Duchess Anne, requesting that the soldiers might not be permitted to enter her plantations, Monmouth instantly gave orders to that effect. About 1200 men were taken prisoners on the spot.

NOTABLE EVENTS.

The Hamiltons were great opposers of the Union. In 1707, when that event took place, 500 troops assembled at Hamilton to resist it by force of arms. It was expected that 7000 or 8000 would have met; but the Duke of Hamilton disapproved of the measure.

On the death of the Duke of Douglas in 1761, the house of Hamilton, as male representatives of the Douglases, laid claim to the estates, under a persuasion that Mr Douglas, son and heir of Lady Jane Stewart, sister of the Duke of Douglas was a suppositious child taken at Paris from the real parents. A long lawsuit was the result. It was decided in Paris and in the Court of Session in favour of the Hamiltons; but, on an appeal to the House of Peers, was ultimately decided in favour of Mr Douglas, afterwards created Lord Douglas—the Duke of Hamilton retaining the titles.

In 1777, Douglas, Duke of Hamilton, coming of age, raised in Hamilton, for the service of the country, the 82d Regiment of Foot, which afterwards highly distinguished itself in the American War.

On 11th June, 1782, the Duke of Hamilton, as Duke of Brandon in England, was called to take his seat in the House of Lords as a British peer. This paved the way to all the Scottish nobility who have since obtained similar honours and privileges.

The parish has been the birthplace and occasional residence of many eminent characters. The celebrated Dr Cullen, sometimes represented as born at Lanark in 1712, appears distinctly from the session-books of Hamilton to have been born two years later in the parish of Hamilton. Dr Cullen was magistrate of Hamilton for several years. The celebrated Lord Cochrane spent many of his early days in the parish. The father of the late Professor Millar of Glasgow was parochial clergyman; as was also the father of the late Dr Baillie of London, and of his celebrated sister, Joanna Baillie. Principal Cunningham, the theologian, was baptised in Muir Street Secession Church on 2d October, 1805; and Dr Livingstone, the African traveller, was a reader in the library of the same congregation.

ANTIQUITIES.

The Castle of Cadzow is the most prominent antiquity in the parish. It stands in Hamilton wood, amidst the softest and most picturesque of sylvan surroundings, on the summit of a precipitous rock, the base of which is washed by the Avon. Who its founders were is unknown, although it is surmised that Caw or Cay was the first of the royal race who took up their residence in this quarter. The Castle continued in the possession of the Crown until it was granted by Robert the Bruce to Sir Walter Fitz-Gilbert. With only two short interruptions, it has ever since continued in the hands of his descendants. The first of these interruptions was about the year 1581, when it fell for a short time into the hands of Captain Stewart. The other suspension, equally short in duration, was in 1654, when by Cromwell's act of grace and pardon,

William Duke of Hamilton deceased, was exempted from all benefit thereof, and his estates forfeited, there being reserved out of them £400 per annum to his Duchess during her life, and after her death to each of his four daughters and their heirs for ever. The Castle of Cadzow seems to have been repaired at different times. The keep, with the fosse around it, a narrow bridge on the south over the fosse, and a well inside, are still in good preservation, and are all of polished stone of a reddish colour. Several vaults and the walls, probably of the chapel, are still visible. Cadzow Castle is celebrated in Scott's fine ballad—

> "When princely Hamilton's abode,
> Ennobled Cadzow's Gothic towers,
> The song went round, the goblet flowed,
> And revel sped the laughing hours.
>
> Then, thrilling to the harp's gay sound,
> So sweetly rung each vaulted wall,
> And echoed light the dancer's bound,
> As mirth and music cheered the hall.
>
> But Cadzow's towers, in ruins laid,
> And vaults by ivy mantled o'er,
> Thrill to the music of the shade
> Or echo Evan's hoarser roar."

The Castle of Darngaber (*i. e.*, the "house between the waters," or, as some have supposed, the "hiding place of the goats,") in the S.E. side of the parish is said to have been built by Thomas de Hamilton, son of Sir John de Hamilton, Dominus de Cadzow. Its ruins stand on a small knoll at the extremity of a tongue of land where two rivulets meet. The foundations only of this ancient fortress can now be traced. They are entirely of flat shingly stones, without lime, and seem never to have been subjected to a tool. Small vaults have been discovered, which are not arched, but drawn together as conduits sometimes are.

It is probable, therefore, that Thomas de Hamilton did not build, but only repaired this castle.

The most perfect, and indeed the only tumulus, properly speaking, in the parish is at Meikle Earnock, about two miles south of Hamilton. It is about 12 feet in diameter and 8 feet high—it was formerly much larger—and hollow at the top. When broken into, several urns were found containing the ashes of human bones, some of them accompanied by the tooth of a horse. There was no inscription seen, but some of the urns, which were all of baked earth, were plain, and others decorated with moulding, probably to distinguish the quality of the deceased.

In the haugh to the north of the Palace there is an ancient moathill or seat of justice. It is about 30 feet in diameter at the base, and about 15 or 16 feet high, and is flat at the top. When it stood formerly in the midst of the town, the hill formed part of the garden of an alehouse, and was dressed with the spade and adorned with plants. It cannot be less than eight or nine hundred years old, as no erections of the kind have been in use since the reign of Malcolm Canmore. Near the Moathill is an ancient stone cross about four feet high, bearing no inscription. It is said to have been the cross of the Netherton.

In the south of the parish a remarkable stone, about six feet high, but leaning considerably to one side, gives the immediate locality the name, "Crooked Stone." It is of freestone, and evidently very ancient. Mr Chalmers notices these bended stones as cromlechs of Druidical origin. A neighbouring farmer (says Mr William Patrick in his Statistical Account of Hamilton, written in 1847) lately set the stone upright, leaving posterity to wonder why it was called crooked stone.

The Barncluith gardens may be noticed amongst the antiquities of the district. The flower garden is cut out of the steep banks of Avon, two or three hundred feet high, and is divided into five terraces. These are flanked by terrace walls, covered with espaliers of various descriptions. The borders of the walls are crowded with a variety of evergreens cut into fantastic forms. In the centre of the great walk is a handsome pavilion fitted up with rustic chairs, and other curious pieces of furniture. The gardens and buildings have afforded infinite scope for the pencil of the artist and pen of the poet. They are believed to have been constructed by John Hamilton of Barncluith, commissary of Hamilton and Campsie, in 1583. He was son of Quinton Hamilton, who was killed fighting in the Queen's cause at the battle of Langside; and is reputed by tradition to have been deeply skilled in mathematics.

THE NOBLE FAMILY OF HAMILTON.

After the defeat of the English at Bannockburn the Barony of Cadzow changed hands for the last time, passing into the possession of the ancestors of its present owner. With the history of the Hamiltons, and their accession to wealth, honour, and dignities, the inhabitants were henceforth to be completely identified; and it may justly be said that wherever there appears a patriot, statesman, or warrior in the annals of the family, there also are found recorded proofs of the loyal support accorded them at every crisis by the "good men of the West," their retainers and dependants.

The English origin of the family is undoubted; how or when it took root north of the Tweed is not so clearly ascertained. Their lineage has been traced to Robert (Blanchmains) third Earl of Leicester, who died 1190. Though it has not been proved, there is nothing improbable in this descent; for the Earl's second son was Bishop of St. Andrews, other relations figure in Scottish history of the period, and the cinquefoil on a bloody shield, the heraldic bearing from an early period of the Scottish Hamiltons, was also that of the house of Leicester referred to. The name, obviously territorial, is believed to have been taken from some one of the numerous manors of Hambleden, situated in Bucks and other English counties. There is a legend connected with the origin of the family, which, though fabulous, having been quoted by Sir Archibald Alison, we do not apologise for including in our narrative. Sir Gilbert de Hemelen, Knight, was a warm admirer of the Bruce, and at the English Court he ventured with chivalrous boldness to give vent to his admiration. He was at once challenged by a parasite named de Spencer to mortal combat. He slew his antagonist, and escaping to the Scotch Court, met King Robert at Cadzow at the head of a hunting party. As a modern minnie-singer relates—

"Bold was the foremost hunter's look—majestic was his air;
  Most firmly knit his head and limbs, and sable dark his hair."

After revealing himself to the Scotch King, and telling his story, he is embraced by the Bruce:—

"Enough, enough, Sir Gilbert, we give thee welcome here;
  Look round thee, and where'er thine eye traverses far and near,
  These acres broad shall be thine own, whilst thou that sword
      shall bring
  To aid broad Scotland's cause and mine, for I am Bruce the
      King."

Subsequently the King bestows on the Knight the hand of his niece, Isabel, in marriage. As connected with this legend, it is explained that the family motto "Through," and the crest with Oak and Saw arose from Sir Gilbert taking in his flight the dress of a wood-cutter and practising that primitive art, crying to his servant "Through" to distract his attention from his pursuers.

All legend to the contrary, the pedigree of the family cannot be carried beyond (1) Walter Fitz-Gilbert of Hamilton, who, in 1296 held lands in Lanarkshire, and swore fealty to King Edward I. of England as Overlord of Scotland, and in 1314 kept the Castle of Bothwell for the English. His early surrender of the fortress and of the English knights and nobles who had fled to it from the field of Bannockburn, was rewarded by King Robert Bruce by grants of the lands and baronies of Cadzow and Machanshire, Kinneil, &c., lands forfeited by the Cumyns and other adherents of England. He attained the rank of knighthood, and married Mary, daughter of Sir Adam of Gordon of Huntley, by whom he left two sons. The elder (2) Sir David Fitz-Walter Fitz-Gilbert was taken prisoner at the battle of Neville's Cross, in 1346. He founded a chantry in the Cathedral of Glasgow in 1361, and appears among the barons in the Scottish Parliaments in 1368, 1371, and 1373. His eldest son (3) Sir David of Hamilton of Cadzow died before 1392, leaving by his wife, Janet of Keith, only daughter and heiress of Sir William of Keith of Galston, five sons and a daughter. The eldest son (4) Sir John of Hamilton of Cadzow, married Janet, daughter of Sir James of Douglas of Dalkeith, by whom he was the father of (5) Sir James of Hamilton of Cadzow, who, about 1422, married Janet, daughter of Alexander of Livingston of Callander, by whom he had (6) Sir James of Hamilton of Cadzow, and four other sons. It was in the person of Sir James that the family was ennobled. By charter of date 1445, he was created

Lord Hamilton, and his manor house of "The Orchard," in the barony of Cadzow was erected into his chief messuage, with the name of Hamilton which it still bears. In 1474, when at an advanced age, Lord Hamilton married the Princess Mary, eldest daughter of James II., King of Scotland, and widow of Thomas Boyd, Earl of Arran. By this connection his descendants came to be declared in Parliament, on the demise of James V., in the event of the death of Mary Queen of Scots, next heirs to the Crown, and have, in consequence, been ever since regarded as a branch of the royal family. Buchanan and some of his followers represent the Hamiltons as dependants on the Douglases, and as becoming great by betraying them to James II., who murdered the Earl of Douglas in Stirling Castle with his own hand, although he had a safeguard. It is further asserted that James III. forced the wife of Boyd, Earl of Arran, to forsake her husband, and marry Lord Hamilton. These statements, there is reason to believe, were invidious on the part of Buchanan, and made in order to please his patron the Earl of Murray, a great enemy of the Hamiltons. Boetius says, that the first daughter of James II. was married to Lord Boyd, who had by her a son and a daughter, and that after the death of Lord Boyd, this daughter of James II. was married to Lord Hamilton; in that way the Hamiltons are "decorit in the King's blood." This edition of Boetius was translated by Bellenden, who, being contemporary with the lady, is better authority than Buchanan, who lived a century after. It is to the praise of the first Lord Hamilton that in 1460, he founded a college in the University of Glasgow—the first college in Scotland founded by a layman.

The death of King James V. in 1542 left only an

infant of five days old between James, third Lord Hamilton, second Earl of Arran, and the throne. He was at once chosen regent of the Kingdom and tutor to the young Queen, and declared to be "second person in the realm"—a position which carried with it something of royal style. He signed or subscribed his name as "James G.," or simply "James," and wrote himself, "James, by the Grace of God, Earl of Arran and Lord Hamilton, Governor and Prince of Scotland." He held his high offices till 1554, when he resigned them in favour of the Queen-mother, Mary of Guise, receiving in return from King Henry II. of France a grant of the Duchy of Chatelherault. His nearness to the throne, his great following, and large possessions, left him still a person of such mark that his eldest son, the Earl of Arran, as he was called, was proposed at one time as the husband of Queen Mary of Scotland, and at another time as the husband of Queen Elizabeth of England. The career which opened with such high aspirations came to a sad and untimely end; the Earl was afflicted with madness in 1562, and never recovered his reason, although he lived till 1609. His father, the first Duke of Chatelherault, dying in 1575, his second son, Lord John Hamilton, the lay abbot or commendator of Arbroath, became virtual head of the house, and as such was, in 1599, created Marquis of Hamilton. He died in 1604, being succeeded by his son James, the second Marquis, who, in 1619, was created Earl of Cambridge in England, and died in 1625. He was succeeded by his eldest son James, the third Marquis, who led an army of 6,000 men to the support of King Gustavus Adolphus of Sweden in 1631-32; and a few years later acted a conspicuous part in the great contest between Charles I. and the Scottish Covenanters. In 1638 he was appointed his

Majesty's Commissioner to the famous General Assembly which met at Glasgow, the proceedings of which are well known. In 1639, when the Scots nation were compelled to defend by arms their civil and religious liberty, the Marquis was sent to Scotland with a well equipped fleet, and a force of 5,000 men, while the King, at the head of 25,000 foot and 3,000 horse, advanced by land. The treaty of Berwick, concluded on the 18th July, prevented hostilities at that time. It was on this occasion that his mother, Ann Cunningham, appeared on horseback on the shore near Leith, armed with pistols, and declared that she would shoot her son should he attempt to land and attack his countrymen. During the hostilities at this time between the Royalists, headed by the Marquis, and the Covenanters, aided by Lords Fleming, Montgomery, Loudon, Boyd, Lindsay, and others, the latter party seized the Castle of Strathaven, and compelled all the gentlemen in Clydesdale, who were suspected of favouring the Royal cause, to give security that they would not rise in arms. "As a reward for his services," says Douglas, "to the King, he was created Duke of Hamilton, Marquis of Clydesdale, Earl of Arran and Cambridge, Lord Aven and Innerdale, by patent dated at Oxford, 12th April, 1643, to him and the heirs male of his body; which failing, to his brother and the heirs male of his body; which failing, to the eldest heir female of the Marquis's body without division, and the heirs male of the body of such heir female, they bearing the name and arms of Hamilton, which all failing, to the nearest legitimate heir whatsoever of the Marquis." In 1648, the Duke promoted with all his power "the engagement" entered into by the Scots Parliament to raise an army for relief of King Charles, who was then in the hands of the

Parliamentary army. He was appointed general of the forces, which were hastily raised, amounting to about 10,000 foot and 4,000 cavalry. With this army he marched into England, and, being joined by the English Royalists they were met at Preston by Cromwell at the head of a strong reinforcement. A battle took place on the 17th of August, when the Royalists were defeated and their army dispersed. The Duke of Hamilton capitulated with General Lambert on assurance of safety to himself and his followers. He was afterwards taken to Windsor Castle and confined under a strong guard. On the 21st of December, when King Charles I. was carried through Windsor on his way to his trial in London, that affecting interview mentioned by historians took place between Charles and the Duke.

After the king's execution the Duke made an escape from Windsor, under night, but entering London he was re-taken, and brought to trial 6th February, 1649, and sentenced to be beheaded on Friday, the 9th of March following. In terms of the sentence, he was decapitated in Palace Yard, Westminster, in the 43d year of his age, and his remains were, according to his desire, conveyed to Scotland, and deposited in the burial place of the family at Hamilton. As the body came by sea to Scotland, it appears to have been landed at Borrowstouness, and taken to Kinneil House, as it is stated in the Kirk Session books of Hamilton that the corpse of James, first Duke of Hamilton, was carried in a coach from Kinneil to Hamilton, and deposited in the family vault at the Old Church, attended by a great assemblage of people.

His Duchess, Lady Mary Fielding, died on the 10th of May, 1638, by whom he had three sons, Charles, James, and William, and three daughters,

Mary, Anne, and Susanna. The three sons and eldest daughter all died young. His Grace having, therefore, no male heirs, was succeeded in his titles and estates, in terms of the patent, by his brother William, Earl of Lanark. He died in 1651 of the wounds which he had received at the battle of Worcester. The duchy of Hamilton, in terms of the patent of creation, now devolved on the daughter of the first Duke, Lady Anne, whose husband, Lord William Douglas, Earl of Selkirk, was, in 1660, created Duke of Hamilton for life. He died in 1694. The Duchess Anne, who survived till 1716, had, in 1698, resigned her titles in the King's hands in favour of her eldest son, James, Earl of Arran, who was anew created Duke of Hamilton with the precedency of 1643. In 1711, he was created Duke of Brandon in England, but the House of Lords refused him a seat or vote in Parliament, on the ground that the crown was disabled by the Act of Union from granting a peerage of Great Britain to any person who was a peer of Scotland before the Union. The Duke was killed in a duel in Hyde Park with Lord Mohun in 1712. He was succeeded by his eldest son, James, who, dying in 1743, was succeeded by his eldest son, James, who, in 1752, married the famous beauty, Elizabeth Gunning, and died in 1758, being succeeded by his eldest son, James George, an infant of three years old. On the death of the Duke of Douglas in 1761, the male representation of the "red" or Angus Branch of the Douglases, with the titles of Marquis of Douglas, Earl of Angus, &c., devolved on the Dukes of Hamilton, as descendants of the Duchess Anne's husband, William, Earl of Selkirk, third son of the first Marquis of Douglas. Dying in 1769, in his 15th year, James George, seventh Duke of Hamilton, was succeeded by his only brother, Douglas, who, in 1782, took his seat in Parliament as Duke of Brandon, the House of Lords being now satisfied, after consultation with the twelve Judges, that the Act of Union did not prohibit the Crown from making a peer of Scotland a peer of Great Britain. Duke Douglas died without issue in 1799, when the titles and estates passed to his uncle, Archibald, the second son of James, the fifth Duke. Duke Archibald dying in 1819, was succeeded by his eldest son, Alexander, who, in 1810, married a daughter of Mr Beckford of Fonthill, and died in 1852; when he was succeeded by his only son, William Alexander Anthony Archibald, eleventh Duke of Hamilton in the peerage of Scotland. He died in 1863, and was succeeded by William Alexander Louis Stephen Douglas Hamilton, the present Duke, who was born in 1845.

The French monarchs always recognised the right of the Dukes of Hamilton to the Duchy of Chatelherault. At the time of the Treaty of Utrecht, in 1713, the Earl of Abercorn preferred a claim for the fourth part of the revenues as heir male of the first Duke of Chatelherault, which was overruled. In 1819, when the grandfather of the present Duke resumed the title, and again in 1823 and 1825, the Earl of Aberdeen, as guardian of the second Marquis of Abercorn, then a minor, through the British Ambassador, sent a remonstrance to the French Government, to which evasive replies were given. Duke Alexander and his Duchess in 1826 were received at the Court of Charles X. as Duke and Duchess of Chatelherault. In 1853, Lord Aberdeen revived the Abercorn pretensions by causing a representation on the subject to be made by the British Minister. There had been no public recognition of the title on the part of the Imperial Court; but, in

April 1864, the Emperor Napoleon III., granted a new patent in favour of the 12th Duke of Hamilton, enjoining "the maintenance and confirmation of the hereditary title of Duke of Chatelherault, created by Henry II. of France in 1548, in favour of James Hamilton, Earl of Arran;" and in April 1866, by a solemn finding of the French Law Courts, the question was finally settled, the title being declared to belong indisputably to the Duke of Hamilton.

It is somewhat remarkable (observes our well-informed local antiquary, Mr Andrew Hamilton, Quarter) that of all the numerous families of the name of Hamilton, who at one time owned lands in Lanarkshire only two who possess estates now are really Hamiltons, by male descent—viz., John G. C. Hamilton of Dalzell, who represents the Orbieston, Rosehall, and Dalzell families; and James Hamilton, who has lately established his claim before the House of Lords, and assumed the title of Lord Belhaven and Stenton, and who represents the families of Udstoun, Wishaw, and Stevenstoun. All the others are descended from heirs-female whose husbands assumed the name of Hamilton. The head of the house, the Duke of Hamilton, is a Douglas; the representative of the Broomhill, Dalserf, and Millburn branches, a Campbell; Raploch, a Macneill; Fairholm, a Stevenson; Barncluith (Lady Ruthven), a Campbell; Blantyre Farm, a Coats; Newtoun, a Gray; and Letham, in Avendale, a Napier.

Since writing the above paragraph, it has been suggested that Andrew Hamilton of Drumclog, Avendale, and Thomas Hamilton of Shawtonhill, Glassford, may be lineally descended through heirs-male, and therefore also Hamiltons; but of this we are not certain, not knowing to what branch they belong, and cannot trace their descent further back than the beginning of the 17th century, although, to all appearance, there has been a regular succession of heirs-male in both families from that period to the present time.

Other two families—viz., those of Silvertonhill, and Avendale and Gilkerscleugh, who once owned extensive possessions in Clydesdale are, we believe, represented at the present time by heirs male lineally descended; but the former, Sir Robert North Collie Hamilton, enjoys only the title of Silvertonhill, without any lands; and the latter, George John Hamilton, Major, 26th Foot, has now no lands whatever in the county, his grandfather, Daniel Hamilton of Gilkerscleugh, Sheriff-Depute of Lanarkshire, having sold Gilkerscleugh about fifty years ago to Sir Edward Colebrooke.

HAMILTON PALACE.

The Palace of Hamilton was originally a square tower about 20 feet long and 16 feet wide. The old part of the house as it now stands was erected about 1591, and about 1717 it was almost entirely rebuilt. The front, facing the south, was ornamented with pillars of the Corinthian order, and two deep wings were added, in the form of a Roman H, much in the style of Greenwich Hospital. In 1822 additions on an extensive scale were carried to completion by Alexander, tenth Duke (the present Duke's grandfather), with Mr Hamilton, as architect, and Mr Connell (builder of Burns' Monument at Ayr) as builder, which have rendered the Palace of Hamilton one of the largest and most magnificent structures of the kind in Britain. The modern part consists of a new front facing the north, 264 feet 8 inches in length, and three stories high, with an additional wing to the west, 100 feet in length, for servants' apartments. A new corridor is carried along the back of the old building, containing baths, &c. The front is adorned by a noble portico, consisting of a double row of Corinthian columns, each of one solid stone surmounted by a lofty pediment. The shaft of each column is upwards of 25 feet in height and about 3 feet 3 inches in diameter. These were each brought in the block from a quarry in Dalserf, about eight miles distant, on an immense waggon constructed for the purpose and drawn by thirty horses. The Palace stands close upon the town, on the upper border of the great valley, about half-a-mile west of the conflux of the Clyde and Avon. It is recorded as a curious statistical fact that there were employed in building the addition to the Palace, 28,056 tons $8\frac{3}{4}$ cwt. of stones, drawn by 22,528 horses. Of lime, sand, stones, wood, &c., 5,534 tons, 6 cwt., 1 qr., $7\frac{1}{2}$ lbs., drawn by 5,196 horses. In drawing 22,350 slates, 62,200 bricks, with engine ashes and coal-culm to keep down the damp, 731 horses were employed. Total days during which horses were employed for other purposes, $658\frac{1}{2}$. In the stables there are 7,976 tons of stones, drawn by 5,153 horses. Of lime, sand, slates, &c., 1,361 tons, drawn by 1,024 horses; besides 284 days of horses employed for other purposes. The stables, according to plan, are not yet completed.

INTERIOR EQUIPMENTS.

The interior equipments of the Palace are not less tasteful or magnificent than its exterior, and are a fair counterpart of the gorgeous pile in which they are contained. Amongst the works of art, " Daniel in the Lion's Den" is a noble picture—the subject of Wordsworth's sonnet—

> "Amid a fertile region, green with wood
> And fresh with rivers, well doth it become
> The ducal owner, in his palace home
> To naturalise this tawny lion brood;
> Children of art, that claim strange brotherhood,
> Couched in their den, with those that roam at large
> Over the burning wilderness, and charge
> The wind with terror while they roar for food.
> Satiate were these; and still—to eye and ear;
> Hence, while we gage a more enduring fear!
> Yet is the prophet calm, nor would the cave
> Daunt him—if his companion now bedroused,
> Outstretched and listless, were by hunger roused;
> Man placed him here, and God, he knows, can save."

The portrait of Charles I. in armour on a white horse, and of the Earl of Denbigh in a shooting dress standing by a tree, with the muzzle of a gun grasped in his right hand, and the butt of it resting on the ground, with a little black boy on the opposite side of the tree pointing out the game—both by Vandyke —are also masterpieces of art. Without going into detail, there may be mentioned an Entombment of Christ, by Poussin; an Ascension piece, by Georgione; a dying Madonna, by Corregio; the Circumcision, signed Lucas Cortonensis; the Misers, Quinten Matsys; Assumption of our Lady, Sandro Bottocelli; painted for the Church of San Pietro, Florence, on the commission of Matteo Palmieri, who gave the whole scheme of the work. The Assumption contains a representation of the zones of heaven, the patriarchs, prophets, apostles, evangelists, martyrs, confessors, doctors, virgins, and hierarchies. Matteo and his wife are represented on their knees in the foreground; in the distance is a view of the city of Florence. Vasari says envious detractors of the painter charged him and his patron with heresy, and the work was interdicted and covered from view. A laughing Boy, by L. Da Vinci; and an admirable portrait of Napoleon by David, painted from life, by permission granted to the Duke of Hamilton—are well-known works of art of great value. The west stair-case contains a large altar-piece by Girolami dai Libri from San Lionardo nel Monte, near Verona, of the Castieri family, with a Madonna and a child, placed in a chair above them. In the breakfast room is a picture by Giacomo da Puntormo of Joseph in Egypt receiving his father and his brothers; into which is introduced the portrait of Beronzino. In the same room is a portrait by Antonelli of Mycena in 1474. This is still in a state of admirable preservation. The great gallery and principal apartments contain also a large collection of family portraits and other paintings by Vandyke, Kneller, Rubens, Corregio, Guido, Rembrandt, Titian, Poussin, Spagnoletti, Reynolds, Hamilton, &c. Here, if anywhere, is

> " An art akin to nature's self,
> So mighty in its means, we stand prepared
> To see the life as lively mocked, as ever
> Still sleep mocked death."

A number of antique vases adorn the principal rooms, particularly one in the new dining room, of Giallo-Antico, in the form of a tripod, of great beauty, and of extraordinary dimensions, being 5 ft. 3 in. in height, 14 ft. 3 in. in circumference, and $9\frac{1}{2}$ in. deep. The vase itself is supported by a circular central pillar of beautiful form, richly carved and fluted, and with three square fluted pilasters at the sides, each resting on a lion's foot, and terminating with a lion's head—the whole standing on a vase of beautiful African marble. In the breakfast room and small drawing room are two slabs of porphyry upon gilt bronze legs—formerly comprising part of an altar-piece at Rome. Both slabs are of oriental porphyry, of equal size, and of great beauty. In an adjoining room there is a cabinet covered with a slab of malachite of most splendent lustre. There are also a great many antique cabinets in the different apartments, enriched with Mosaic and all sorts of precious stones; particularly, a casket of ebony ornamented with gilt bronze, and oriental stones in relief, formerly belonging to the Medici family. At the upper end of the gallery is Duke Alexander's ambassadorial throne, brought from his embassy at St. Petersburgh; and on the walls on each side of the throne are two capital portraits of George III. and Queen Charlotte, painted soon after their marriage. Fronting the throne, at the other end of the gallery, is a magnificent large architectural door of black marble, the pediment being supported by two oriental columns of green porphyry, unique in their kind, and supposed to be the finest of that material in Europe. The two oriental black porphyry columns were purchased by Alexander, tenth Duke of Hamilton, at Rome, from an individual who had them as a favour in gift from Braschi Pius VII. They were taken by his Holiness's orders from the Church of St. Georgio in Viterbo, which church was built out of the ruins of the Basilica di Semproneo. These columns originally formed an ornament to that ancient Basilica, one of the most celebrated of Ancient Rome. The collection of pictures numbers not less than 1000 pieces, of which 100 are at Chatelherault. The value of the prints alone, none of which are exhibited to strangers, has been estimated at from £10,000 to £15,000. Some of them have never been unfolded. Many of the cabinets are worth £1,500; and a single table has been estimated at £4,000. The value of the plate is over £50,000. In the drawing room are two marble columns from Astracan, said by geologists to be unique, and which are valued at £40,000. The present Duke, when recently in Venice, acquired two magnificent bottle-shaped vases, composed of tortoise shell inlaid with ivory, and studded with turquoise and other precious stones. The vases are four feet in height. They are placed on pedestals two feet in height, supported by three negroes in a kneeling posture. His Grace, at the same time, procured two figures of negresses, five feet in height, beautifully painted in full Eastern costume; mounted on pedestals two feet high, and which are placed on the Eastern staircase.

GREAT HALL.

The principal apartments besides the entrance hall, are—the tribune, a spacious saloon with lofty and highly ornamented lantern roof, from which many of the principal rooms enter; a dining room, 71 feet by 30; a library and drawing room. Next the drawing room is the Great Hall, entered from the steps under the portico of the north front; it is 54 feet square and 42 feet high from the floor to the roof; the walls, from floor to ceiling, being of polished sand-stone. Over the two fire-places are the ducal arms, carved in stone. The upper portion is enriched with carved cross beams and cornice, supported by sixteen fluted pilasters with capitals all of polished sand-stone. The floor is paved with Sienna and black marble. There are here five colossal bronze statues of L'Apollon du Belveder, La Diane, Le Gladiateur, L'Hercule Commode, L'Antinous Belveder, each on a black marble pedestal three feet high. These statues were cast in Italy early in the sixteenth century by order of Francois I. in moulds taken from the original statues in Rome. They were afterwards acquired by Nicolas Merville, Secretary of State. At the Revolution they were removed to Paris, and purchased there by Alexander, Duke of Hamilton, and placed in the palace. There is also here a colossal bronze bust of Alexander, Duke of Hamilton, by Thomas Campbell; besides other busts, vases of porphyry, rare marbles, &c.

GRAND STAIR-CASE.

The steps, balusters, and rails are all of pure black marble from Galway in Ireland. The stairs branch right and left from the first landing, terminating at a landing leading from the Great Hall to the tapestry rooms. This is also of black marble. Each rail is formed of one piece, and the first landing is a solid slab, measuring ten feet by seven feet. The long landing or passage is supported from below by two colossal figures in bronze by Soyer of Paris. The floor is paved with Sienna and black marble, and the walls are of polished sand-stone, similar to the Great Hall, carried to the roof. The ceiling is arched and richly ornamented with plaster work, the family arms, &c. On the side walls are hanging full length portraits of the Emperor Napoleon III. and the Empress Eugenie by Winterhalter. There are also here three antique busts—Vespasian in basalt and oriental alabaster; the Emperor Augustus, in Egyptian porphyry and gilt metal ornaments; Tiberias, in Egyptian porphyry with gilt metal ornaments. These busts are on ebonised pedestals, ornamented with pietra dura and gilt metal work.

TAPESTRY ROOMS.

The walls of these rooms are hung with very fine Italian tapestry, the subject of which is taken from Tasso's "Jerusalem Delivered." The ceiling is in compartments richly gilt and coloured. The doors, windows, &c., are white and gold, the chairs and sofas richly gilt and covered in tapestry, the cabinets, tables, vases, &c., are of the choicest kind, corresponding with the other portions of the Palace. We may mention a Damascene table of Milanese work of the sixteenth century, purchased at Prince Soltykoff's sale at Paris for 800 guineas. It would be beyond our sphere to attempt to enumerate all the precious and costly articles of furniture in this princely Palace.

GALLERY AND OLD STATE ROOMS.

The gallery is 120 feet by 20, and 20 feet high. The ceiling is in compartments, with portions of the family arms, richly gilt and coloured. The walls are covered with dark oak panels. Leaving the gallery, entrance is obtained to the old state rooms, the walls of which are panelled to correspond with those of the gallery. These magnificent chambers contain a superb variety of costly cabinets, in Mosaic work, Japan Lac, Buhl, &c.; besides a collection of sumptuous furniture and pictures.

THE BECKFORD LIBRARY.

Adjoining the old state rooms is the Beckford library. The room was specially arranged for this celebrated collection, after the decease, in 1844, of Wm. Beckford. Esq., of Fonthill (the author of "Vathek") whose daughter married Alexander, tenth Duke of Hamilton, and by whom it was formed. The collection consists of over 15,000 volumes, amongst which are many rare editions of the early authors—all in the finest condition. The room is T shaped. The ceiling is arched, pierced for lights from the roof. All round the room over the cases (which are entirely of cedar wood) is a rich scagliola cornice, supported by polished Peterhead granite pilasters on a scagliola base. Over the centre of the T is a circular dome with a light in roof, around which are painted allegorical figures representing literature, music, painting, and architecture. There are here four full-length portraits of the Beckford family—Miss Beckford (afterwards Duchess of Hamilton), by Phillips; William Beckford, Esq., by Romney; his father, Alderman Beckford, by Sir Joshua Reynolds; and Peter Beckford, their ancestor, Governor of Jamaica in 1692. These pictures are fixed in panels to the wall over the fire-places, supported below on rich marble slabs; above is a cornice of scagliola, supported from the marble slab at the back by pilasters of Aberdeen granite; in front by columns of antique Egyptian granite, with gilt metal capitals. Besides this library there is the family collection of books—altogether upwards of 25,000 volumes, and 800 volumes of MSS. In the wing leading from the other end of the gallery are the

DUCHESS' PRIVATE APARTMENTS.

These are most tastefully decorated in white and gold, and are richly furnished. Included amongst the valuable furniture is a secretaire, a bureau, and a work table, formerly belonging to Maria Antoinette of France, and said to be the finest specimens of inlaid-work extant. They were manufactured by Reisner of Paris, the metal work by Goutière. The catalogue of the South Kensington Loan Exhibition says—"In the three specialities is displayed the utmost perfection of French decorative art; and, in all probability, the suite of furniture as a whole is the most important and beautiful work of its kind produced in the age of Louis XVI."

THE CHARTER ROOM.

The charter room contains, besides the family charters, a number of valuable manuscript letters, including the correspondence of Charles the First, the Duke of Lauderdale, and others, with the first Duke of Hamilton and his brother, the Earl of Lanark. Many other curious relics are deposited here, as, for instance, the ring given by Queen Mary previous to her execution, to Lord John Hamilton, afterwards Marquis of Hamilton, and the veritable gun with which Hamilton of Bothwell Haugh fired the shot which proved fatal to the Regent Murray at Linlithgow.

MISCELLANEOUS.

The Palace and main avenues are lighted with gas. The Duke Alexander, amongst other improvements, at considerable expense provided a copious supply of pure water for the use of the Palace. A large tank and filter were constructed on the heights at Chatelherault. The water is conveyed by pipes into cisterns on the roof of the Palace. Pipes are also laid round the exterior of the building as a provision in case of fire. Recently the town's gravitation water has also been added, so that should unfortunately a fire ever take place, it is expected the provision will be equal to the emergency.

The stables stand between the Palace and town, and are in every way worthy of the splendid edifice of which they are an appropriate accompaniment.

The gardens belong to a recent date. During the season of 1861, a new geometrical flower plot was formed at the eastern wing of the Palace. It covers nearly an acre of ground, and is surrounded by a massive balustrade wall, with a handsome fountain in the centre. The new kitchen and forcing garden was formed about the same time. The garden is about 5½ acres in extent, and contains a range of hot houses 370 feet in length and 14 in breadth. Situated on a gently sloping bank, as seen from Cadzow Bridge the stretch of greenhouses, &c., present an imposing appearance.

QUEEN MARY AT THE PALACE.

The associations of the Palace are many of them necessarily interesting. A touching episode is furnished in the narrative of the visit of the unfortunate Queen of Scots after her escape from Loch Leven and at the time of the Langside disaster. The Queen, after her delivery from the keep of Kinross, rode to the Castle of Niddry, near Linlithgow, and next day, the number of her followers increasing, she went on to Hamilton Palace. According to Hill Burton, among the chiefs who had here assembled, besides Seton and the Hamiltons, were Herries, Sommerville, Argyle, Cassilis, Fleming, Ross, Eglinton, and Rothes. They had soon around them six hundred men in fighting array. Hamilton Palace had the aspect of a Court well guarded by troops. The opportunity was taken to revoke the Queen's abdication, with all the business that had followed upon it. The Queen's followers naturally looked around for some stronger position than Hamilton, and an attempt to gain Dunbar Castle having failed, Dumbarton, held by Lord Fleming, was the next recourse. It involved a march close by Glasgow, where the Regent Murray was stationed; but, as the Queen's force was the larger of the two, it was resolved to take this risk. After the battle, the decisive character of which sealed the fate of Scotland, the Queen rode off towards the Border, and in a short time was a prisoner in the hands of Elizabeth. Albeit, her son, James VI., is said to have frequently enjoyed the sports of the field at Cadzow, and the Hamiltons in subsequent reigns were prominent figures. Until recent years, there is no further notable event connected with royalty and the Palace to record—

> Old times were changed, old manners gone,
> A stranger fill'd the Stuarts' throne.

OTHER ROYAL VISITORS.

Of distinguished visitors at the Palace in recent years, may be mentioned the Duchess of Kent (the mother of Her Most Gracious Majesty), in 1851; the late Queen of Holland, 1857; the Empress Eugenie, in 1860; the Duc de Bordeaux (Henry V.); and the Emperor Napoleon.

VISIT OF THE PRINCE OF WALES.

On 13th January of this year (1878), H.R.H. the Prince of Wales arrived at the Palace on a visit to the Duke and Duchess of Hamilton. The Princes Imperial of Austria and France, with other distinguished personages, were invited to meet H.R.H., and for a week the Palace was once more the centre of gaiety and festivity. The early meeting of Parliament curtailed the royal visit to one of four days, but the most was made of the brief space, and before his departure the Heir Apparent had seen enough of the district to charm him with its scenery—its fine timber especially exciting surprise and admiration—and of the inhabitants to gratify him with the sincere heartiness and cordiality of their loyalty. The Prince's well-known agricultural proclivities led him to Merryton, where Mr Drew showed his famous Clydesdales, passing under royal review, "Prince of Wales," "Lord Harry," and over one hundred mares, colts, and fillies, and providing a sight which, in the words of H.R.H., could nowhere else be seen in the world. The Prince Imperial of France got on the back of "Lord Harry," which had never been ridden before; and the bystanders looked on as he scampered round the yard, hardly knowing whether to admire or reprove the wildness of the feat. On Monday, the royal party shot over the home policies, and on Tuesday found their way to the High Parks. In marked contrast to the previous day, rain, accompanied by a high wind, fell all the morning, and continued during the remainder of the day. Undeterred, the Prince of Wales, the Crown Prince of Austria, the Prince Imperial, Prince Esterhazy, Count Jaraczewski, Count Bombelle, the Duc de Bassano, and three other gentlemen, left the Palace at eleven o'clock. Mr Tait, the head keeper, and assistants had gone on to Larkhall an hour before. Along the route to the shooting ground the royal cavalcade attracted much attention, and were cheered at different points where crowds had assembled. Entering the grounds at Larkhall, the party shot through the Captain's Wood on to Belvedere, which they also exhausted. So plentiful were the game, the services of the beaters were hardly needed, and the difficulty was to shoot the animals that came within range. At Chatelherault a halt was called for lunch. The storm was at its height, and the party remained at the *chateau* for some time. A start was eventually made, the party having to drive for some distance. After crossing the river at the ornamental bridge, the peeps of scenery from both sides of which were greatly admired, they lingered for a time amid the hoary ruins of the Castle of Cadzow, which here crown the precipitous banks of the stream, and then they passed on to the Oaks and the White Cattle in the chase beyond. It would be difficult to describe the surprise of the sportsmen in unexpectedly finding themselves surrounded by so many grand specimens of the monarch of the forest. In the White Cattle, too, they evinced the greatest interest. They concluded the day's shooting in Ramsay's cover. The roe deer which were met with were very wild, some of them leaping over the keepers' heads. The Prince of Wales brought down one of the deer, the Prince Imperial of France another, and three fell to other guns. The Duke of Hamilton was present, but confined himself to attending to the wants of his guests. The bag for four hours' work and ten guns was the largest ever made in a similar space of time within the memory of the oldest keeper. In the evening, the Duke and Duchess gave a ball in the Tribune of the Palace, which was attended by the royal party and several hundred guests. Such a galaxy of beauty and fashion had not assembled in the same noble chamber for years before; and

"When to the trembling string
The dance gaed thro' the lighted ha."

with the bright dresses of the ladies and the blaze of uniforms the scene was brilliant and dazzling. On Wednesday the party for a short time were out on the Logans, and at night took their departure.

The inhabitants—the private character of the visit, and the brief intimation of the hour of departure leaving little time for preparation—yet succeeded in making a most creditable display of loyalty. The public buildings were illuminated, and private houses lighted up. In honour of their noble Colonel, the Queen's Own Yeomanry furnished a guard of honour, and at the Central Railway Station the 16th Lanark Rifles, under Colonel Austine, were drawn up. Inside the platform was a most respectable crowd of three thousand people. Opposite the saloon carriage in which His Royal Highness was to travel were posted the Provost, Magistrates, and Town Council, it having been previously ascertained that the Prince would be pleased to receive an address from the Corporation. The address, which was presented in graceful terms by Provost Forrest to His Royal Highness, ran :—

"We, the Provost, Magistrates, and Town Council of the burgh of Hamilton desire to avail ourselves of this opportunity of renewing the assurances of our attachment and loyalty to your august mother and to your Royal Higness, and the other members of your illustrious family, under whose enlightened and paternal government the people of these realms have enjoyed so much prosperity and happiness.

"We learned with much pleasure that your Royal Highness was to visit the Duke and Duchess of Hamilton, and our regret is that circumstances have prevented you from prolonging your stay; but it is our hope that you will at no distant date renew your acquaintance with a district fraught with many interesting associations, and characterised by devoted loyalty to the throne.

"We desire to express the hope that your Royal Highness and your illustrious and most estimable wife, and your Royal children, will long continue to occupy your elevated social positions, and, endowed with health and other blessings, that you will be enabled to discharge the duties which these positions entail.

"Signed, in name and by appointment of the Magistrates and Town Council of Hamilton, this 16th day of January, 1878,

"J. C. FORREST, Provost."

His Royal Highness expressed the pleasure it afforded him to receive the address, to which he stated a reply would be forwarded in the usual way. He then entered the carriage amidst loud cheers, which he repeatedly acknowledged, and was followed by the Prince Imperial of France. The train was then backed out of the station, and having been shunted on to the centre line of rails, it slowly steamed past the platform, the public on both sides having the while a good view of the occupants of the train. The Prince of Wales and Prince Imperial held their hats in their hands until the train was clear of the station, and acknowledged the hearty cheers with which they were greeted. The band played the National Anthem, and the cheering was renewed again and again. Provost Forrest afterwards received the following reply to the address :—

"Sandringham, King's Lynn,
19th January, 1878.

"Sir,—I am desired by the Prince of Wales to thank you, and through you the Magistrates and Town Council of the Burgh of Hamilton, for the expressions of loyalty towards the Queen, himself, and the Royal Family contained in your address to His Royal Highness of the 16th inst.

"The Prince further commands me to thank you for the reception you gave him at Hamilton, and to say how he regrets that important duties in England prevented his making a longer stay in your loyal burgh.

"His Royal Highness hopes, however, at some future period to renew his acquaintance with a district which, as you rightly say, is fraught with many interesting associations.

"I have the honour to be, Sir, your most obedient servant,

"D. M. PROBYN, Major-General,
Comptroller and Treasurer of the Household of
His Royal Highness the Prince of Wales.

"To J. C. Forrest, Esq., Provost of Hamilton,"

The annexed table shows the total results of the royal and ducal sport :—

	Policies.	High Parks.	Logans.	Drafan.	Home Farm.	Quarter.	Dechmont.	Total.
Pheasants,	83	171	59	25	101	96	110	615
Partridges,	..	1	2	19	20	4	20	66
Hares,	10	64	87	500	228	121	223	1249
Rabbits,	626	1002	641	520	121	345	121	3376
Woodcocks,	2	14	6	3	1	3	1	30
Deer,	..	5	3	..	..	1	..	33
Sundries,	1	7	3	9	6	1	6	33
Total,	731	1264	801	1076	477	571	486	5402
Guns,	9	13	11	10	12	7	5	66

This had never been equalled in any previous season. The following took part in the shooting : — H.R.H. The Prince of Wales, H.I.H.

Crown Prince of Austria, H.I.H. Prince Imperial of France, Prince Louis Esterhazy, Duke of Hamilton, Duke of Manchester, Duke de Bassano, Lord Rendlesham, Lord Mandeville, Count Jaraczewski, Count Bombelle, Mr Montague Guest, Mr Vaughan, Mr Cooper, Colonel Campbell, Major Coghill, The Hon. Hanbury Lennox, Colonel Teesdale.

THE MAUSOLEUM.

The Mausoleum, another of Duke Alexander's creations, is situated on a beautifully formed terrace, raised to the north-west of the Palace, from which it is distant about a quarter of a mile. It is to a considerable extent enclosed by rows of stately beeches, varied at intervals by luxuriant shrubbery, but from its great altitude, being nearly 120 feet high, it towers far above the objects by which it is surrounded. The base covers an area of somewhere about 110 feet diameter. The structure is a composition of Roman architecture, most of the details being developed in the purest style. The mausoleum may be said to consist of three several storeys or compartments placed upon a surbase formed by colossal steps rising several feet, above which is a massive stylobate or basement, in the western portion of which is the entrance to the chapel. From this stylobate rises a dado, whose sides are panelled and pilastered. This is perhaps the most pretentious of the three storeys and exhibits great skill and elaborate finish. The panels are formed by single slabs, of gigantic proportions, and the effect produced is strikingly imposing. The super-structure is a huge plinth of plain polished stone, with the guilloche or fretband boldly indented and channelled. The whole is surmounted by a dome which rises eighteen feet above the plinth. The vaulted basement constitutes what may be termed the ground storey of this splendid temple of the dead.

In deference, it is understood, to popular ideas, the entrance to the catacombs is placed in the east. This portion forms the front of the mausoleum, and is built in a piazza-like form. It consists of three massive arches executed in rustic work, the frontage stretching some 80 or 90 feet. On the keystones are exquisitely carved masks, the work of Mr Handyside Ritchie of Edinburgh, representing Life, Death, and Immortality. Life is adorned with a chaplet of fruit and flowers; and on the lower portion of the stone is part of a clock-dial, with the indicator pointing to the hour of twelve. Death is crowned with poppy heads and a variety of flowers; over the mouth is placed the dread seal of everlasting silence, a finger rising obliquely upwards over the lips; the eyes are for ever closed in "the sleep that knows no waking," and the expression of the face is awe-striking and effective. Immortality forms a vivid contrast to the other masks, especially that of Death; the head is crowned with lilies, and the brow encircled with the serpent, emblematic of eternity; while immediately above is the Greek symbol of immortality, a butterfly.

Passing through the centre archway we are speedily in the vaults or catacombs. Mr David Hamilton planned this portion of the basement; and the groving and vaulting are certainly splendid models of masonry. A solid pillar of stone in the centre receives the springing of all the arches, thus supporting the fan-groining. By the dim light emitted through the door-way, the visitor is made aware that many of the recesses are occupied by the remains of Scotland's premier Dukes. Early in 1852, the bodies which had previously rested for centuries in the old Church of Hamilton—once situated in the immediate vicinity of the Palace, but now levelled to the dust, and every trace of its existence removed—were transferred to the vaults of the new Mausoleum, where they now repose. There are thirteen of these, and there have since been interred the body of the late Duke in 1863 and that of his mother some few years before.

Leaving the vaults, we find the piazza terminated on each side by handsome stairs, which lead to the chapel of the Mausoleum. At the top of these stairs are two colossal lions, beautifully cut in freestone by Mr A. H. Ritchie, which surmount the piazza, and are placed so as to command the arches that lead to the catacombs beneath. To these majestic guardians of the dead, the spirit of sentinelship has been imparted by the artist in a most masterly style. The entrance to the chapel is from the western side. In approaching, the eye is attracted by an inscription, in bold raised characters, and by the elegance of the door of the chapel. The inscription is as follows:—

HOC MONVMENTVM
SIBI ET SVIS
EXTRENDVM CVRAVIT
ALEXANDER
DVX HAMILTONII DECIMVS

"Alexander, tenth Duke of Hamilton caused this monument to be erected for him and his." The chapel door is in bronze, is a superb work of art, and reflects much credit on Sir John Steell, R.S.A., by whom it was executed. It comprises *fac-similes* of various panels forming the celebrated gates of Ghiberti, in the Baptistry of Florence. Critics who have seen both original and copy, bear testimony not only to the beauty, but the correctness of the counterfeit presentments. There are six panels, each of which illustrate, in mixed alto and basso-relievo, interesting Scripture subjects: the Queen of Sheba's reception by Solomon;

David Slaying Goliath, and Flight of the Philistines; Isaac blessing Jacob, and Esau entering from the Hunt; Joseph and his brethren in Egypt, and the finding of the Cup in Benjamin's sack; Moses on the mount, and the carrying of the Ark across the Jordan. The castings are the first of the kind executed in Scotland, and are not the least creditable of the great sculptor's work.

Inside the chapel the *tout ensemble* is exceedingly imposing and solemn. The chapel is circular, the walls being effectively broken up by numerous niches, wreaths, and other appropriate decorations. A "dim religious light" is admitted from the dome by means of an immense sheet of plate glass, from 12 to 15 feet in diameter. The subdued rays streaming in through this opening fall with an awe-inspiring influence which is deepened by the immense altitude of the chapel, while the powerful echo from the dome responds to the slightest whisper or the gentlest footfall. A splendid effect is produced by the ornate character of the floor. It is laid in mosaic, arranged in a geometrical design, and is composed of jasper, white and yellow marbles, with radiations of red and green porphyry, and divisional bands of black marble. The whole is picturesque and artistic, both in colour and arrangement. In the first storey, so to speak, there are four principal recesses with pilasters surmounted by a plain frieze. In the largest recess, and exactly opposite the entrance to the chapel, is placed the sarcophagus which contains the embalmed body of the tenth Duke. It rests upon a plain but massive pedestal of black marble. The sarcophagus consists of two ponderous pieces of basalt, and is one of those precious Memphian relics of antiquity which have from time to time been recovered from the land of the Pharaohs. It was originally intended for the

British Museum, but owing to a dispute about the price, it fell into the hands of the Duke Alexander. On the upper portion or lid, a female face of colossal features, but noble expression, looks upward, while the surface from head to foot, is covered with various figures and hieroglyphics. The sarcophagus and portion of the marble upon which the sarcophagus rests bears the following inscription :—

ALEXANDER,
HAMILTONÆ, BRANDONII, ET CASTELLEROTII,
DUX,
NAT. D. III. OCT., A. MDCCLXVII.
OBIT. D. XVIII. AUGUST, A. MDCCCLII.

Above the recess in which the sarcophagus is placed, the Hamilton arms are sculptured. Immediately above the pilasters previously alluded to, there are a series of oval shields, with mottoes, surmounted by exquisitely carved cherub heads, also the work of Mr A. H. Ritchie. The stone used was selected from quarries near Glasgow, the lower portion having been built with blocks from the Duke's own quarries.

The architect was Mr David Bryce, R.S.A., and the cost over £100,000.

CHATELHERAULT.

The chateau or summer palace of Chatelherault is finely situated on a commanding eminence on the banks of Avon, opposite the ruins of Cadzow Castle. It fitly terminates the fine avenue of trees which stretches in direct vista from here to the Palace, and thence on to Bothwell. The chateau, with its turrets and extended front, looks more spacious than it really is. The principal gamekeeper occupies one wing and the other is reserved for the use of the Duke when out shooting in the neighbourhood. The kennels are also located here. The walls of the chief apartments exhibit exquisite specimens of French decorative art, of the era of Louis Quatorze, in wood-carving and stucco. The truth-to-nature, lightness, delicacy, and elegance of these plaster pictures are exceedingly pleasing and impressive. They consist of scenes of rural life, of fruits and flowers, of mythologic figures, and others

> Smacking of Flora and the country green,
> Dance and provencal song, and sunburnt mirth.

THE OAKS AND ABORIGINAL BREED OF CATTLE.

The venerable oaks of Cadzow—the remains of the great Caledonian forest, which in olden times extended over the whole of upper Clydesdale and the valley of the Tweed as far as the English Border—are well-known to all lovers of leafy solitudes, for their boundless contiguity of shade. But besides the ancient ruin of Cadzow Castle, which overhangs the steep banks of the Avon, this umbrageous forest affords shelter to other relics of the past, in the shape of the last surviving descendants of the wild cattle that formerly roamed through the forest solitudes of Northern Britain. Their claim to be the last of the race is perhaps shared with the white cattle at Chillingham, in Northumberland, but owing to the erratic fancy of a park-keeper about the beginning of the present century, the specific distinction of black muzzles and ears, which are the beauty of the Cadzow cattle, was weeded out from the Chillingham herd—preference being given to an accidental pink-eared strain. Formerly herds of these white wild cattle existed at Gisburne, at Wollaton, at Chartley, and in the chase of Drumlanrig—all of them possessing the distinguishing characteristic of black ears and muzzle. But these have gradually disappeared. Sir Walter

Scott, when passing a summer in the Upper Ward, availed himself of Cadzow to introduce these denizens of the forest into his spirited ballad of "Cadyow Castle"—

> "Mightiest of all the beasts of chase
> That roam in woody Caledon,
> Crashing the forest in his race,
> The mountain bull comes thundering on."

These verses Thomas Campbell speaks of as "perpetually ringing in his imagination." But although the white cattle of Cadzow retain at the present day many of the instincts and habits of their wilder progenitors, they have assuredly become much more discreetly behaved than in Scott's days. The "mountain bull" seldom, except at certain seasons of the year, displays much disposition to attack strangers, and when, according to annual custom, some of the herd are shot down in the winter, the slaughter is a very matter of fact performance. It is quite in the fitness of things that, as relics of antiquity, these white steers should be slain among venerable oaks at Christmas-tide. The oak was the sacred tree of Druidical worship, and at the festival of the winter solstice in honour of the Sun-god, the ancient Britons, accompanied by their priests, sallied forth to gather the mistletoe from its branches. "When the oak was reached on which the mistletoe grew, two white bulls were bound to the tree, and the chief Druid, clothed in white, ascended, and, with a golden knife, cut the sacred plant. The bulls, and often also human victims, were then sacrificed." The oaks cover several hundred acres. Many of the trees have attained to an enormous size, measuring 36 feet in circumference; others are gnarled and in the last stages of decay. Permission to visit the oaks and white cattle is by order, which can be had on application to the Duke's officials. Pic-nic parties occasionally frequent the grove, and to all such the famous "boss tree," which is capable of containing at one time eight individuals, is an object of interest and attraction.

In Sir William Jardine's "Naturalist's Library" there is a very interesting account of the Hamilton breed of white cattle, for which the learned baronet acknowledges to have been indebted to Robert Brown, Esq., Chamberlain to His Grace the Duke of Hamilton, and which we extract:—

"This very ancient and peculiar breed of cattle has been long kept up with great care by the noble family of Hamilton, in a chase in the vicinity of their splendid seat at Hamilton, in the Middle Ward of the County of Lanark. They are generally believed to be the remains of the ancient breed of white cattle which were found on the island when the Romans first visited it, and which they represent as then running wild in the woods. The chase in which they browse was formerly a park or forest attached to the Royal Castle of Cadzow, where the ancient British kings of Strathclyde, and subsequently kings of Scotland, used frequently to reside and to hold their courts. The oaks with which the park is studded over, are evidently very ancient, and many of them are of enormous size. Some of these are English oaks, and are supposed to have been planted by King David, first Earl of Huntingdon, about the year 1140. The chase is altogether of princely dimensions and appearance, amounting to upwards of 1300 Scotch acres. The number of white cattle at present kept is upwards of sixty. Great care is taken to prevent the domestic bull from crossing the breed; and if accidentally a cross should take place, the young is destroyed. In their general habits they resemble the fallow-deer more than any other domestic animal. Having been exposed, without shade or covering of any sort, to the rigours of our climate from time immemorial, they are exceedingly hardy; and having never been caught or subjected to the sway of man, they are necessarily peculiarly wild and untractable. Their affection for their young, like that of many other animals in a wild or half-wild state, is excessive. When dropt they carefully conceal them among long grass or weeds in some brushwood or thicket, and approach them cautiously twice or thrice a day, for the purpose of supplying them with the necessary nourishment. On these occasions it is not a little dangerous to approach the place of retreat, the parent cow being seldom at any great distance, and always attacking any person or animal approaching it with the utmost resolution and fury. The calves, when unexpectedly approached, betray great trepidation, by throwing their ears back close upon their necks, and lying squat down upon the ground. When hard pressed they have been known to run at their keepers in a butting menacing attitude in order to force their retreat. The young are produced at all seasons of the year, but chiefly in spring. The mode of catching the calves is to steal upon them whilst slumbering or sleeping in their retreat when they are a day or two old, and put a cloth over their mouths to prevent them crying, and then carry them off to a place of safety, without the reach of the herd, otherwise the cry of the calf would attract the dam, and she by loud bellowing would bring the whole flock to the spot, to attack the keeper in the most furious manner. These cattle are seldom seen scattering themselves indiscriminately over the pasture like other breeds of cattle, but are generally observed to feed in a flock. They are very chary of being approached by strangers, and seem to have the power of smelling them at a great distance. When any one approaches them unexpectedly, they generally scamper off to a little distance to the leeward, and then turn round in a body to smell him. In these gambols they invariably affect circles, and when they do make an attack—which is seldom the case—should they miss the object of their aim, they never return upon it, but run straight forward without ever venturing to look back. The only method of slaughtering these animals is by shooting at them. When the keepers approach them for this purpose they seem perfectly aware of their danger, and always gallop away with great speed in a dense mass, preserving a profound silence, and generally keeping by the sides of the fields and fences. The cows which have young, in the meantime, forsake the flock and repair to the places where their calves are concealed, where, with flaming eyeballs and palpitating hearts, they seem resolved to maintain their ground at all hazards. The shooters always take care to avoid these retreats. When the object of pursuit is one of the older bulls of the flock, the shooting of it is a very hazardous employment. Some of these have been known to receive as many as eleven bullets, without one of them piercing their skulls. When fretted in this manner, they often become furious, and, owing to their great swiftness and prodigious strength, they are then regarded as objects of no ordinary dread. The White Urus, or Hamilton breed of wild cattle differs in many respects from any other known breed. As compared with those kept at Chillingham Park, Northumberland, by Lord Tankerville, they are larger, and more robust in the general form of their bodies, and their markings are also very different. In the Tankerville breed, the colour is invariably white, muzzle black, the whole of the inside of the ear, and about one-third of the outside, from the tip downwards, red. The horns are very fine, white, with black tips, and the head and legs are slender and elegant. In the Hamilton *urus* the body is dun-white, the inside of the ears, the muzzle, and the hoofs black, and the fore part of the leg, from the knee downwards, *mottled with black*. The cows seldom have horns; their bodies are thick and short; their limbs are stouter, and their heads much rounder than in the Tankerville breed. The inside or roof of the mouth is black or spotted with black. The tongue is black and generally tipped with black. It is somewhat larger in proportion than that of the common cow; and the high ridge on the upper surface, near to the insertion of the tongue, is also very prominent. It is observable that the calves that are of the usual markings are either entirely black or entirely white, or black and white, but never red or brown.

"The beef, like that of the Tankerville breed, is marbled, and of excellent flavour, and the juice is richer and of a lighter colour than in ordinary butcher-meat. The size of the smaller cows does not exceed fifteen stones tron weight; but some of the larger sort, especially the bulls, average from thirty-five to forty-five stones. The circumstances of their breeding *in-and-in*, of being chased so much when any of them are to be shot, of being so frequently approached and disturbed by strangers, and of having been exposed so long to all the vicissitudes of the seasons, and constantly browsing the same pasture, have no doubt contributed greatly to the deterioration of the breed, and must have reduced them much in size and other qualities.

"The ancient history of this breed is involved in much mystery. From fossil remains, chiefly found in marl-pits, it appears that two species of the ox tribe formerly prevailed in Scotland, namely, the *Bos taurus* and the *Bos urus*. Some heads of these, of very large dimensions, are still preserved in the collections of the curious. Professor Fleming of Aberdeen informs us that he has a skull of the former in his possession, measuring $27\frac{1}{2}$ inches in length, 9 inches between the horns, and $11\frac{1}{2}$ inches across at the orbits. The accounts of ancient authors certainly allude to a species of wild cattle, very different in their character and dimensions from those of the present day. The favourite haunt of these animals in ancient times seems to have been the Caledonia Sylva, or Caledonian Forest, which extended from Stirling through Menteith and Stratherne, to Athol and Lochaber. It is described by old authors, as dividing the Picts from the Scots; and, being well furnished with game, especially with fierce white bulls and kine, it was the place of both their huntings and of their greatest controversies. Some say it took its name from Calder which signifies a hazel, or common nut-bush. The Roman historians delight much to talk of the furious white bulls which the Forest of Caledonia brought forth. In these early days they are represented as of large size, and as possessing *jubam densam, ac demissam instar leonis;* or as Holinshed has it, crisp and curled manes like feirs leonis.

At what period this great forest was destroyed, and the white cattle extirpated is uncertain. Sir Robert Sibbald describes them in his time, as denuded of their manes. In the sixteenth century, they seem to have become entirely extinct as a wild race, and, as we learn from Gesner, were all slain except in that part which is called Cummernad. Another author informs us that thocht thir bullis were bred in sindry boundis of the Colidin Wod, now be continewal hunting and lust of insolent men, they are destroyit in all parts of

Scotland, and nane of them left but Allenerlie in Cumernald. At what period the present breed were introduced to the royal chase at Cadzow cannot now be well ascertained. It is well known that the Cummings were at one period proprietors of Cadzow and Cumbernauld, and it is likely that in their time the white cattle were in both places. But be that as it may, they have long been extirpated at Cumbernauld; while they have been preserved in great perfection at Hamilton. The universal tradition in Clydesdale is that they have been at Cadzow from the remotest antiquity; and the probability is, that they are a part remaining of the establishment of our ancient British and Scottish kings. At present they are objects of great curiosity—both to the inhabitants and to strangers visiting the place. During the troubles consequent on the death of Charles I., and the usurpation of Cromwell, they were nearly extirpated; but a breed of them having been retained for the Hamilton family, by Hamilton Dalzell, and by Lord Elphinstone at Cumbernauld—they were subsequently restored in their original purity. A tradition prevails in the country, that, about a hundred years ago, when it was found necessary for a time to remove them from one pasture to another, several hundred individuals belonging to the different baronies on the ducal estate were called out, and that they only effected their purpose with much difficulty and danger. Instances are recorded of their having been taken when young and tamed, and even milked. The milk, like that of most white cattle, is described as thin and watery. The usual number of ribs is thirteen on each side; some have been slaughtered with fourteen pair of ribs, but this is exceedingly rare. There is no other park of cattle in Scotland of a similar description."

THE TOWN OF HAMILTON.

The town of Hamilton stands on a rising ground, gently sloping towards the east, about a mile west of the conflux of the Avon and the Clyde. Cadzow burn runs nearly through it. The ancient town stood farther to the east, in the Duke's pleasure grounds, and was called the Netherton. Mr Patrick says that part of the present town which stands near the flesh-market and the public green appears to be the most ancient. The rocks behind the flesh-market are about twenty feet high, and were once occupied by a mansion, called the Ha' or Hall, of which an antique dove-cot (which gives the name of doocot-ha' to the place) is the only memorial now remaining. On the opposite side of the burn stood a mill called the Ha' Mill, which has given the name of "Sheilling Hill" to the street where it stood. When the *tun*, *ton*, or town, collected round this place it was called Ha-mill-ton. So says tradition, but history, which is more to be depended on, gives, as we have already seen, a different and more satisfactory account. The date of the foundation of the lower part of the town cannot now be ascertained. It has been long swept away. That the upper part is also of great antiquity appears from the fact that it was considerable enough to be erected into a burgh of barony in the year 1456 by James II. In 1548, Hamilton was created a royal burgh by Queen Mary; but Bailies James Hamilton and James Naismith consented to resign that privilege in 1670 by accepting of a charter from Duchess Anne, by which

Hamilton was constituted the chief burgh of the regality and dukedom of Hamilton. A law-suit was entered into by the magistrates, &c., in 1723, before the Court of Session, for the restoration of their ancient rights; but it was not till 1832 that the inhabitants were re-invested with the privilege of sending a member to the House of Commons. Hamilton is the capital of the Middle Ward of Lanarkshire, and is 10¾ miles S.E. of Glasgow, 36 W. of Edinburgh, 15 N.W. of Lanark, 7 N. of Strathaven, and 8 miles S. of Airdrie.

ECCLESIASTICAL HISTORY.

The ancient parish of Cadzow included the chapelry of Machan (the "little plain"), now the parish of Dalserf. The church with its pertinents was granted by David I., with consent of his son, Earl Henry, in perpetual alms to the church and bishops of Glasgow, and this grant was confirmed by the bulls of several Popes *inter* 1170 and 1186. Afterwards, with the lands of Barlanerk and Baldernock, it became the appropriate prebend of the Dean of the See of Glasgow. One of the rectors was William Frazer, who became Chancellor of Scotland. Another, in 1454, was Andrew Muirhead, a son of Muirhead of Lauchope, who became Bishop of Glasgow. The parish, by the influence of the first Lord Hamilton, was in 1454 made a collegiate charge, and a new edifice with a choir, two cross aisles, and a steeple— all of polished stone and highly ornamental—was erected. The patronage of this establishment was vested in Lord Hamilton, that of the parish church continuing as before with the Bishop of Glasgow. Manses, gardens, and glebes were provided for the Provost, and eight prebends, besides a manse, garden, and glebe, for a chaplainry dedicated to the Virgin Mary. There is a farm at Eddlewood still called the Chapel. At the epoch of the Reformation, Mr Arch. Karry, "the vicar pensioner," had twenty merks yearly; and the Dean had £349 in money, 16 bolls of meal, 24 bolls of oats, and 24 capons yearly. The old collegiate church continued till 1732, and one of the cross aisles remained and was used as a burying-place by the Hamilton family prior to the completion of the noble mausoleum within the last thirty years.

By the Act establishing Presbyterianism as the national form of worship, two ministers were settled in Hamilton upon a provision of eighteen chalders of victual. Readers or catechists seem also to have existed. The former arrangement was not, however, lasting; for, though in 1590 Mr John Davidson is mentioned as first minister, and Mr Gavin Hamilton as second minister of Hamilton, there was only one minister for many years afterwards, with a stipend payable out of the deanery of Glasgow. Episcopacy took the place of Presbyterianism in 1606, and continued the Established faith—with brief interruption during Cromwell's rule—down to 1689, when Presbyterianism was fully restored. Mr Robert Wylie in 1692 became first minister, on the understanding that, as "formerly," he was to have a colleague. After a good deal of opposition, this arrangement was implemented in the appointment of Mr Alex. Findlator from Avondale.

TWO DISTINGUISHED ROMAN CATHOLIC RECTORS.

At the death of Alexander III, a distinguished man, William Frazer, was, as we have already noticed, rector of the parish. He afterwards became Lord Chancellor of Scotland and still later Bishop of St. Andrews. He was a guardian of the kingdom during the brief reign of Margaret the Maiden, but being a crafty self-seeking ambitious man, on the first rumour of the Queen's death, he sent an invitation to the English King to approach the Border. This was ostensibly to prevent bloodshed, but really to forward the Baliol interest of which he was a partisan. One of Rector Frazer's successors was, Alexander, fourth brother of Robert the Bruce. He espoused the cause of the Bruce, and was taken prisoner along with his brother, Thomas, while fighting against the M'Dowalls, a Galloway sept. His captors carried him to Carlisle, where, by order of the English King, he was hanged, his head being afterwards cut off and suspended at the gate of the merry border town.

REFORMATION ASSOCIATIONS—THE ATTITUDE OF THE HAMILTONS—JOHN KNOX.

The ties which knit the House of Hamilton and their burghers in feudal times had not lost any of their strength when the Reformation period dawned on Scotland. The head of the house was James, the second Earl of Arran and Duke of Chatelherault. He was of a vacillating and uncertain disposition, Popish and Protestant by turns, but neither long; and the peoples' motto would appear to have been "like master like man." When he joined the Lords of the Congregation, he appointed Robert Hamilton of Bothwell—in the ancient church Rector of Torrens and prebendary of Bothwell—minister of the parish, and thus through his influence Hamilton was one of the few parishes that had from the first a regular pastor of the Reformed faith. Hamilton was the friend of John Knox and it is notable that of one of the Duke of Chatelherault's chaplains—Thomas Gwilliam, formerly a black friar—Calderwood relates " that he was the first man from whome Mr Knox received ane taste of the truthe." We need scarcely add that subsequent to 1566 the Hamiltons lost favour with the Reformers by supporting Queen Mary and her cause, and that after the assassination of the Regent Moray by Hamilton of Bothwell Haugh there was no language too abusive or forcible that could be heaped upon them.

CHURCH DISCIPLINE 200 YEARS AGO.

About the year 1648, a Mr Naysmith was appointed to the parish. He was a red-hot zealot for Kirk and Covenant, and set himself to purge the parish of its wickedness. After clearing his session of certain adherents of Montrose, the worthy minister set himself to deal with the prevalent immorality— Sabbath-breaking, drinking, swearing, &c.—of the day. His course of procedure will be best illustrated by extracts from the records of kirk-session of the period. One entry is—" The qlk day James Struthers comperit and confest the breach of Sabbath, by strykeing his neighbor, making that actioun his daylie custome, and being censured, was ordained to make his repentance in public place." Another— " The qlk day ordains to summond Arthur Hamilton in Merritoun for his absence from the church and taking his barne to ane other church, the minister being at home." A few days afterwards Arthur duly appeared and promised never to be absent from church in time coming, otherwise to be censured as a breaker of the Sabbath. Arthur Hamilton of Auchingramont was accused of kissing Isabell Granger betwixt the doors on the Sabbath; he denied the charge, and witnesses were brought up against him on several occasions. Finally, the following entry appears :— " The qlk day comperit Arthur Hamilton of Auchingramont, and confest his misconduct with Isabell

Granger, . . . and thairfore being censured, was ordained to make his repentance in the public place." There was a good deal of bad feeling about Montrose in the parish. Here is an entry bearing on the subject—"The qlk day John Scott in Merritoun comperit and denyit that he sklanderit Patricke in saying that he did raise the people to ryde with James Grahame." There was a Jean Lang who had disobeyed the session, and been very refractory, and "the last of Appryll, 1646, the qlk day the Sessioun requests the baillies to take Jeane Lang and put her in the tolbuith till Satterday, and yrafter to put her on the cross, with ane paper upoune her heid." Besides Jean Lang, there were many other troublesome women in Hamilton, particularly of the name of Naysmith and Hamilton. "The qlk day Joane Naysmithe comperit and confest that she callet the people of God drytting puritans, was ordained to make her repentance in her awin seat." There was a great deal of drinking in Hamilton. Here is one of the Session's regulations on the subject—"The qlk day the Sessioun renewit their former act anent drinkers after ten of the clocke at night, and the baillies for that occasioun to cause ringe the ten hours bell at night." The following is a most excellent resolution: "The qlk day the Sessioun, taking to consideration the great prejudice to the gospell by selling of drink till men be drunken, thairfore the Sessioun ordains that quhosoever sells drink till men be drunken sal be punished with that same punishment that the druken man is punished with." Swearing also prevailed. The following is one of the entries on the subject:— "The qlk day the Sessioun, taking to their consideration the great disdaine done to the name of God by swearing, ordained that if any sall fall in the lyke sin, sall go to the publict place of repentance."

PREACHING AT THE GREAT DUKE.

Previous to setting out in command of the Forces sent to England to support King Charles I., the Duke of Hamilton attended church in Hamilton. The clergy were vehemently opposed to the expedition, and Mr Naysmith preached on the occasion, his text being Jeremiah xxii and 10—"Weep not ye for the dead, neither bemoan him; but weep sore for him that goeth away, for he shall return no more." It is related that he used much freedom with the Duke in the course of his discourse, and pointedly applied the text to his Grace's case. The expedition, we need not add, ended in the defeat and capture of his Grace, who bravely suffered death in the following year.

Naysmith refused to take the oath of allegiance and was ejected from his living in 1662. Modifying his views a few years afterwards, he ended his life in 1674 as an "indulged" minister at Glasford.

PRESENT ECCLESIASTICAL CONDITION.

Past ecclesiastical divisions have multiplied the number of churches, but there is at the present time amongst the clergy of all denominations a pleasing absence of sectarian jealousy and bigotry. The parish church stands on a high ground adjoining Cadzow Street. The body of the church is a circle with four cross aisles. The design, which is generally accounted elegant, was by Adams, the elder. By decreet of modification and locality, dated 1st March, 1867, the stipend payable to the minister of the first charge is 182 bolls of meal, and 146 bolls, 1 peck and 2½ lippies of barley, Linlithgow measure, with £63 14s in money, including £10 for Communion elements. There was formerly a manse attached to the living, which was situated within what are now the policies of the Duke of Hamilton, and which was acquired by his Grace, who, instead of building a new manse, granted the then incumbent an annual allowance in name of house rent. This arrangement was continued with successive ministers. During the incumbency of the late Dr Keith the glebe was let to the Duke; and, for 15 years, the annual sum paid by his Grace, as rent therefor, and in name of house rent in lieu of manse, was £155. In 1875, the mineral underneath the glebe was let to the Bent Colliery Company (Limited) on lease for thirty years from 1873. The rent, in the option of the lessors, is a fixed sum of £300 per annum, or a lordship, and 10 per cent. of the annual produce is to be paid to the incumbent for the time being, in respect of injury to the amenity of the glebe, and personal inconvenience and trouble, and the residue, after paying expenses, is to be deposited in bank and invested for behoof of the living. The Court of Teinds, on 13th March, 1876, granted power to the present incumbent to feu the glebe, £20 per acre being fixed as the minimum rate. The income of the minister, it is expected, when the feuing, which has commenced, is completed, will be increased by about £500 per annum, and this would make the living one of the most desirable in the Church. The feuing of the glebe necessitated that the incumbent should get it into his own hands, and that there should be a new arrangement with the Duke of Hamilton in respect of allowance for a manse. In the negotiations which followed, Mr Padwick, his Grace's Commissioner, repudiated all obligation on the part of the Duke to provide a manse and offices or continue the annual money allowance therefor. Mr Hamilton, the incumbent, acting on the advice of counsel, thereupon called on the heritors to erect a manse and make him a money allowance until this was done. The request at once raised a question of no small moment to the parishioners, as the assessment for defraying the cost of a manse would fall on the small feuars as well as upon the wealthy heritors, and this in all likelihood would raise an agitation which it was the interest of the friends of the Established Church to avoid. No solution of the difficulty has yet been arrived at. The committee of heritors, to whom it was referred, have, however, obtained an opinion of eminent counsel (the Lord-Advocate and Mr Lee, Sheriff of Perthshire) that the ultimate liability rests not upon the heritors but upon the Duke of Hamilton as representing his grandfather, and they suggest that the most expedient course is for the heritors to meet the minister's claim with an action of declarator directed against him and the Duke, concluding to have it found that the Duke is bound to erect a suitable manse and offices for the accommodation of the minister, and in any view that the heritors, if liable to furnish that accommodation in the first instance, are entitled to relief of their obligations at the hands of his Grace. It is to be hoped that the Duke's advisers will see their way to withdraw from the position they have taken up. The minister of the second charge has a manse but no glebe. His stipend is understood to yield £500 annually. Auchingramont Church, a handsome Gothic edifice, was erected about eighteen years ago, the accommodation in the Parish Church having been for long insufficient. The first and second ministers conduct the services in both churches, preaching alternately forenoon and afternoon. Two years ago, Cadzow Church was erected at Woodside Walk, and its endowment is being carried through the Court of Teinds. In connection with the National Church there is an unendowed chapel at Quarter, and mission agencies at Burnbank and elsewhere.

Non-conformity, from an early period, played an important part in the ecclesiastical polity of the parish. The Blackswell U.P. congregation, now worshipping in Saffronhall Church, dates back to 1755. Twenty-one years later, in the spring of 1776, the second charge of the parish being vacant, a large body of parishioners to whom the presentee was unacceptable, formed the Relief Church, and built the place of worship in Muir street, now used as a volunteer store, and which was evacuated upon the congregation removing to the new and elegant structure now occupied by them in Auchingramont Road. The Chapel Street United Presbyterian Congregation was founded about the end of last century, and the Brandon Street congregation—a split off Muir Street—in 1831. A new church in Duke Street was erected in 1835 in connection with the Establishment, which, since the Disruption, has been the leading—indeed, until a few years ago, when a church was built at Burnbank Road —the only Free Church in Hamilton. Besides these there is a Congregational Church in Auchingramont Road, which was formed in a building in Blackswell about seventy years ago; an Episcopalian Church in the same thoroughfare; an Evangelical Union Chapel in Park Road; a Roman Catholic Chapel in Cadzow Street, formed in 1846. At Burnbank, a neat and commodious wooden structure has been built for the United Presbyterian Mission to the mining population of that quarter. There is a missionary labouring in the same district in connection with the Free Church.

MARTYRS OF THE COVENANT.

Hamilton has in precious keeping dust of martyrs of the Covenant. Into the east wall of the Churchyard, there is built a monument, which, from its grotesque appearance, is one of the first objects to arrest the eye of the visitor on entering the enclosure. It is a slab of freestone, four feet two inches in length, by two feet eight inches in breath. It has the following inscription :—

AT HAMILTON
LIE THE HEADS OF
JOHN PARKER, GAVIN HAMILTON,
JAMES HAMILTON,
AND
CHRISTOPHER STRANG,
WHO SUFFERED AT
EDINBURGH,
DEC. 7TH 1666.

FOUR HEADS IN BASSO-RELIEVO.

Stay, passenger, take notice
what thou reads.
At Edinburgh lie our bodies,
here our heads.
Our right hands stood at Lanark,
these we want,
Because with them we sware
the Covenant.

Renewed
MDCCCXXVIII.

The four heads in basso-relievo are sculptured in the rudest manner. Indeed (says the Rev. Mr Thomson in his "Martyr Graves of Scotland"), so grotesquely criminal are the features, that they look like the work of an enemy rather than a friend.

John Parker was a waulker, *i. e.*, a fuller of cloth in East Kilbride; Gavin Hamilton, a tenant in Carluke; James Hamilton, a tenant in Killiemuir; and Christopher Strang, tenant in East Kilbride. All four were taken prisoners at Pentland. They were tried at Edinburgh before the Council. Sharp was president, and with his native ferocity, urged on their condemnation. It was pleaded on their behalf that since quarter had been given them by such as had the king's commission to kill or save, and Grotius, in those days the great authority upon such matters, had, in his treatise, "De Jure Belli et Pacis," determined that "faith is to be kept even with rebels," they could not be put to death. But Sharp secured that this pleading be put aside, and that the trial take place. It is said that even Dalziel, bloodthirsty as he undoubtedly was, when he heard of this pressing on of the trial, cursed and swore terribly, and declared were he to serve the king ever so long, he should never bring in a prisoner to be butchered. The record of the trial is given at length in Wodrow, book II. *c. i. s.*, 3. Its replies, its duplies, its triplies, and quadruplies, are interesting as a specimen of the mode of procedure in a Scotch Court in the seventeenth century—a mode of procedure which actually continued to the beginning of this century—as well as for their able reasoning. The advocates for the prisoners seem to have done what they could in their defence; but all was of no avail. They were sentenced to be hanged at Edinburgh on the next Friday, December 7th, 1666; and after they were dead, their heads "to be cut off," and "affixed at Hamilton"; and "their right hands on the "public ports" of Lanark, "being the place where they took the Covenant." "Naphtali" contains the "Joint Testimony" of the four and other six condemned along with them, a second testimony, and three other individual testimonies. The close of the first testimony is remarkable for its confidence in the ultimate triumph of the cause for which they suffered and died. It is:

"And further, we are assured, though this be the day of Jacob's trouble, that yet the Lord when He hath accomplished the trial of His own, and filled up the cup of His adversaries, He will awake for judgment, plead his own cause, avenge the quarrel of His Covenant, make inquiry for blood, vindicate His people, break the arm of the wicked, and establish the just; for to Him belongeth judgment and vengeance, and though our eyes shall not see it, yet we believe that the sun of righteousness shall arise with healing under his wings; and that He will revive His work, repair the breaches, build the old wastes, and raise up the desolations; yea, the Lord will judge His people, and repent Himself for His servants, when their power is gone, and there is none shut up or left. And therefore, rejoice, O ye nations, with His people; for He will avenge the blood of His servants, and will render vengeance to His adversaries, and He will be merciful to His land and people. So, let thy enemies perish, O Lord! but let them that love Him be as the sun when he goeth forth in his might."

Mr Dodds has ferreted out, in the State Paper Office, a letter from Main, the postmaster in Edinburgh, to the Government in London, giving an account of their death. "All of them died adhering to the Covenant, declaring they never intended in the least any rebellion, and all of them prayed most earnestly for his majesty's interest, and against his enemies." "They prayed to forgive the judges and the noblemen, and declared their blood lay only at the prelate's door—would not be hindered to express themselves in such a manner—which expressions had too great dipping in the hearts of the commonality."

EDUCATIONAL.

Hamilton, from remote to present times, has been unusually well served educationally. The grammar school is of ancient date. In 1588, we find Lord

John Hamilton granting a bond, still in possession of the corporation, settling for ever on that school the yearly sum of 20 pounds Scots. In the old schoolhouse, which still stands, and which gives the name to a spacious square in the old town, Pillans, Whale, Gillies, and other eminent men taught; James, Duke of Hamilton, grandson of the good Duchess Anne, received part of his education, as did Dr William Cullen, Dr M. Baillie, Professor Miller, Lord Dundonald; and there were sent from it pupils who, in the town and spheres far beyond, have made their mark, and are even now sustaining well their part in the world. The old grammar school, in its time, did much for the cause of secondary education in the district. In 1847, new premises were erected on a commanding site near the Leechlee, and opened under the name of the Academy. It included the parish school, and represented the old grammar school. The teaching staff more than sustained the high character inherited from the older institution. When, on the passing of Lord Young's Education Act, the School Board was brought into existence, the Academy was the only existing school which passed under the Board. Being in a most prosperous condition, the future of the institution became a source of anxiety to the members of the School Board. It taught many branches besides the elementary; and the scale of fees charged deprived it of assistance from the grant. It had always been essentially a higher-class school in the sense of the Act, and the Scotch Education Department so designated it after considering the flattering report of the inspector who reported on it. It was so in the estimation of the Board, who, after long deliberation, resolved, in terms of the statute, that it should be so regarded, and that the Board of Education should be asked to sanction its being so enrolled and treated. This resolution was the result of very much and anxious thought to the Board, who deprecated the possibility of the status of the School being lowered, and also considered that, for the sake of the town and district, it should be ranked as a high-class school. In their resolution on the subject, the Board redeemed a pledge which they gave to the parish Board—that, in respect of the latter Board foregoing their claim to the parochial part of the Academy, the Board should do what they could to have the Academy ranked as a higher-class school. The want of any endowment, which was the great obstacle in the way, was eventually overcome, and the Academy, still under its able head (Mr Blacklock), but equipped with an almost entirely new staff of highly-trained teachers, began the session of 1876-77 as a higher-class school. The success attending it has been most gratifying, and has evidently not yet reached the highest point. Last session, its examiners were Mr Andrews and Mr Smith, the Government inspectors of the district. They conducted the examination, not in virtue of their official position, but at the invitation of the School Board. Their ability and perfect impartiality are, therefore, beyond question, and Mr Andrews concluded a highly flattering report in the following terms :—

"I would conclude my report in remarking that what impressed me as the leading feature of the school, a feature running through all its departments, and down into the minutest detail of its working, was the thoroughness with which everything attempted was gone into, the downright honesty and soundness of all the teaching, and the utter absence of anything like educational quackery or sham. Healthy vigour and genuine work pervade its whole atmosphere, and as, under the fostering care of the School Board, it gradually widens its aims, and reaches up to higher levels of study, I have no doubt that the Hamilton Academy will come to occupy a leading position among the secondary schools of the country."

St. John's Grammar School, conducted by Mr Adams and an efficient staff of masters, has been an incalculable blessing to the town. Conducted with unflagging energy and zeal—teaching at a moderate rate the higher as well as elementary branches—its pupils are to be found in every walk of life, many of them adorning the professions. The Quarry School, under the Orphan and Charity Society, and St. Mary's School, in connection with the Roman Catholic Church, impart instruction of excellent quality to the very poorest class in the community. There are two elementary schools under the management of the School Board, which are faithfully doing their work. When the Board was brought into existence six years ago, the number of children between five and thirteen years of age was found to be 2,211, and of these 824 were not attending school. There was a deficiency of school accommodation for 1062 children, and allowing for the opening of schools in suitable districts by the Parish Board, the Board resolved to provide accommodation for 750. To meet this, they erected a building in Beckford Street to accommodate 350, and another at Townhead Street for 400. Beckford Street School was opened in August, and Townhead School in November, 1875. Under the management of the Parish Board, there are schools at Greenfield, Low-waters, Motherwell, Quarter, Beechfield, and Ferniegair.

Of private establishments, the Clydesdale College is efficiently conducted by Messrs Wood and Kinmond. Miss Neilson, in Clydesdale Street, and the Misses Spence, at Earnock View, have establishments for young ladies.

MUNICIPAL.

From 1832, down to the present year, the town was governed by a Provost, three bailies, a treasurer, a town clerk, and seven councillors. The town latterly was divided into four wards, and a representative of each retired annually. The gas works, having been acquired from a private company, are managed by the Town Council, and are in course of being greatly extended. The water works, from their erection, until the November of this year, were managed by a body of Commissioners. From time to time the state of the old town forced the question of improvements into prominence, and application to Parliament was long talked of. Some of the worst evils connected with the old town disappeared before the rapid increase of workmen's houses, which, prompted by high rents, private enterprise was providing in other and better parts of the town, and the need for an Improvement Bill was becoming less and less urgent when new causes for going to Parliament presented themselves. The Water Commissioners, though they had been in Parliament so recently as 1875 for borrowing and other powers, were again requiring money to bring the abundant supply of water which they had collected at the ponds at Townhead down to the town. There was scarcity in the high-lying parts of the burgh, and the new suburbs at Burnbank and Greenfield were calling out for a supply. These suburbs had almost sprung up in a night, and were the direct result of the opening up of the coalfields in that direction, stimulated by the speculation mania which had just spent itself in Glasgow, and which settled here after for a time casting about for fresh fields. These suburbs not only wanted water and gas, but they required drainage, and streets to be formed, &c. They applied to be taken into the municipality, and were refused, and they then asked the Sheriff to form them into a burgh under the Police Act. The Town Council, with the prospect of having a divided jurisdiction so near their borders, and requiring to go to Parliament for water purposes at any rate, after taking a plebiscite of the inhabitants—with whom it was distinctly stipulated that the benefits of the common good should not extend beyond the old boundaries—resolved to make application for a Bill for the extension and improvement of the burgh. The Bill was determinedly opposed in both Houses of Parliament, but ultimately passed, and with it greater and more important changes have been brought about than since the Reform Act of 1832. The portion annexed, including Burnbank, Greenfield, and Low-waters, is constituted the Fifth Ward of the burgh, with three representatives in the Town Council, which is thus increased to fifteen members. A fourth bailie is added to the magistracy, who is to be Dean of Guild. The Dean's Court consists of a Depute-Dean and three Councillors, and enlarged powers are conferred upon it. The Water Commissioners ceased to exist on 11th November, 1878, and the management of the works passed into the hands of the Town Council. Power is also given to elect a Chamberlain, who is not to be a member of Town Council, and to carry out several important improvement works.

Hamilton unites with Falkirk, which is the returning burgh, Lanark, Linlithgow, and Airdrie, in sending a member to Parliament. The constituency for 1878-79 numbers 1292, the part recently annexed being, so far as Parliamentary representation is concerned, still in the county. The population of the burgh in 1871 was 11,496; the present population (inclusive of the extended portion) is estimated at about 17,000. The total valuation for 1878-79 of the old and extended burgh, including railways, is set down at £77,297 13s.

The following names appear in the minutes of Council, being those of Provosts or Chief Magistrates and Bailies :—From 1735 to 1787—J. Porterfield, James Semple, Wm. Cullen, Thos. Cunison, Quintin Hamilton, Thomas Duning, William Mather, John Naismith, John Aitton, James Syme, John Bryson, James Hamilton, George Wands, Wm. Brown ; from 1801 till the present time—John Hinshaw, John Torrance, James Haldane, Will. Hamilton, James Henderson, Robert Henderson, Thomas Anderson, James Naismith, Walter Black, Alexander Gibson, John Meek, Robert Henderson, James Nisbet, John Dykes, W. A. Dykes, John Clark Forrest.

BURGH REVENUE.

The Town's Lands were acquired from James, Lord Hamilton, by charter, dated 14th October, 1474, and they are also contained in a charter by Anne, Duchess of Hamilton, with consent of William, Duke of Hamilton, her husband, dated the 1st day of June, 1670. No part of these lands, so far as known, has been alienated by the town since the date of acquiring them, except the ground feued out for an annual feu-duty, and certain small parts given in exchange as after-mentioned.

By disposition granted by Anne, Duchess of Hamilton, dated 22d August, 1695, she, in lieu of an acre of the Muir of the Burgh, which had been imparked with her Laigh Park, disponed to the town an acre of her field land, next to the east side of the Muir of Hamilton; and in this acre, with the teinds thereof, the Magistrates and Council were infeft conform to instrument of sasine, dated 11th, and registered 12th September, 1695. The acre of ground thus disponed, comprehends those feus belonging to the town on the east side of Muir Street.

By the disposition last mentioned, Duchess Anne also dispones in excambion of the old common green of the burgh, all and haill, these homes and haill ground betwixt the burn of Hamilton and the lade that leads the water to the mill thereof from the Mill-dam-back down to the Shealing-hill. The town also acquired, in lieu of the old green, for a price paid by Duchess Anne, from James Lowdon, litstor in Hamilton, all and whole that acre of land called Ducot acre, lying on the south side of the wynd called St John's Wynd or Muir Wynd, and on the west side of the yard called Ducot-hall Yard, conform to disposition dated 22d August, 1695, and in which the Magistrates and Council were infeft conform to instrument of sasine, dated the 11th, and recorded on the 12th day of September, 1695, and which writs are confirmed by charter from Duchess Anne, dated 22d September, 1695.

This acre, with the holms and ground above-mentioned, and certain parts of the lands of Rogerscroft, feued by the town from the heirs of Archibald Weir, and from John Campbell of Saffronhall, form the present common bleaching green of the burgh.

No part of these has been alienated by the town except those parts feued out to the late Mr George Wands and Dr Wharrie, and a small part to the Relief Congregation. The extent of the present bleaching green and holms is 2 acres 1 rood and 24 falls.

By agreement entered into between the Magistrates and Council and the Duke of Hamilton, dated in October, 1829, His Grace discharged certain arrears of feu and teind duties due by the town, with the valued price of the teinds, for which decree of sale was obtained on 3d July, 1799, the whole amounting to £453 12s 6d sterling. The town has now right to the teinds of these lands, but no regular disposition to the same has been yet obtained.

The Council house tenement was acquired by disposition from Duchess Anne, dated 3d August, 1707, and in which the town was infeft, conform to instrument of sasine dated 16th September, and recorded 2d October, 1707. The old Flesh-market of the burgh formerly occupied the site of this tenement. The present tenement was built in the year 1796.

The Meal Market tenement was acquired by the town by disposition from John Muir, maltman in Hamilton, and in which the town was infeft conform to instrument of sasine, dated 17th and recorded 19th June, 1699. The titles of the town are confirmed by the superior conform to confirmation dated 14th July, 1713.

The Grammar School and rector's house were acquired by disposition from Duchess Anne, dated 15th February, 1714, and instrument of sasine following thereon in favour of the town, dated the same day, and recorded 18th February, 1714.

The site of the present fleshmarket and slaughterhouse and adjoining ground was acquired from the doers of the deceased Douglas, Duke of Hamilton and Brandon, in exchange for a small piece of ground lying next the gate to the entry to Hamilton Palace, at Gallowhill. The agreement was settled by missives, dated 6th February, 1784, and both parties have since possessed the respective pieces of ground got in exchange. The transaction was completed by a regular contract of excambion. The town stands infeft, conform to instrument of sasine, dated 2d, recorded 11th June, 1829. The present fleshmarket and slaughter-house were erected in 1794.

That derived from mineral is now by far the largest

item of revenue. Despite gloomy presages to the contrary, we hope the coal may realise the large expectations formed of it: the benefit to the town will be great and obvious, as taxation will not only be remitted, but the Town Council will be furnished with the means to carry out many useful improvements. In Treasurer Mackie's financial statement for the year ending 15th October, 1878, the land and mineral rents are shown to have amounted to £2765 18s 9d, making a total from this source, since the coal began to be worked, of £3140 12s 4d. During the year in question, there was derived from feu-duties, £1023 1s $6\frac{1}{2}$d; from house rents, £246 5s 4d; town hall, £156 9s; and the miscellaneous revenue was £174 11s 6d. Few towns in Scotland are fortunate enough to possess such a valuable common good.

CHARITIES.

I. Robertson's mortification, or what is called the town's hospital. James Robertson, sheriff-clerk of Lanarkshire by deed of mortification, dated 4th Sept., 1657, disponed the lands of Airdrie, Rawyards, and Arbuckles, in the parish of New Monkland, to the magistrates and town council, and to the ministers and kirk session of the parish of Hamilton; and bequeathed certain moveable funds for the purpose of endowing an hospital. The deed was reduced as far as regards the heritage by Mr Robertson's heir-at-law. The moveable funds, with the addition of a sum bequeathed for a similar purpose by a Mr Lyon, came into the hands of the town, and yield £38 yearly, which is paid to nine old men, who receive £4 each— £2 of salary being paid to a factor. The hospital is under the management of the magistrates and town council and ministers and kirk session. They nominate alternately.

II. Mr John Rae, Mr Hamilton of Floors, and Miss Mary Mathie, severally mortified funds to the town, yielding £9 12s 4d, to be paid to poor persons. It is distributed yearly, according to a list made up by the magistrates and council.

III. Anne, Duchess of Hamilton, mortified one hundred pounds to the kirk session of the parish, for behoof of certain schools in the parish.

IV. Mr Michael Naismith mortified £100 to the town; the interest of which was to be applied in educating twelve poor children. The children on this mortification are nominated by the magistrates and Council, or rather they appoint one of their members, who sees that the number of children is full. (The Hamilton Orphan Society also educate about 70 children yearly.)

V. Aikman of Ross burdened his lands of Burnhouse with a fund for endowing an hospital in Hamilton. A house was accordingly built for the accommodation of four old men. They are elected alternately by the proprietor of Ross, the ministers of the parish, and the magistrates of the burgh, who are managers of the hospital. Besides a house, the old men receive each £5 yearly, with a hat and pair of shoes, and a suit of clothes every second year.

VI. Mr John Roxburgh of Bothwell Shields, burdened certain parts of his property with £10 10s yearly, to be paid to poor inhabitants of the town. The managers are—the eldest bailie of Hamilton, and certain of Mr Roxburgh's relations. The money is drawn and distributed yearly among poor persons, according to a list made up by the managers.

VII. Major Burns, in 1844 or 1845, mortified to the town the sum of £500, the interest of which was to be paid to three aged persons. The magistrates, council, and ministers of the parish, and certain trustees, are joint patrons.

VIII. Mrs Andrew Simpson, Haddow Street, Hamilton, in 1867 mortified £803 3s 2d, yielding £40 yearly, to be paid to poor persons belonging to the town of Hamilton. Ten old females receive £4 each yearly, and are appointed by the Town Council.

PUBLIC BUILDINGS—THE TOWN HALL.

The architectural character of the public buildings has made great advances. The new Town Hall was opened in 1863. It occupies the south-east corner site at the intersection of Duke and Quarry Streets. The style adopted by the architects (Messrs Clarke & Bell, Glasgow) is that of modernised Scotch baronial. The facade to Duke Street, though plain, is extremely fine, but the most prominent object of the building is the tower which stands at the corner of Duke and Quarry Streets, and which rears its tall and beautiful form to a height of nearly 130 feet. On the basement floor are situated the town clerk's office, police court, office, cells, &c. A stair leads from the principal public entrance in the tower to the Council Chambers and large hall, which is 63 feet long by 36 feet wide, and capable of accommodating from 400 to 500. The hall is fitted with a splendid organ, a public memorial to the late esteemed Provost John Dykes. There are ample retiring accommodation, and a commodious lesser hall 29 feet by 19 feet.

The Corporation, eighteen months since, acquired, at considerable outlay, a site near Gateside for new municipal buildings, the erection of which has not, however, yet been resolved upon.

THE OLD TOLBOOTH.

The old jail, now within His Grace's policies, was

built in the reign of Charles I. In its front balcony stood many a culprit as a spectacle to the gaping crowd. Strange associations are connected with this ancient structure, and stranger still the many scenes which have been enacted within its walls. Restrictions in feasting and drinking were winked at in those days. It was not unusual to see the bottle handed out and in at pleasure, and if the funds permitted, the debtor might drink his fill without let or hindrance. There were then no first, second, or third rate diets, no special wards, no turnkeys, save one; no cranks, no oakum-picking, or hard labour. The jailer himself was a hearty "old buck," occupying a shop underneath the belfry and the bell, where he could see all that was going on. Jokes, toasts, songs, jigs, were the rule, and grief or *ennui* the exception. It is reported that on one occasion the jailer allowed a prisoner his freedom for a few hours to attend the funeral of a relative. Not very far from the prison, another place had the endearing appellation of the "Deil's Elbow," and further down was the "Back Burn." In the building opposite there still stands what was once the town hall, where feasting and drinking were carried on at the public expense. Whisky was then cheap and stomachs strong. Francis Wakefield knew this when he presented the Town Council with the capacious punch bowl still so much prized.

THE COUNTY BUILDINGS.

At a period comparatively remote, the Sheriff-Court business in the Lower Ward of Lanarkshire was of so little importance that it was all taken to Hamilton, which was then the seat of the Court for the Lower Ward, including the City of Glasgow, as well as for the whole of the Middle Ward. The late Sheriff Aiton was wont to tell that within his recollection the office of Sheriff-Substitute was filled by a weaver, and his salary was only £30. "During his time," says the Sheriff, "I learned from my fellow practitioners (two of whom had been doing business in the Court for more than 50 years prior to 1798) the practice was to hold the Court in a public-house kept by a tailor, who was then head sheriff-clerk, and in these patriarchal days the Judge was employed in making and distributing the toddy amongst the practitioners and their clients whilst the business of the Court was going on. The ordinary routine of a process was then as it continued to be for many years afterwards : (1) summons or petition ; (2) defences ; (3) answers ; (4) replies ; and (5) sometimes duplies. I have seen an original process in which all these pleadings were written on a single sheet of paper, and the sum charged for drawing and extending seemed to be 2s 6d for each. If the parties and procurators had been so disposed and the bench not too potent, all these pleadings might have been written and interchanged, and the whole process ready for decision at a single sitting. Later, the practice was to write long papers. On one occasion, when there was laid on the Court table an action of damages against the owner of a hen that had strayed into a bowl shop and broken some coarse crockery, one of the octogenarians referred to, after looking at the number and size of the papers which had been prepared by young practitioners who wanted to show off, held up his hands and exclaimed in the way of soliloquy—'All that about a hen ; what if it had been a cow ?' And on another occasion, when a short defence had been made with a very long answer, the old-fashioned agent told his client in a voice shaking with astonishment and consternation, that the opposite agent had given in a paper as thick as ——, and after looking round and groping with both hands for a suitable simile, he gave up the attempt in despair, and filled up the hiatus with the words, 'as thick as his head,' meaning them to be taken in their literal sense, and never dreaming that they could admit of any other interpretation." It is needless to say what a different state of things now exist. There have been established courts at Glasgow and Airdrie, and yet the business before the Hamilton Court is one of the largest in the county. It has advanced with the onward march of commerce and population in the district. This was well illustrated by Sheriff Spens in taking leave of the bar on his removal to Glasgow in December 1876. His Lordship said that when he took his seat on the bench in 1870, the population of the district was between 70,000 and 80,000. Since then it had increased in a marvellously rapid way, and he believed now the population could not be less than nearly 110,000. The reason of this was partially, or rather, he should say, chiefly, due to the immense impetus given to coal and iron development by the abnormal prices and demand during the years 1872, 1873, and 1874. With the increase of the population, there had been an increase in the work of the Court. In the year 1870 there were 1063 Small Debt cases in Wishaw and Hamilton, 103 Debts' Recovery cases, and 104 cases on the Ordinary roll. In 1875, although the Wages' Arrestment Act was in force, the number of Small Debt cases had risen to 1630; Debts' Recovery cases, 199; Ordinary cases, 279. The increase has been going on steadily every year since.

The buildings were begun in 1834, and have since been altered and enlarged. Their Grecian aspect and pillared facade and pediment are calculated to favourably impress strangers, but internally the accommodation is quite inadequate, and the ventilation, drainage, and general sanitary condition, of the worst description. The officials, practitioners, and Court-house Commissioners have each made representations on the subject to the Government, who have caused an inspection to be made, but nothing further has yet been done.

THE PRISON.

The prison is situated behind the Court-house. The two buildings were erected together in 1834-35 at an outlay of £7000—the half of which may be considered the cost of the prison. The population of the burgh was then between seven and eight thousand. A few years afterwards the cells were reduced in number, but increased in size and improved in ventilation; and, at the same time, a bath-room, wash-house, and six stone-breaking sheds were erected, and half an acre of additional ground acquired to provide for future requirements—all at an additional cost of about £1000. The accommodation of the prison has never been sufficient, and in 1873, when trade was good and Hamilton becoming the centre of a large working population, it was evident that a considerable extension would require to be made. The Prison Board took up the question, and, after mature deliberation, finally, in 1876, approved of a plan which would have provided accommodation for the whole of the southern district of Lanarkshire, leaving the prisons of Airdrie and Lanark in their existing state for the detention of short-sentenced prisoners. When this plan was submitted to the authorities in Edinburgh it was rejected, as the Government had then a legislative measure in contemplation, which was shortly afterwards introduced into Parliament, though not passed into law until the following session. This Act, which applied to the whole country, came into force on 1st April, 1878. Under its provisions the Prison Board was abolished, and the entire prison administration vested in the Home Office, with a Department in Edinburgh controlling the management of the Scotch Prisons. It is believed that a new prison will ultimately be erected at Hamilton for the southern district of the county.

MILITARY.

The Barracks in Almada Street cover a large area, which is surrounded by a high wall. The cavalry element formerly predominated, but the erection of the Maryhill Barracks, and changed ideas at headquarters led, much to the regret of the inhabitants, to the withdrawal of the horse soldiers in the summer of 1877. Under Lord Caldwell's Army Organisation scheme, Hamilton was selected as a double depot, and was constituted the 59th and 60th sub-districts, the regiments linked in the former being the 26th (Cameronians) and 74th (Highlanders), and in the latter the 73d and 90th. For the accommodation of the foot soldiers, the horse barracks have been utilized; also the buildings formerly the stores of the 1st Royal Lanark Militia; and fine new quarters for officers and men built, and the hospital greatly enlarged. The head-quarters of the 1st Royal Lanark Militia are at Hamilton, and the barracks and erections connected therewith adjoin those of the Regulars. The Queen's Own Yeomanry meet annually for training in Hamilton, finishing up their week's drill with a review and races. The head-quarters of the 16th Lanarkshire Rifle Volunteers are also here.

POORHOUSE AND HOSPITAL.

There is a commodious poorhouse in Bothwell Road for the accommodation of paupers belonging to the parish, and to the adjoining parishes of Dalserf, Stonehouse, Glassford, Avondale, Cambuslang, Blantyre, and East Kilbride. The parish and burgh local authorities have joined in the erection of a fever hospital in Beckford Street, which is just approaching completion. It will be utilized for accident and other emergency cases.

RAILWAYS.

Through the influence of the ducal family, the Caledonian main line was diverted from Hamilton, which continued up till 1876 to be indifferently served by a branch line from South Side, Glasgow, with a terminus at Clydesdale Street. There was a 'bus required for conveyance from the railway station to the centre of Hamilton on the one hand, and to the centre of Glasgow on the other. After a severe struggle in Parliament, the Caledonian Railway Company obtained powers to construct a line connecting their terminus in Clydesdale Street with the Lesmahagow Railway, and an independent company, a railway from the North British system at Shettleston to Hamilton by way of Uddingston and Bothwell. By the one, the district to the south of Holytown and in the Lesmahagow direction are brought within easy access, and by the other a most interesting country is opened up and passengers set down in the centre of Glasgow. The Caledonian stations are at Quarry Street and Clydesdale Street; those of the Glasgow, Bothwell, Hamilton, and Coatbridge Railway in Cadzow Street and adjoining Peacock Cross. For unequalled facilities and cheapness, Hamilton, as regards travelling, would probably rank with the most highly-favoured town in the Kingdom.

RETROSPECTIVE.

To hark back for a brief space to those days, a few generations ago, when life was more simple and homely than it is now, the condition of the burgh, as illustrated by the public records of the time, may justly claim passing reference. Take the epoch of the Rebellion, or one hundred and forty years ago. The Palace was in the centre of the town, and its noble possessor knew everybody and everybody knew him. It is said of an old woman that she was in the habit of exulting over the fact that she "lived next door to the Duke," and that His Grace often called on her for a "light of his pipe." Upwards from the old Tolbooth, towards the west and south, there stretched the Castle Wynd, the New or School Wynd, and the Muir Wynd. Along this last road, from the Dovecothall and manse upwards, in the Bothwell direction, there seem to have been no houses, except, perhaps, one on the Muirbrow at Saffronhall, belonging to Mr Campbell; and through the wilderness of whins which overspread the Muir, both below that house and beyond it, there led the rough, narrow old road to Bothwell Bridge, along which many then living remembered to have met the fugitives from the famous battle, as after the fighting and the preaching of that eventful day they fled from Monmouth's army and the revengeful pursuit of Claver's dragoons. Branching off the road to Bothwell Bridge, there seems to have been a track through the whins nearly in the line of what is now Almada Street and Burnbank Road, and in 1736 there was the first attempt to make this track into something like a road for foot passengers and horses. By order of Town Council it was to be a "road or casway of an elne wide," or if Jackson of Bardykes, the laird of Westburn, and other proprietors in that direction subscribed liberally, the Bailies and Council promised to extend the width to four feet. At the head of the School Wynd, near the mill and the miller's house, and beside the Shieling Hill, the Grammar School then stood alone, and past it there led a path to the then new kirk. In 1751, the Duke feued the ground west of the Grammar School, and in the same year the first houses in the Church Road were built by James Bishop and others. At an early period the Duke's almshouse was set down at the Old Cross; and the Grammar School Square, under the name of the Hawk Hill, was the place where the noble family kept their falcons. At a later period a Quaker's burying-ground was laid out exactly at the place where the Edinburgh Road enters Hamilton. There was the Castle Wynd Port, and near it, projecting awkwardly into the street, an open draw well. It cost the Council much labour to get led away and down the Blackswell the water from Woodside and Quarryloan, which had a perverse but not unnatural inclination to run down the Castle Wynd and "damnify the casway," as the minutes tell us. The houses did not extend far up the Quarryloan, but they were to be found in straggling fashion along Townhead and out towards Broken Cross. Away east and north from the old Tolbooth across the haugh there were several roads and streets of which there is now no trace. There was the Netherton Wynd leading northward to the Muir Wynd; the High Street or Hie Town, leading eastwards from the Tolbooth towards the old front of the Palace; the Langloan branching southwards from this towards Huttonbank, and crossing the road to the Ross, and there was the causeway leading to the Boathouse and the boats. The Boathouse was at the mouth of the Hamilton Burn; and, at the junction of the burn with the Clyde, a quay was formed where lay two boats, one for cattle and carriages, which in these days were rare, and a little one for passengers. The boathouse and boats were let for a considerable period of time to some worthy man or woman, who took the management and drew the "customs" for the ferry.

THE COUNCIL AND THE FERRY FOLKS.

Very kind, says the late Provost John Dykes, the bailies and Council always were to the ferry folks, especially when Isobel Naismith was the tackswoman, and she held the ferry for a good many years. When Isobel's chimney smoked the treasurer had to see about it; and when, by reason of the long frost, the people crossed on the ice, to her great loss and detriment, she got, as was reasonable, an allowance out of her rent; and when there was a long drought, and they forded the water, her case was considered; and on all occasions the repair of her house and her personal comfort were looked after with a care and liberality which speaks volumes for the gallantry of the bailies towards the lone woman at the ferry. It was after her time, however, that the greatest misfortunes of any befel the boats. On the 11th of November, 1760, by "an extraordinary great flood in the water of Clyde," as the minutes tell us, "the large boat was so much shattered and broken that it could not be mended, and so must be made of new, without which there could be no passage in the winter season for horses and heavy carriages." Seven years afterwards the boats were both carried away by the ice; and altogether it must have been a great relief to the town when in 1780 the New Bridge, as it is still called, was opened, and the boats were sold off by public roup. The customs for the boats, as fixed in 1761, in sterling money, were as follows :—

Each foot passenger, a halfpenny stg.	½d.
Each horse or cow, one penny	1d.
Each loaden single cart, fourpence	4d.
Each unloaden single cart, twopence	2d.
Each double loaden cart, eightpence	8d.
Each fourwheel chaise with 2 horses, eightpence,	8d.
Each fourwheel chaise, with 4 horses, one shilling fourpence	1s 4d.
Each coach with six horses, two shillings	2s
Each single horse load that requires to be unloaded on boating, one penny, besides the horse freight	1d.

POSTGATE OR POSKITE.

Before leaving the topography of old Hamilton, it may be mentioned in regard to this street that the proper name is Passgate. It is the remains of an old Roman road or gate from the Langloan that passed along the Castle Wynd, leading directly from the old boathouse through the Muir to Bothwell Bridge. In times of danger, there was a sentry placed here, and a barricade erected, communicating with a fort at Castlehill, with another at the watchtree, and finally with the Castle of Cadzow itself. This was, therefore, the Passgate, and was known as such long before ever a Post was known in Scotland.

THE UNREFORMED TOWN COUNCIL.

The affairs of the town were managed by a Council of twelve, including two bailies and a treasurer, who were elected annually in a sort of perpetual succession, the old appointing the new. Yearly a list of six was named by the expiring Council, and carried down to the Palace, out of which list the Duke named two bailies, generally the old ones. On a stated day these bailies appeared in the Court-house in the Tolbooth, and took the oaths, and then adjourned with the old Council to the Council-house, and there "choiced" a new Council, consisting commonly of their own noble selves without any change. In their nomination, the bailies are authorised to "administrat justice to the inhabitants of the burgh, and all others His Majesty's lieges, and to uplift and receive the fynes and emoluments pertaining to the said office, *and employ the same to their own uses.*"

CONVIVIALIA.

The magistrates exercised great diligence in exacting fines, but as there is no trace of any of them finding their way into the public purse, the inference is that they were applied to the purposes of refreshment during the many consultations held for the public welfare. If they were so applied it is clear they did not suffice for the purpose, for we have the tavern bills regularly and punctually settled every year along with the rest of the town's accounts. These were the times when vintners in name were vintners in reality, and when gentlemen and burgh magnates had the best of claret at the change house for some 18s or so a dozen. One William Simpson seems to have been the favourite vintner about the time of the Rebellion, and his wine account would come to from £20 to £30 yearly. But the Council did not confine their patronage to the regular dealers. They got their wine where they could get it best, and they seem at one time to have dealt regularly for the article with a medical gentleman, who, whatever he might know of the constitution of the body corporate, must have been qualified to judge of the appropriate stimulants for the bodies of the corporation. This gentleman was a James Naismith, chirurgeon, and his accounts are regularly settled year after year, with, in one instance, in the year 1731, "three shillings and fourpence money foresaid farder, as the price of two bottles whyte wine omitted out of the account, and which was drunk by the Baillies and Councill, with John Hamilton, one of his Graces's Commissioners." In the times somewhat later, we find the effect of the duties imposed on the juice of the grape indicated by the change of tipple to what is vaguely called "liquor," and by entries of expenses "for sugar and lemons." The harmonising effect of this generous system would seem to have been complete, as the authority we have already quoted leaves it on record that, in an examination of the Council minutes for a period of over 30 or 40 years, he could find no trace of any division in the Council.

THE COUNCIL AND PRINCE CHARLIE.

In 1745, Prince Charlie in his progress northwards stayed some days at Hamilton Palace, the noble owner of which was understood to be not unfavourable to his cause, and it is also well known that levies were made upon Glasgow for clothing and all sorts of supplies for the rebel army. The Council with great caution and prudence kept a "calm sough" as long as the enemy was at their door. No sooner had the last of the Highlanders crossed the Forth with the Duke of Cumberland's army in pursuit, than their loyalty was made to shine brilliantly forth, and, on the 4th of February 1746, "they appoint their treasurer to pay to Bailie Cunison four guineas for defraying his expenses in going in to Edinburgh to advise with the Lord-Justice Clerk as to the best way of behaving in the present conjuncture—how the town should behave most for the interest of the Government." This "four guineas" was all that the great Rebellion cost the town of Hamilton.

A TROUBLESOME JAILER.

John Hepburn was appointed town officer in 1731, and for many years held the four dignified appointments of town officer, jailer, keeper of the clock, and ringing of the bell, with all the fees and emoluments thereto belonging. John, however, was rather a convivial spirit, and did not always in his cups remember the propriety of demeanour due to the important offices he filled. Thus, on the 13th September, 1743, "Bailie Cunison represented to the Council that John Hepburn, jayler, hath several times, especially when drunk, been very abusive to the said Bailie, and that within these few days, being drunk, he gave the said Bailie a great deal of abusive language, and at the same time gave the Bailie the keys of the prison, which he had put into the hands of John Telfer, officer; and the Council considering the same, they are of opinion that some fit person should be thought upon against next meeting of Council for supplying the office of jayler." John seems to have got a fright at his behaviour being thus seriously taken up, and to have made his peace with the Bailie and the Council, for there is no farther allusion to the affair, and, thirteen years afterwards, we find John Hepburn is still jailer, and town officer to boot, in all the glory of the coat and hat and ribbons, which awed the youth of ancient Hamilton into respect for the constituted authorities.

The other subordinate officers of the town at this time were—1, The town's officers—two in number—whose wages were raised in 1761 to 20s each per annum, besides the coats and hats and ribbons. 2, The town's drummer, who made all the more important announcements, and received 10s per annum for his services, besides a hat and coat, and 1s on the annual rouping days. 3, A town crier, first appointed in 1754, when his stations were fixed by the Council, and his remuneration settled at 1d stg. for each notice proclaimed. 4, A lamplighter, whose salary was £1 sterling, besides a "froak," which the town allowed him, no doubt, to save his clothes from the oil.

MAKING PROGRESS.

On the 29th of October, 1737, we find that "The Bailies and Council, in regard, it will be convenient, for the Burgh to have lamps through the town, appoint their treasurer to buy and put one on for a trial, and provide oil for the same, and to report the expense thereof betwixt and the next council day, and to put up the same at the corner of Bailie Muirhead's house. This lamp must, no doubt, have been considered a great success, and have been much admired by all the good burghers and their wives and bairns, for a dozen more were ordered, for the other parts of the town, before the winter was over. They were pretty dear, Bailie Muirhead's one costing £42 16s Scots, and the others £213 13s; but, no doubt, this was thought a cheap price for so great an improvement. Occasionally we find the Council making a grand exertion towards what we would call sanitary improvements; and, from what the minutes disclose, they seem to have had good reason. Thus, on 23d October, 1756, we find it recorded that "The Bailies and Council, having this day along with the sworn men of the burgh, visited the common loans, sheughs, and marches, in the Haugh, they, in the first place, find the Langloan is scarce passable by carts; therefore agree that the treasurer shall amend the same by gravelling the road up the Langloan from the Barns upwards, to where the road towards Ross crosses the Loan; they appoint intimation to be made by tuck of drum, on Monday next, that the possessors of the lands in the Haugh do cast sufficiently the sheughs in the Haugh against the Monday following, certifying such as neglect that the Bailies will cause do the work at the possessor's charge, and the sworn men are to visit the same after cast, to see that the same is sufficiently done, so as to carry off the whole water. They find there should be a covered syver for carrying the water across the road at *Solomon's Vineyard."* Then, after the various details about the sheughs, the minute goes on—" And appoint the midden, now lying in the street opposite to Golder's and James Burnes's houses in the Townhead, to be removed, and the same to be filled up with rubbish, and all other dunghills gathered on the High Street, to be removed." The Council had a proper estimate of the value of the commodity thus stored in the public street, and it was only on a written petition, and on his undertaking that he would send all his fodder to be consumed in the town that Mr John Campbell was allowed to remove some of it for the cultivation of his land on the Muirbrow.

TREATMENT OF SOCIAL PROBLEMS.

There were paupers in those days, too; and this is how the increase of beggars was dealt with. On 2d February, 1738, "The Magistrates and Town Councill, considering that of late the poor of this paroch have considerably increased, and many of these appear to be strangers from oyr. paroches, who ought to be inhibited to the charity of this paroch, for preventing and remeiding whereof, they do yrfor appoint strict enquiry to be made with respect to the poor who are strangers, and have not resided three years in the paroch, that reports thereof be made to the Councill to the end that such persons be turned out of the paroch: And farder, prohibit and discharge the heritors of this burgh, in time coming, to set houses to strangers from other paroches, till such time as they apply to one of the Magistrates of the Burgh who may judge if the person who wants to take the house have wherewith to maintain ymselves and family, without being burdensome to the paroch; and that under penalty of Twenty punds Scots, to be exacted of the heritor who shall neglect to make such previous application before settling; and likeways appoint the officers of the burgh to seize and apprehend all such strolling vagrant beggars as do not reside within the paroch, and to the end the persons who are proper objects of charity may be distinguished from vagrants, they appoint publick intimation be made through the Town of Hamilton by tuck of drum, and placarding copies of this Act in the public places, ordering all the persons who resolve to beg in the paroch, that they present themselves and appear before the Magistrates and Town Councill, in the Tolbooth of Hamilton, the 13, 14, 15, and 16 days of Feb. inst., at ten o'clock forenoon, that ye said Baillies and Councill may enquire into these circumstances; and, upon finding them proper objects of charity, give such persons badges to intitule them to beg, which badges they appoint their treasurer to have in readiness against that time, certifying all such persons as shall be found begging in this Burgh in time coming, not having such badges, that they shall be punished as vagrants with the utmost severity; and recommend to the Baillies to wait upon the ministers and Kirk Session, and acquaint them of, and lay before them this Act, and desire them to make up lists of the poor of the country part of this paroch, and give in the same to the said Bailies and Town Councill, that they may likeways receive badges." Accordingly, on the 22d of February, we find it recorded that "The beggars being convened," the badges were given to the persons therein named, twelve in all, authorizing them to beg. The difficult problem of pauperism, however, was not to be so easily solved; and, in a few years afterwards, we find again the same complaints of the increase of the poor; and their character seems to have got worse, for the grievance is the "Allowing people to beg who can earn their bread without the charity of others, and allowing people to reside who are under the character of thieves and resetters of theft, and entertainers of vagrants and banished persons;" and the Council remit to Bailie Semple, and others, to make up exact lists of all such persons, and report them on the next Wednesday.

MERCANTILE AFFAIRS.

Protection was the leading rule of trade. No hides were allowed to go out of the town until the town's tanner and shoemakers were first supplied. So also the price of bread was fixed from time to time, according to the price of wheat. Bakers were obliged to put their names, or initials, on their loaves —a practice still to some extent prevailing. Fines were imposed on butchers for cutting and hacking hides of the animals they killed, as well as for some operation called "tawing and blawing" in killing butcher meat. The same power and practice of regulation seems to have been applied to other trades. and where there was no law to warrant interference, the Bailies and Council passed resolutions, which they called Acts of Council, and which served the purpose nearly as well as Acts of Parliament. As one instance of this, amongst many, we may refer to a minute of date 14th October, 1736:—"The Baillies and Councill agreed to the following rates to be paid to every horse-hyrer (in name of hyre) in manner following, viz. :—That every man that is in use to let horses for hyre be obliged to hyre his horses when demanded, unless they can show that they are oyrways necessary employed in journeying : That no horse-hyrer pretend to demand more in name of hyre than two shillings Scots for each mile single, and three shillings Scots for each double horse, besides half a-merk for every night the horse is kept, after allowing the proper time for journeying in an ordinary way, and that the owner of the horse who shall demand more, or exact any higher wages or hyre than is a stipulat, shall, upon conviction yrof, be lyable in a fyne of fourty shillings Scots money for each refusal or contravention. They therefore appoint this Act to be promulgat by tuck of drum, and placarded, that none may pretend ignorance."

On market days and fair days, the various dealers in the town, and the class called merchant travellers, had stations assigned to them in the various streets, and there they exposed their goods on stands for sale. Thus, so late as 1766, we find it recorded that "The Baillies and Councill agree to the following regulations with regard to the merchants' stands at the fairs, viz. :— The merchant travellers dealing in softwares shall have their stands from the entry to the third shop below the Tolbooth, and so eastward all upon the north side of the street, leaving proper passage to closes and shops—and the woollen cloth merchants east of them. The merchants dealing in hardware shall have their stand all upon south side of the High Street, from the entry to John Mather's closs eastwards, and the nailers east of them. That the shoe market shall be held on the south side of the School Wynd, above the well. That the crockery merchants shall stand to the west of the shoe market, south side of School Wynd. That the dealers in sweetmeats shall stand on the north side of the School Wynd, from Alexander Wilson's house door westward."

Previously to 1732, the market for "horse and nolt" was held on the high ground above the town, now occupied by the Parish Church and churchyard, and surrounding buildings; but in that year this market had to be removed down to the streets of the town on account of the building of the church, and because, as the minute says—"the rest of the ground will be taken up with houses which the town's people will probably build for the conveniency of being near the church." In 1736 there was a sheep market instituted, to be held in May and June yearly on the Muir, and so much of the Muir was ordered to be cleared of whins as would be sufficient for the sheep to stand and pasture upon it. This market place was fenced in shortly afterwards "with a pale dyke three feet and a half high, with stoups and double rails"—the neighbouring tacksman, Thomas Scoular, furnishing half of the nails necessary for the dyke, according to express arrangement with Bailie Porterfield.

The old burgess privileges were in full force. No craftsman or merchant was allowed to carry on business on his own account within the town unless he were a duly admitted burgess; and this privilege was necessarily of much value, and considerable fees were paid on admission—the amount of which, however, was occasionally, in special circumstances, reduced, and sometimes for the encouragement of trade, or to confer special honour, a few favoured applicants were admitted gratis. Thus, on 18th December, 1753, "The Baillies and Councill appoint a gratis burgess-ticket to be given to William Guthrie, skinner and breachmaker, as being the first professor of that trade in the Burgh." And ten years before, there is another special case which, in the minutes of 12th March, 1743, is thus stated :—" It being represented by John Telfair, weaver in Hamilton ; Archd. Telfair, taylor, there ; and Thomas Craig, weaver, there, to the Baillies and Councill that Martinmas fair, 1741, the said Baillies being attacked by some of the Duke's servants, and they being very assistant to rescue them, the Baillies and Councill, for their reward, allow the Clerk to give them their burgess-ticket."

FIRES.

As the houses in the town had all, or nearly all, thatched roofs, there was, of course, great danger from fire, and the Bailies and Council occasionally enacted some laws to be observed for the public safety. One of these was passed on 21st January, 1740, and as it is very elaborate and somewhat peculiar in its provisions, we give its terms in full :—" The Baillies and Councill considering that the town of Hamilton consists generally of thatched houses, and that frequent accident fires happen on account of the foulnes of the vents, therefore, to prevent as much as possible such accidents, they authorise and appoint ———— to go through the town of Hamilton three times in the year—viz., Candlemass, Whitsunday, and Hallowmass—and to sweep and clean sufficiently the whole used vents in the town, at the following rates—viz., for each vent of the length of one storey, a penny ; and for those of a greater length, three halfpence ; and to discharge all other ordinary sweepers to use that imployment, and appoint this Act to be intimat by tuck of drum throw the town of Hamilton, with a certification to such persons as shall refuse to allow their vents to be swept on pretence that they are not foull, if, upon a visitation, these vents are actually found to be foull, the person so refusing shall be lyable in a fyne of fourty shillings

Scots ; and the said authorised sweepers are by their acceptation of the office bound to make a careful visitation of all the vents, and to report to the Magistrates such persons as refuse to admit their vents, when foull, to be swept, under the penalty of being punished at discretion of the Baillies." Notwithstanding this rigid exactment, a very serious fire occurred in the town a few years later—a fire which history says raged for eight days, and burned down Barrie's Close and other adjacent parts of the town, and caused great misery to the inhabitants. It would seem that, on the usual principle of the precautions coming after the calamity, it led to the town getting its first fire-engine. In September 1748, "the Baillies and Councill considering the great use of a water engine for extinguishing fire, especially in this town where the houses are mostly thatched," agreed to buy one which was for sale in Edinburgh, and which cost £15 sterling, besides new leather pipes, which were got from Glasgow. A few months later, we find it noticed that collections had been set on foot in Edinburgh, and elsewhere for behoof of the sufferers by the late fire, and the Town Treasurer is authorised to receive the money, which was then to be issued forth at the direction of the Magistrates and Council.

A TIME OF SCARCITY.

It was in 1740, when "the Baillies and Councill, considering the present scarcity of meall, and the great hardships the inhabitants, and particularly the poor, now labour under, and understanding that John Mather is going to Perth Fair, where he may probably be informed where a quantity of meall may be bought at a reasonable rate, they therefore give commission to John Mather to contract for ane hundred bolls of sufficient meall upon the credit of the community, providing the same can be bought so as to be delivered at eight pounds Scots per boll at Borrowstowness free of sea carriage."

HOUSE RENTS.

Shop and house rents were much less a century ago than now. From the treasurer's abstract of accounts we take the following sample:—Adam Roxburgh's shop for one year, from Whitsunday 1785 to 1786, £1 12s; Andrew Hamilton's do., £1 1s; Janet Russell's house, £3 15s; Wm. Buchanan's, £4 10s; Wm. Wilson's shop 16s 8d; Janet Hyslop's shop, £1 1s. These figures may well excite envy amongst a community overridden with exorbitant rents, and striving hard to release themselves from the burden.

A PIOUS BELLMAN.

If, at one time, Hamilton had her inebriate John Hepburn, she was at another time famed for a bellman or church-officer of another sort. He was a rigid observer of family worship. In his devotions, however, he had an eye to this world as well as the next. One morning his wife had neglected to bar the door, and when Sandy had got about half-way through his prayer, a person entered to purchase a pennyworth of something from the mistress, who kept a small shop. The ounce weight had gone amissing, and could not be found. The modern Pharisee, with the view of helping his better half out of her difficulty, paused, and by way of parenthesis said, in a less whining tone of voice, "As for the ounce weight, Jenny, ye shall find it amongst the wee bits o' ben leather on the window bottom; may the Lord preserve us frae formality and carnality!" and then he resumed his long prayer.

CHARITY SCHOOLS A CENTURY AGO.

So far back as 1789, a charity school was erected in Hamilton, of which Mr James Bruce was schoolmaster. This school was kept up for many years. Annual premiums were distributed, and, as they are rather novel, we give a few specimens. For the boys —To the best reader in the Bible, a scarlet bonnet with a silver button; for the best reader in the New Testament, a scarlet bonnet; for the best reader in the A B C, 2d. For the girls—To the best reader in the Bible, a mutch of Holland, with a head suit of ribbons; to the best reader in the New Testament, a necklace; to the best reader in Proverbs, a new Testament; to the best reader in the Question Book, a napkin; to the best reader in the A B C, 2d. These children met every Sabbath day between sermons, when the bell rung, and repeated their questions before the congregation. About the same period, another school was instituted by the Duchess of Hamilton for little maiden orphans, where they were taught to spin and work lace. The lace, under the name of Hamilton lace, rose into high repute, so much so that the trustees for encouraging fisheries and manufactures in Scotland, destined £75 for encouragement to young beginners—every young scholar to have £1 at the end of the first year of their apprenticeship, and £15 to be divided into prizes amongst them. A large house and garden, rent free, newly mounted—now the old manse of Hamilton—was set aside for the purpose of a school-house. A number of subscribers also contributed to the "Orphan Hospital." About £3 yearly was considered a sufficient sum to maintain each orphan in meat, clothing, &c. After much labour on the part of its promoters, the scheme was laid aside.

TRANSITION.

The population of the parish, which in 1755 was 3815, had increased in 1841 to 10,861, being at the rate of nearly 82 per annum. The means of communication with the outer world had more than kept pace. "Davie Hamilton's Caravan"—a lumbering, covered one-horse cart—gave way to the stage-coach, which in turn was replaced by the iron horse. Apropos of the "Caravan," it started from Hamilton at 6 A.M., and reached an old inn in the Gallowgate, near Charlotte Street, at 11. Davie drove himself, and never allowed his Rozinante to trot except for a short distance down hill. The return journey was made at 4 P.M., and the party reached Hamilton about 8. In winter, the company were sometimes favoured with a "bawbee" candle. As time went on, the town began to spread its wings to the south and west. The great highway between Glasgow and London, ran through the burgh, and for the purpose of avoiding the brae in Muir Street and cutting off the awkward elbow at the Cross, about the year 1847, the road was diverted into the present line of Cadzow Street. The new road is upwards of 700 yards in length, and it is carried over the Cadzow burn above the public green by a bridge of three arches, each 60 feet span, which Mr Patrick, writing at the time, not inaccurately described as stupendous, the top of the parapet wall being 60 feet above the bed of the burn. The town began to lose much of its pleasant rural appearance. No longer was the quiet of Muir Street to be disturbed by the din of the stage-coach in its daily passage through the burgh, and Castle Street, as the leading thoroughfare, was doomed. Along the new line of route, handsome banks and shops sprung into existence, and Cadzow Street became the centre of trade and business. The opening of the Caledonian Central Railway Station threatens to raise in Quarry Street a formidable rival, and already first-class shops are occupied by energetic, pushing tradesmen—some of them from Cadzow Street and Townhead Street; and after the improvements which are in contemplation have been carried out, there are not wanting signs that ere long this neighbourhood will become the centre of the burgh. Forty years ago there were no buildings on the west side of Cadzow Street, except a few one-storey thatched houses near the foot of Campbell Street. Auchingramont Road, Park Road, and Clydesdale Street were not in existence, while nearly all the properties along the line of Union Street and west-end of the town have been subsequently built. Hand-loom weaving was the staple trade of the town, and the nearest coal-pit was several miles away. Now all is changed, the weavers with the appliances of their craft are almost totally extinct, and there are no less than 12 pits almost within the bounds of the burgh, and fully as many more within a mile of it. Glasgow merchants were attracted by the woodlands and the pure air, and made their homes in the suburb of villas in the west-end. The geological situation of the coal measures—and probably also Hamilton Palace—were a guarantee that the neighbourhood would not soon share the fate of so many pleasant districts in the west. Here was still an oasis where the eye could wander over undulating fields and tree-clad heights yet untouched by the indomitable mercantile spirit which has converted the Clyde valley into a teeming hive of industry. The abnormal prices and demand for coal and iron during 1872-73-74 changed all this, and now the amenity of the district has to be sacrificed for the good of the country at large. Railways have cut it up in all directions; its romantic rocks serve but for piers to the unromantic girder bridge; and over the trees rises the coalpit head-gear, with its attendant chimney stalk, darkening the air with smoke and smudge.

THE COAL INDUSTRY.

In the new statistical account of the parish of Hamilton, written in 1835 by the Rev. Wm. Patrick, the coal field of the district is thus described:—" Coal is chiefly wrought at Quarter, about three miles south of the town of Hamilton. The same bed also extends a great way northwards in the direction of Glasgow, but owing to a slip in the coal metals between the farms of Simpsonland and Carscallan, a little to the north of Quarter, the coal is sunk nearly 100 fathoms below its usual level; an accident which puts it almost beyond the reach of the inhabitants of Hamilton, Blantyre, and part of Bothwell: the strata not rising up again till near Cambuslang. The existence of this remarkable fracture is indicated by the coal metals on the banks of the Avon, and the other burns below where the break occurs, all dipping to the southwest; whereas above that particular spot they, and indeed the whole strata of the district, with this single exception, dip to the north-east. The coal strata here resemble those throughout the county. At Quarter, the first bed worth working is the ten feet or woman's coal, so called because it was once wrought by females. This is a soft coal, which burns rapidly; and although called the ten feet coal, is in reality from 7 to 14 feet in thickness. Fifteen fathoms lower down, the ell coal occurs, so called because it was first found of that thickness; but it is frequently from 4 to 6 feet thick. In the fire it cakes, or runs into a mass, and is much esteemed by blacksmiths. Ten or fifteen fathoms below the former is the seam called the main coal. This, at Quarter, is 5 feet 6 inches thick, and consists of four distinct varieties of coal—1st, The ground coal, undermost, 20 inches thick, gummy and sooty: 2d, immediately above it the yolk, or jet coal, 6 inches thick, of a fine clear vitreous texture, like cannel coal, affording abundance of light; 3d, parrot coal, 10 inches; 4th, splint coal, about 30 inches. This is the coal now wrought, both by shanks and ingoing pits. The shanks at Quarter are about 30 fathoms. The mouths of the ingoing pits are on the banks of the Avon, about two miles above Hamilton. These pits communicate with each other. The coal is brought from Quarter by a railway along the banks of the Avon, and is laid down at Avon bridge, half-a-mile from Hamilton, at 3s 9d a ton. Upwards of 10,000 tons are here sold annually. About half that quantity is disposed of at Quarter to people in the upper side of the parish, and the adjacent parishes of Glassford, Avondale, and Kilbride."

EARLY MINING OPERATIONS.

Coal has been wrought at Quarter from an early period for the use of the surrounding district. As an evidence of the antiquity of the workings, it may be stated that, about forty or fifty years ago, some workmen penetrated into an old mine which entered from the banks of the Avon, and on exploring it they discovered a pick and shovel of a very primitive construction, being made of wood, and shod or pointed with iron. The mine was in good order, and the mode of working it had been very secure. The coal was hewn out in the form of an arch, having "a heat coomceiled roof," as one of the exploring party described it to Mr Andrew Hamilton. It has been supposed that these old workings date as far back as the time when Cadzow Castle was inhabited--some 300 years ago. As the uppermost seam, called the soft coal, crops out here, it appears to have been wrought first by running a mine into the face of a brae, which was called " an ingaun ee." By cutting a *gatten* or gutter in the pavement of this mine it formed a drain to carry off the water from " the faces " or " rooms," as the working places were named. This mine was called a " level," and the coal thus drained was said to be "level free," which was considered a great advantage by miners in the olden time, when there was no pumping apparatus. The coal was taken to the mouth of the mine in corfs or hutches, which were drawn along the pavement. As the road soon became rough and the draught heavy after the mine was driven in a certain distance, it was deemed more expedient and profitable to sink a pit to the coal, and thus save the heavy labour of drawing. These pits being ebb (from 8 to 10 fathoms) the coals in the hutches were raised to the surface by a hand windlass, and emptied in cartloads on the *hill*, as they were sold by measure before the introduction of the weighing machine. When it became necessary to sink a deeper shaft the gin superseded the windlass, and after the introduction of steam the gin gave place to the winding engine.

RECENT OPERATIONS AT QUARTER.

The Quarter collieries were till within the last thirty years held in the possession of the proprietor, the Duke of Hamilton, and were under the charge of a " grieve," or manager, who sold the coals, paid the workmen, and transacted all the business of the works, for which he was accountable to the Chamberlain at Hamilton Palace. One pit at Quarter was sufficient to supply the country sale up to the year

1854, when the mineral field was leased by the Messrs Dunlop of Clyde Ironworks, after which its resources were fully developed. Boring operations were then commenced, and a bed of excellent blackband ironstone discovered about 15 fathoms below the main coal. The seams called the slatey and clay band were also found at Darngaber and Boghead. Pits were sunk to them, a large quantity put out and calcined, and more pits were sunk to the coal. In 1856 two furnaces were built for the manufacture of pig iron, and put in blast in March 1857. A third was built in 1867, a fourth in 1869, and a fifth in 1875. Owing to the depression of trade, only three are in blast at present. The average production of pig-iron from each furnace is about $8\frac{1}{2}$ thousand tons a year. The ironstone at Quarter has been wrought out, but the company have pits at Boghead, Blantyre, and Drummine, from which large supplies of ore are brought to the furnaces. The limestone required is also brought from Blantyre and Lesmahagow.

Of five coal pits four are in operation just now, the output from which may be stated at 120,000 tons yearly. Besides supplying the furnaces, a large quantity of coal is sent to the market. After the opening of the Hamilton and Strathaven Railway, in 1862, a branch line was made to the works, which greatly facilitated the mineral traffic. As it requires about 150 men to supply material for each furnace, upwards of 500 hands of all kinds are employed in connection with the works.

OVERCOMING THE "ACCIDENT."

The "accident" mentioned by Mr Patrick, by which the coal was sunk almost beyond the reach of the inhabitants of Hamilton, Blantyre, and Bothwell, has been successfully overcome by the aid of capital, improved machinery, and modern appliances for the working of mines. In 1856, twenty years after Mr Patrick wrote, the mineral under Dykehead and High Merryton, extending to 597 acres, was leased by his Grace the Duke of Hamilton to the Summerlee Iron Company, by whom the field is still wrought. A still more conspicuous proof that the "accident" had been overcome, was the leasing in 1858-59 of the mineral in connection with the estate of Greenfield, to the west of the town, by Mr Lewis Potter to Mr James Nisbet. The need of mechanical appliances and engineering skill of the first order was very emphatically demonstrated in the Greenfield case. The quantity of water and other physical difficulties that were encountered and had to be overcome in the act of reaching the coal exhausted Mr Nisbet's considerable means. After his withdrawal from the concern, operations were continued by the Hamilton Coal Company, by whom the colliery is worked at the present time. The Ferniegair Colliery, on the Larkhall Road, extending to 230 acres, was successfully worked on lease from his Grace the Duke of Hamilton by Mr James Nisbet from 1859 to 1861; by Messrs James Nisbet & Co. till 1866; and since that date by Mr A. Russell, who a year or two ago acquired the additional right to work the mineral lying underneath Chatelherault Park. In the same locality, the Merryton Colliery was opened up by the Duke, who in 1860 granted a lease of the same to Messrs Cochrane & Brand. The colliery in their hands has been remarkably successful. Three years ago it was closed for six months—fire, believed to be the result of spontaneous combustion, having broken out in the workings. The firm acquired an additional field under the High Parks in 1865. In 1862, the Allanton field, still in the same neighbourhood, extending to 340 acres, was leased by his Grace to Messrs Austine & Co., who also in 1865 had an additional field in the High Parks added to their workings. This fruitful part of the Clyde basin was not yet exhausted, and in 1864 the Duke leased the Merryton Home Farm field, of 160 acres, to Messrs Hamilton, M'Culloch & Co. The unparalleled inundation, which in a few hours, on a dark January morning of 1877, ruined the working of the colliery, and deprived four men of life, is elsewhere noticed. With unflagging zeal and energy, the acting partner of the firm, Mr Kirkwood, has had the chasm, which was created by the action of the water, pumped dry, and the workings are being redd with good prospects of operations at the colliery being again resumed. In 1865, Messrs John Watson & Son leased Bog and Highlees, about 320 acres, and transferred the colliery in 1871 to Messrs Hamilton & M'Culloch. A year later, in 1866, a lease of the South Haugh field or Haughhead, about 100 acres, was taken up by Messrs Merry & Cuninghame, and in 1877 was transferred to the present lessee, Mr John M'Donald.

THE COAL IN THE TOWN'S LANDS.

That one day coal would be found in the town's lands was the fond belief of more than one generation of Hamiltonians, and the prophecy was indulged that the town would yet become a Coatbridge. At last, in 1838, a citizen of great public spirit, Mr Daniel M'Arthur, lace manufacturer, made application to the Town Council for a lease of the mineral. His application, which came before the Council on 13th January, 1838, was in the following terms :—" I hereby make offer to the Magistrates and Town Council of Hamilton for a twelve years' lease of the coal within the burgh lands of Hamilton, and to pay therefor of fixed yearly rent the sum of £100 stg., or in the option of the proprietors, one-ninth of the coal sold or removed from the pit-mouth or coal hill of lordship, payable said rents half-yearly at Martinmas and Whitsunday, and in respect that it has yet to be ascertained whether there are coals in said lands, and whether they may be worth working, it is understood that I am to have full power and liberty to bore, search for, use means for ascertaining what metals are in the lands, and that only at my own expense; and that the said rent or lordship shall not commence until the workings are begun and a regular output of coals given. Further, that I shall not be bound to continue the lease should the coal or mineral turn out impracticable and unprofitable, and it is also understood that should the experiment prove successful that I shall enter into a regular lease containing all the usual clauses contained in those most approved of in the county consistent with this offer, and that I shall have right to use the roads connected with the town's lands, as well as to drive levels, shank pits, and make railroads or other roads necessary for said work, and erect engines for carrying on the same. I shall be bound in addition to said rent to pay all surface damages that I may occasion, the same to be ascertained by men to be mutually chosen; and it is understood that any engines, implements, or effects, which I may lay down or erect shall belong to me, and be at my disposal at the termination of the lease, the proprietors having the first offer thereof on a fair valuation." This offer being taken into consideration, the Council, after due deliberation, " and considering that coal may not be found, and if found that it is likely to be attended with heavy expense in the working thereof," unanimously accepted of the same, accompanying their acceptance with five conditions, the principal of which was that the trial for coal was to be made and completed by Mr M'Arthur within six months. The likelihood of coal being found seems to have strongly impressed itself on the minds of the members of Council, as at this same meeting they passed a resolution directing the clerk in all future feu contracts to be granted by the Magistrates and Council to insert a clause reserving the metals and minerals to the town. Hitherto there had been no such reservation, and at the present time a committee of Town Council is engaged negotiating with those feuars who are lucky enough to hold their charters from a date prior to the passing of this resolution for the purchase of their rights in the coal.

Mr M'Arthur appears to have vigorously prosecuted the necessary boring operations during the six months allowed him, though not successfully. On 19th August a special meeting of Town Council was held, to consider a motion relative to the operations. On behalf of Mr M'Arthur, Mr Gowans informed the meeting that he had bored to a depth of 75 fathoms, whereby he had expended about £200, that both the appearance of the metals and strata throughout indicated the prospect of there being coal in the lands; but the six months allowed him for the trial having expired, he was not inclined at his own expense to proceed further at present. He, however, recommended the town to carry the bore down other ten fathoms, giving it as his opinion that before that depth was reached the coal would be found, if it was in the lands capable of being wrought to any advantage; and he accompanied his recommendation with an intimation of his willingness to present to the town gratis, if they continued the bore for the ten fathoms, his windlass, triangle, lever, ropes, and other implements used by him in making the trial. The Council did not deem it advisable to follow out the suggestion made to them. They passed a resolution placing it on record that they were sensible of the exertions and perseverance of Mr M'Arthur in proceeding so far, and incurring so much expense in the trial, and unanimously voted him their thanks on that account. The resolution not to continue the trial, it should be explained, was only carried by a majority of three votes, and Mr M'Arthur's bore was ordered to be plugged up and secured "so as at any after period the town might have recourse to it in facilitating the trial for coal or other minerals" in their lands.

After this, all idea of developing the mineral resources of the town, if not abandoned, was allowed to go to sleep. For twenty years the Council records make no mention of the subject. The long silence was at last broken by the receipt of a letter, which was considered at the monthly meeting on 6th June, 1859, in these terms:—

"Drumpark, Coatbridge, 2d June, 1859.—Dear Sir,—I have been requested by a party to inquire if the coal in the town's lands of Hamilton are to be let, and should that be the case to inform me as to the mode or principle upon which an offer might be framed. Your early answer will oblige, &c.,
(Signed) "WM. M'CREATH."

The Council appointed a committee to report how far it would be expedient to entertain any proposal for letting the mineral. Next month the committee reported in favour of letting the mineral, the town to be at no expense in boring or otherwise testing the coal field, or in the putting down of shafts or pits. The Council were not satisfied with the information laid before them, and the committee were re-appointed with instructions to report further details, and employ an engineer if they saw fit. The committee consulted Mr William M'Creath, M.E., who stated that the surface under which the town had it in their power to work the minerals, including roads, railway, &c., was about 85 acres Imperial, under all of which the several seams of coal contained in the Clydesdale basin might be confidently expected, and of quality and thickness similar to what was found both on the east and the west of the burgh. The position of the blackband ironstone was also throughout the whole field, but its lay was more capricious than that of the coals, and its being found in the lands was more uncertain. The Town Council followed up this procedure by advertising the let of the minerals. At their meeting on 5th December an offer was produced from Mr James Nisbet, Provost of the burgh, and at the time engaged in his Greenfield undertaking. The offer does not appear to have come up to the Council's expectations, and a committee appointed to consider and report upon it having recommended to the meeting on 5th March, 1860, that the offer be not entertained, all further reference to the subject vanishes once more from the records, and does not again appear for more than ten years afterwards.

For a third, and, as it proved, last time, the question was brought before the Council on 7th March, 1872. It was seriously taken up, and that Mr James Mackie, who has since been appointed burgh chamberlain, had the matter in charge, was a guarantee that nothing would be left undone to successfully carry it out. The form of the Council's action was to appoint Bailie Cassels and Mr Mackie, the latter convener, a committee to consider if, and in what way, the minerals could be made available. The negotiations were tedious and protracted, and extended over a period of two years; but the untiring perseverance of the committee eventually surmounted every obstacle. On 19th February, 1874, an offer by Dr Thomson, Jerviston House, Motherwell, and Mr R. L. Alston, Newfield House, Hamilton, " to take on lease the whole coal down to and including the splint seam in the town's lands of Hamilton, to be worked along with the coal in the lands of Wellhall, which we have purchased, and that in the lands of Nether Auchingramont, which has been leased by us," was accepted. The arrangement included a fixed rent of £350 per annum, commencing to run at Whitsunday, 1878, to be increased by £50 annually until it reached £500, at which it was to remain during the remainder of the lease, or, in the option of the proprietors, a lordship of 10d for each $22\frac{1}{2}$ cwt. of coal and dross unscreened that was put out. The lease was to be for 31 years from Whitsunday, 1873, with breaks in the tenants' option at the end of the sixth and every third year thereafter. The arrangement was an important and favourable one for the burgh, and the committee were awarded a vote of thanks for carrying it out.

In addition to Wellhall and Nether Auchingramont, the lessees acquired the right to work the coal under Backmuir and Barmichael Plantations, belonging to the Duke of Hamilton, and extending to 300 acres. The collieries more than two years ago were taken up by the Clyde Coal Company (Limited) who have also pits in course of being sunk at Spittalhill, Cambuslang. Those at Hamilton admit of an output of 1200 tons a day restricted, on account of dull trade, to 700 tons. Above ground the works have been planned on an extensive scale. The permanent buildings, which have all been constructed of red brick with white facings, include the necessary engine-houses for the winding gear and pumps; engineers', joiners', and blacksmiths' shops, a pay office, with enclosed yard, round which are sheds to protect the men in wet weather, while waiting for their turn at the window, and the general offices of the company. The machinery which has been put up is of a very powerful description, commensurate with the heavy work it has to perform in raising coal hutches from such a depth. Each of the winding engines has a 24-inch cylinder with a 5-feet stroke, all the boilers being of the tubular type, with the latest improvements for securing economy of fuel. The shafts, it may be said, are 24 feet by 7 feet in section, and are each divided into three parts by strong wooden partitions technically known as brattices; the pumping gear working in one division and the "cages" in the others. The sides of the shafts are strongly lined with wood. As it is estimated that the hutches pass up and down at a speed of 20 miles an hour, it was necessary that the framework over the pit mouth should be of a most substantial character. This has not been lost sight of, and all the head-gear, here as elsewhere, has a very durable appearance. To ventilate the pits, a fan of large dimensions, driven by steam, is employed, and is powerful enough to keep air circulating freely in the three pits. A private line connects the colliery with the Hamilton branch of the Caledonian Railway, and every convenience in the shape of stages and separating screens for loading the waggons has been provided.

In connection with their pits at Hamilton, nearly 300 houses for the accommodation of workmen have been built by the Company in a field at Burnbank, half a mile west from the colliery. The houses, which are of brick, with stone facings, are all two storeys in height, divided into quarter flats, each containing a room and kitchen, having a little strip of garden ground attached.

CADZOW AND OTHER COLLIERIES.

Both for the scale upon which they are laid out, and the large capital embarked in the enterprise, the Cadzow Company's collieries at Low-waters may be selected for special notice. The coalfield, which covers an area of upwards of 500 acres, has been leased by the company from his Grace the Duke of Hamilton. It extends from the Strathaven road to the Avon, being situated almost wholly within the High Parks of Hamilton, and it contains all the usual seams of coal of the district. By bores put down it was known that the first seam, the celebrated household ell coal of the district, would be found at a depth of 244 yards below the surface. For the winning of the coal, three pits were sunk. These consisted of No. 1, the pumping pit, 24 ft. 6 in. × 7 ft.: No. 2, 21 ft. 6 in. × 6 ft.; and No. 3, a round pit, built from top to bottom, 13 ft. 6 in. within the brick work. Commenced in 1872, the work of sinking proved one of unprecedented difficulty. Water was encountered at a depth of only twelve feet from the surface, and two sets of pumps had to be put in, both in No. 1 and No. 2 pits. The obstacle assumed serious proportions when the red rock was reached, and 6000 tons of water fell to be removed from the shaft every twenty-four hours. To accomplish this, the company erected a Cornish engine of great size and power, having an 85-in. cylinder with a 10-ft. stroke, and being one of the largest in Scotland. The pumps of the engine are 26 inches in diameter, the pump rods 18 inches square, strapped with iron $7\frac{1}{2}$ inches broad and $1\frac{1}{2}$ inches thick. Before the indomitable perseverance and energy of the managing partner of the company, Col. Austine, Oak Lodge, Hamilton, every obstacle had eventually to give way, and the mineral was struck in No. 2 Pit on the 3d of February, 1876; in No. 3 Pit a few weeks afterwards, and in No. 1 still later. In No. 2 Pit the ell coal was struck at 123 fathoms. The other two shafts are carried down to the splint seam, which was tapped at a depth of 148 fathoms or 888 feet. One of the shafts—the upcast—is constructed in a circular form, 13 ft. 6 in. in diameter, and is lined with brick instead of wood from top to bottom. The pit fittings are of an advanced description. Three permanent coupled winding engines set on concrete seats have been erected, their cylinders being 24 in., with 5-ft. stroke, and for the purposes of ventilation a Guibal fan, by Haggie & Co., Newcastle, 40 feet in diameter and 12 feet broad, has been set up, and the fan house is connected to the upcast shaft by a tunnel 12 feet in diameter. The fan is driven by a 36-inch cylinder engine, stroke 3 feet; and, in case of repairs being needed, there is a reserve engine of the same size and power which can be connected in a few minutes. A little village has sprung up at the collieries, which are connected with the Caledonian line at Hamilton by a branch line one and a half miles long. The estimated output from all the pits when in full operation is 1500 tons per day—in the present state of trade it is, of course, greatly less.

But a short distance from Cadzow, are the Eddlewood Coal Company's pits, and coming down the hill, within a few hundred yards of each other and half encircling the town, there are the collieries of Barncluith and Silvertonhill (A. Russell), Bent (Bent Colliery Company), Allanshaw (Allanshaw Coal Company), and Earnock (John Watson), Taking up the circle Blantyre wise, and not mentioning Messrs Dunlop's ironstone pits, there fall to be enumerated the new collieries, all recently opened up, of Dykehead (Dunn & Ure), Blantyre (W. Dixon, Limited), Auchinraith (Merry & Cuninghame); and towards Bothwell, the collieries of Craighead and Bothwell Park—collieries just opened up, or in course of being opened up by Messrs Wm. Baird & Co. The list might be greatly extended by continuing it to Cambuslang, where on the lands of that name the Flemington Company have sunk the deepest pit in Scotland—the depth to the splint coal being 212 fathoms, or a quarter of a mile.

In estimating the effect of so many new collieries on the market, one or two important considerations must be kept in view. In the first place, all the fixed rents are large; and next, the amount of capital required to "win" the coal from such depths is very heavy. It is, therefore, only by sending a large supply of coal into the market that these expensive undertakings can be made to pay; and, having that in view, it is estimated that, when all the pits have been got into full working order, and making allowance for bad times and the other contingencies of mining, the output from the Hamilton and Bothwell district cannot be less than 2,000,000 tons per annum. In round numbers, this field has an area of 8000 acres, and as it is computed to contain 300,000,000 tons of coal it will doubtless be one of the principal coal-producing districts in Scotland for two or three generations to come. The capital embarked in the undertaking is estimated at over one million sterling. The following figures, taken from the Valuation Roll for the current year, will throw further light on the value of the coal industry of the district :—

Burgh and Parish of Hamilton,	£55,465
Parish of Blantyre,	9,301
Parish of Bothwell,	19,271
Total,	£84,037

MEMORABLE ACCIDENTS.

An explosion of fire-damp took place on 16th March, 1841, at a pit at Avon Bank, resulting in the death of 13 men. The pit was commenced about 1825 by his Grace the Duke of Hamilton. From 150 to 200 hands were employed, the mode of working being by ingoing "eyes." Such terrible calamities were rare in those days, and the effect of the news on the town was paralysing. As to the circumstances under which the explosion occurred, one man had been burned the day previous. This did not arouse alarm, and the colliers resumed work on the morning of the accident as usual. They were not, however, long in the mine when the explosion took place, killing seven men. An hour after the explosion, an exploring party of nine, including Mr Ord Adams, the manager, entered the workings, and four of their number died from the effects of after-damp. We believe that Mr Adams, and a miner named Michael Forrest, Quarter, are the only survivors of those who formed the exploring party. A widow of one of the victims (Mrs Duffy, Quarter), still lives, and is a pensioner on the Duke's bounty. On Wednesday, 7th August, 1861, the community had again emphatically brought home to them the dangers of the mine by a disastrous and fatal fire, which broke out about 1 P.M. at Dykehead Colliery, Larkhall, in the occupation of the Summerlee Iron Company. The fire, beginning in the air shaft, destroyed the pit-head framework and burned the wooden casing of the shaft. The law had not yet made the double shaft imperative, and all communication with the men in the workings, 50 in number, was cut off. As invariably happens, there were not wanting many willing to risk their lives to rescue those imprisoned below ground, and by the persevering efforts of the managers, workmen, and others, the last of them had been brought to the surface by one o'clock next morning. It was found that 12 had been suffocated by the foul air, and one died afterwards, making the record of victims 13. The year 1877 will ever possess a black eminence in the mining annals of the district. On the morning of the 23d of January a disastrous inundation occurred at Home Farm Colliery. Between 50 and 60 miners had been lowered to the pit bottom, when the water burst into the ell workings, filling them in the course of a few hours with silt and water. The men, with the exception of four were got out in safety. In October of this year the incidents of the catastrophe were recalled by workmen engaged in excavations, with the view to resuming working at the Colliery, finding the remains of the four victims lying thickly imbedded in the sand. The most disastrous of mining accidents, not merely in this district, but in Scotland, took place at Nos. 2 and 3 Pits, High Blantyre Collieries, on the 22d of October, 1877. There had not been lacking warnings of the fiery character of the splint seam of the district, two explosions on a considerable scale having within the previous nine months occurred no farther away than Cadzow, which, while happily unattended with loss of life, resulted in the Colliery on each occasion being for some time closed. Nor had coalmasters failed to profit by these warnings, by attention to ventilation, the use of the most approved safety lamps, &c. Despite of every precaution, the explosion occurred, depriving 212 men and boys of life. Of 233 who were at work at the time but 27 escaped, 4 others who were brought up alive having soon afterwards died. The calamity awakened national sympathy, and that the widows and children of the lost might be provided for, nearly £50,000 was subscribed. In the spring of this year an accident from over-winding occurred at No. 3 Pit, Blantyre Collieries, by which six men were killed.

QUARTER.

(By Mr Andrew Hamilton.)

THE lands of Quarter form a portion of the ducal estate of Hamilton, and are situated on the south side of the wall which surrounds the High Parks of Hamilton. They stretch along the banks of the Avon from that wall to the march of Fairholm on the east, marching with Thinacres and Wellbog on the south and Darngaber and Carscallan on the west, and extend to upwards of 400 acres imperial.

In a rent roll of the Hamilton estates for 1637, in the time of James 3d Marquis of Hamilton, they are designed "The fiftie pund lands of Quarter," and were then divided into 8 "Rooms" or holdings, and possessed by the following tenants :—George Golder, younger; John Thomson, George Golder, elder; William Golder, John Wilson, Andrew Haddow, John Stobo, and John Alstoun."

In the year 1745, a meeting of the heritors and tenants of the parish was convened at Hamilton, to consider a demand made on them for supplies of forage and corn for the use of Prince Charles— Edward's cavalry then occupying Glasgow. The following names from Quarter appear in the list of heritors and tenants then convened :—" Wm. Wilson, in Quarter ; Andrew Haddow, there ; James Wilson, there ; John Hamilton, in Laigh Quarter." It thus appears that the 8 holdings of 1637 had been converted into 4 by the year 1745. The lands are now divided into three farms—named South Quarter, North Quarter, and Knowetop—tenanted respectively by Abram Torrance, Andrew Hamilton, and John Fleming. Part of the old farm of Laigh Quarter is let for grazing.

Part of the old houses of High and Low Quarter are remnants of the farm steadings, or "touns," occupied by the land tenants, when it was more sub-divided than at present. Their architecture is of a very rough order, and that part of them named "The Divoty" indicates the material of which it was originally constructed. They were about twenty in number. After the opening of the mines in Avon braes, about sixty years ago, some 15 or 20 additional houses were built at Low Quarter for the accommodation of the workmen employed there.

As coals in the olden time were only required for household purposes, the demand in summer was limited, and in that season the colliers at Quarter were not regularly employed, so that they had to turn their attention to "country wark," such as working in stone quarries and lime works, and with the farmers at hay-time and harvest. Being economical and thrifty, they were mostly all "bein" and well-to-do. A number of them kept cows for the use of their families, and all of them a pig—a practice which still prevails among the descendants of "the old residenters."

When the works were extended by the Messrs Dunlop, a large number of houses were built in the neighbourhood of the furnaces; so that there are now more than 200 houses in connection with the works, besides a great number rented by the workmen at Darngaber, Wellbog, Limekilnburn, and other places.

Before the extension of the works, the population of the old village of High and Low Quarter was about 200. In 1861 it stood thus—

Quarter Ironworks,	461
High Quarter,	60
Low Quarter,	140
Total,	661

In 1871—

Quarter Ironworks,	544
High Quarter,	76
Low Quarter,	178
Total,	798

The following census was taken in 1877 by Mr Allan, the police constable stationed at Quarter, of the district under his charge, lying on the south and west sides of the parish of Hamilton. With the exception of the farmers and cottars and the inhabitants of Earnockmuir Rows, the most of the householders of the other places specified are employed about the works. 1877—

Quarter Ironworks,	695
High Quarter,	60
Low Quarter,	149
Carscallan Rows,	120
Boghead Rows,	80
Plotcock,	38
Darngaber,	40
Wellbog,	23
Limekilnburn,	99
Earnockmuir Rows,	62
Farmers and Cottars,	418
Total,	1784

On the farm of Darngaber the field is still pointed out where Gordon of Earlston was killed by a party of English dragoons, after the defeat of the Covenanters at Bothwell Bridge. It is called Allows Hill—perhaps a corruption of Earlston's Hill; and I remember a stunted thorn tree, "worn by the knawing tooth of Time," which the old people in the district held in reverence, and said marked the spot where the martyr fell. It is stated by tradition that, after putting him to death in the most barbarous manner, they seized his horse, stripped him of his accoutrements, including a pair of silver spurs, and rode back to Carscallan—a neighbouring farm town—where the English officer demanded refreshments for his men, ostentatiously displaying his spoil with many imprecations, which roused the feelings of the goodwife of the house, who indignantly exclaimed —"It becomes a better man than you, sir, to wear these." After rifling the house of provisions, they rode off towards Hamilton, giving vent to their rage against the Covenanters by oaths and ribaldry. Gordon was buried by his friends secretly in the churchyard of Glassford, about two miles southwards from the place where he fell, where a monument has been erected to his memory by one of his descendants, which tells of his many virtues, and "hard fate."

About half a mile eastward from Darngaber Castle, on the lands of Broomelton, near the public road leading to Stonehouse, stand the ruins of Plotcock Castle, on a jutting point of the banks of the brawling rivulet of that name. This fortlet is said to have been used as a prison by the barons of Cadzow, for their refractory vassals or prisoners taken in war, when the feudal chief possessed "the power of pit and gallows." As it stands at a point where "three lairds' lands meet," and the glen is clothed with umbrageous brushwood, and presents rather a gloomy appearance, popular superstition has tenanted the ravine with ghosts, witches, and bogles—so that the wight who has been overtaken in his travels by nightfall, when passing the place, keeps a sharp outlook for a sight of some of those aerial beings who may be "revisiting the glimpses of the moon," and sporting among the banks and braes around the old dungeon keep.

The name Plotcock given to this place, is very suggestive of its being haunted by the agents and emissaries of the evil one, as it is the old Scotch name of that being, and is a variation of Pluto, who, according to heathen mythology, was god of the infernal regions.

The small estate of Eddlewood lies about a mile north-west from Quarter Iron Works. Like Darngaber the name of this place smacks of great antiquity, and carries the mind back to the days of the native Celtic Chiefs, before the time of Malcolm Canmore, and the introduction of the feudal system, when each family or clan enjoyed all the privileges of freeholders being independent of any superior— even of the Crown. The word Eddlewood probably signifies "The freehold, or free possession in the Wood," and is derived from *Udal*, or *Aedal*, which according to Dr. Jamieson, is "a term applied to lands held in uninterrupted succession without any original charter, and without subjection to feudal service, or the acknowledgement of any superior. "The word is much of the same import as the law Latin term *Allodium*, applied to a free manor, or independent possession. *Wood*, the other constituent part of the word, is easily accounted for, as the lands lay within the bounds of the ancient Caledonian Forest. But although its possessors, at the time the name was imposed, were "Udallers," or freeholders, it seems that before the war of independence they had become vassals or tendants of the Crown, and "the tenandry of Adelwood" were included in the grant of the barony of Cadzow by Bruce to Sir Walter Hamilton immediately after the battle of Bannockburn. This grant is thus narrated by Hamilton of Wishaw, in his "Description of the Sheriffdom of Lanark,"—"The precise time when this lordship was given to the Duke of Hamilton his predecessors, is not clear; but there is one charter extant, granted by King Robert Bruce, in the 7th year of his reign, 1314, to Sir Walter, son of Sir Gilbert de Hamilton of this barony, and the tendry of Adelwood, which formerly belonged to his father, Sir Gilbert, and has without interruption continued in that family ever since." It thus appears to have been a small barony, and like other baronial holdings, it had its Castle, Chapel and Mill. The Castle of Eddlewood was situated on the banks of the Meikle burn, within the wall which surrounds the High Parks of Hamilton. Its site is marked by a mound of rubbish and the fragment of a wall. The Chapel of Eddlewood stood on a farm near the present Eddlewood House, still called, "The Chapel." It appears to have been built for the accommodation of the retainers of the Hamilton family in the upland part of the parish, and was connected with, and served by an official of the Collegiate Church of Hamilton. The only remnant of it is a fine spring of water called "The Chapel Well." Eddlewood seems to have been held in the natural possession of the Lords of Cadzow along with that barony, for a considerable length of time; but latterly a considerable part of it appears to have been given to a cadet of the family of which little is known, "A John Hamilton of Eddlewood" appears in records about 1612.

About the middle of last century it was in the possession of Captain James Gilchrist, a brave and gallant officer of the Royal Navy. He was the son of Mr. Walter Gilchrist, Merchant, Edinburgh, and Grizell Hamilton, the last of the Hamiltons of Neilsland. Captain Gilchrist married Anna, eldest daughter of Major Roberton of Earnock, and had issue two daughters, co-heiresses. After retiring from the navy the Captain resided at Eddlewood, or Annsfield, so named after his lady Anne Roberton. He built the present mansion house, and planted the avenue of beech trees on the west side leading to it, which is said to have been the exact length of the ship he commanded when at sea. The arms of Captain Gilchrist empaled with those of his wife, Anna Roberton are sculptured on a tablet above the front door of the office houses of Eddlewood. These are *Gules*, three cinquefoils, *ermine* for the Hamiltons of Neilsland, of which family the Captain was the representative ; and for the Robertons of Earnock, from which his lady was descended, quarterly 1st, and 4th *Gules*, a close helmet, *argent*, 2d and 3d, a cross crosslet fitcheé, *Gules*. Crest, an anchor, proper. Motto, For Security. The Coat is considerably defaced, and the Motto illegible, but the name Anna Roberton, above the arms is distinct and legible.

Captain Gilchrist's eldest daughter, Grizell, married Mr. Boyes of Wellhall, and after her father's death, got the lower portion of the estate, now called Eddlewood. Anna, his 2d daughter, married, 17th October, 1774, Archibald 9th Earl of Dundonald, and got the upper section, Annsfield and Earnockmuir. She was the mother of 6 sons, the eldest of whom was Thomas, 10th Earl—the famous Lord Dundonald, who was born at Eddlewood House, 14th

Dec., 1775. The room in which he first saw the light is still pointed out. Another son, the Hon. Wm. Erskine Cochrane, was Major in the 15th Dragoons, and served with distinction under Sir John Moore in Spain. After retiring from the army he lived for some time at Eddlewood House and farmed Annsfield, which he inherited from his mother, but latterly sold it to Mr. Dixon, who also purchased at the same time the lower section of Eddlewood. Mr. Dixon resold Eddlewood some time after to Mr. Allan of London, whose heirs are now the proprietors.

QUARTER IRON WORKS.

Proprietors—Colin Dunlop and Company

Individual Partners of the Firm—Colin K. Dunlop, sen.—residence, Garnkirk House, near Glasgow; George Dunlop, Garnkirk House; Colin Dunlop, jun. (managing partner)—residence, Oakenshaw House, near Hamilton

Officials—Alex. G. Reid, general manager; James Galt, manager of furnaces; James Munro, underground manager; James Shaw, cashier; Archibald Macdonald, storekeeper

QUARTER LITERARY AND SCIENTIFIC ASSOCIATION.
(Instituted 1867.)

Hugh Jack, president; Alex. G. Reid and Andrew Hamilton, vice-presidents; James Shaw, treasurer; James Wilson, secretary; William Rodger and Alexander Bell, librarians—with a large consulting and managing committee

FRIENDLY SOCIETIES.

THE OLD QUARTER COLLIERS' FRIENDLY SOCIETY (Instituted 1799).—Annual contributions, 8s. Aliment for sick members, 6s weekly. Funeral allowance, 30s. John Fleming, preses; William Johnstone, treasurer; Francis Gilchrist, secretary, with three key masters and four ordinary masters

QUARTER IRON WORKS PERMANENT FRIENDLY SOCIETY (Instituted 1861). Annual contribution, 13s. Sick aliment, 8s weekly. Funeral allowance, £3. The annual dividend to each paid-up member has averaged from 5s to 7s. William Johnstone, president; James Shaw, treasurer; James Young, secretary, with twelve members of committee.

GOOD TEMPLAR LODGES.

OAKENSHAW LODGE, No. 622 (Instituted 1875)

JUVENILE LODGE, "BUDS OF PROMISE," No. 142 (Instituted 1877)

CRICKET AND FOOTBALL CLUBS.
Instituted 1864 and 1867.

George Moffat, captain; James Brown, secretary

POST OFFICE—Mrs Rodger, postmistress

MISS ANDERSON,

LADIES' OUTFITTER

AND

GENERAL DRAPER,

13 TOWNHEAD STREET,

HAMILTON.

A. T. YOUNG,

General Draper,

SHIRTMAKER, HOSIER AND GLOVER,

69 Quarry Street,

INVITES inspection of his Stock, now complete in every Department, **and in** point of value cannot be surpassed. Every article is marked in plain **figures** at lowest Cash Prices. Some good bargains will be given in

LAMBS'-WOOL HOSIERY AND UNDERCLOTHING,

LADIES' and GENTS.'S SCARFS, UMBRELLAS, GLOVES,

SHIRTS, AND SHIRTING, &C.

Shirts Made to Order on the Shortest Notice.

Note the Address—

69 QUARRY STREET, HAMILTON.

A. PARKER,
Umbrella-Maker,
BRANDON STREET, HAMILTON.

Umbrellas Repaired, Re-Covered, and Made to Order,

Sign of the
RED AND GOLD UMBRELLA,
Opposite the Central Station.

GAVIN CROSS,
TAILOR AND CLOTHIER,
79 QUARRY STREET, BURGH BUILDINGS, HAMILTON.

CARD.
WILLIAM MACKIE,
SADDLER,
10 NEW BUILDINGS, DUKE STREET, HAMILTON.

THE WAREHOUSE FOR
WATCHES, CLOCKS, JEWELLERY, &c.,
46 AND 48 CADZOW STREET, HAMILTON.

Established 1850.

JAMES WISEMAN

Respectfully solicits an Inspection of his Extensive Stock before purchasing elsewhere. The more valuable portion of it is not exposed to public view, but kept in air-tight Safes, clean and untarnished.

Old Gold and Silver Bought or taken in Exchange.

Jobbing done expeditiously by Experienced Workmen.

NOTICE OF REMOVAL.

THOMAS & ROBERT ANNAN

Beg to intimate that they have REMOVED from
BURNBANK ROAD
TO
BOTHWELL ROAD,
(Opposite Palace Gate),

Where they are now prepared to execute all kinds of PHOTOGRAPHY in the Best Style of the Art.

Portraits Taken Daily, from Ten a.m. to Six p.m.

ADVERTISEMENTS.

JOHN STEWART,
DISPENSING CHEMIST,
(From Glasgow Apothecaries' Co.),
8 CADZOW STREET, HAMILTON.

REMOVAL TO NEW PREMISES.

OPENING ANNOUNCEMENT.

JOHN DOBBIE

Has Opened New and Commodious Premises for the Sale of

GROCERIES, WINES, & SPIRITS,

AT

BURNBANK ROAD,

Near Peacock Cross, Hamilton,

And would respectfully request the attention of Families to his Superior Stock. All Orders are delivered per own Van in the Country District six miles round.

Orders now being received for October Brewing of

BASS' AND ALLSOPP'S ALES.

ROBERT MOCHRIE,

Family Grocer and Wine Merchant,

BURGH BUILDINGS,

HAMILTON.

EGGS—WHOLESALE.

WILLIAM CAMERON,
FAMILY GROCER,
QUARRY STREET,
HAMILTON.

JAMES KEITH,

Grocer and Wine Merchant,
86 CADZOW STREET,
HAMILTON.

TEAS.

- 3/2. — A blend of Finest Teas imported.
- 3/. — Assam, Moning and Kaisow.
- 2/10. — Strong, well-flavoured Tea.
- 2/6. — Thoroughly sound, sold by many as the Best Tea.
- 2/. — Good Common Tea, free from rank flavour.
- 1/8. — First-rate Value.
- 3/6. — Pure Black Teas, finest selected.

WINES.

All Wines Imported direct and Guaranteed Genuine.

- 16/. — Tarragona Port.
- 24/, 30/, 36/. — Pure Oporto Wines, sound, and excellent value.
- 38/, 42/, 48/. — Fruity, rich flavour and aroma.
- 54/, 60/. — Tawny, old, silky, and dry.

VINTAGE WINES, 1863, 1868, and 1834.

SHERRIES.

- 20/, 24/, 30/. — Good, sound Wines.
- 36/, 38/, 44/. — Excellent Dinner Wines.
- 42/. — Old East India.
- 48/. — Fine selected Madeira.
- 48/ and 54/. — Dessert Wines.

Manzanilla, Zucco, Marsala.

CLARETS.

- 14/, 18/, 24/. — Sound light Claret.
- 36/, 42/, 48/. — Selected Chateaux.
- 48/ to 96/. — High-class, old bottled Wines.

WHITE WINES.

Graves, 24/.   Barsac, 36/.   Sauterne, 36/.   Haut Sauterne, 48/ to 60/.

Carlowitz and **Max Gregor Hungarian Wines.**

CHAMPAGNES.

36/, 48/.—Sound, fair Wines.
54/.—Ayala.
60/ to 80/.—Ayala, Jules Mumm, Ruinart, Moet, Pommery, Heidseick, Clicquot, Roderer.

FINEST OLD WHISKY,

17/, 18/, 20/ per Gal.

J. K. warrants all Whisky at these prices to be entirely free from patent coffee-still Whisky. They are matured in bond for years, and have the advantage peculiar to Old Whisky of being comparatively, if not altogether, free from fusil oil. No new Whisky whatever is blended with the

TODDY WHISKIES, from 17/ upwards.

BRANDIES, 42/, 48/, 54/, 60/, 78/.

RUM (Old Jamaica).

GIN (Hollands and Old Tom).

HOCKS, LIQUEURS, MINERAL WATERS,

BRITISH WINES,

Bass' and Allsopp's Ale.

REID'S FINEST IMPERIAL PORTER.

GUINNESS' DUBLIN STOUT.

J. K.'s Stock of

GENERAL GROCERIES

Is specially selected for a First-class Family Trade,

And the best quality of everything is sent unless otherwise ordered. Cheaper Qualities of various Articles, such as Butter, Flour, &c., always in Stock, and these can be had at prices much below what is charged for the best article.

Detailed Price Lists sent on application.

JOHN LIGHTBODY,

FAMILY

Bread, Biscuit, and Pastry

BAKER

AND

Confectioner

Soiree and Excursion Purveyor,

58 Cadzow St. |AND| 4 Duke St.,

HAMILTON.

SOMMERVILLE & KINNEAR,

Wholesale and Retail

LINEN & WOOLLEN DRAPERS,

Milliners, Dressmakers, Tailors, &c.

14 and 16 CADZOW STREET,

HAMILTON,

(ESTABLISHED 1792),

Announce that they have always on hand a well-assorted Stock of

GENERAL DRAPERY GOODS.

R. C. MACKILL,

CHEMIST AND DRUGGIST,

56 CADZOW STREET, AND 10 BRANDON STREET.

Medicines Supplied of the Finest Quality, and at Moderate Prices.

Prescriptions Dispensed with the Greatest Care, and in the compounding of which nothing but the finest Medicines are used.

HORSE AND CATTLE MEDICINES.

SHEEP DIP, INCLUDING M'DOUGALL'S, COOPER'S, BIGG'S, &c.

WHEAT DRESSING (COOPER'S), and BLUE VITRIOL.

Agent for
Himrod's Celebrated Cure for Asthma—Price, per Box, 4s 6d, or by Post, 4s 8d.
Mrs Seigel's Curative Syrup.
Cochrane's Eye Ointment.
Greer's Pills, &c., &c., &c.

MINERAL WATERS, HUNYADI DE JANCOS, FRIEDRIHSHALL, CARLSBAD, VICHY, &c., &c., &c.

ADVERTISEMENTS.

HAMILTON & MOFFAT,
JOINERS AND TIMBER MERCHANTS,
BENT ROAD,
HAMILTON.

CURRIE & WILSON,
PLASTERERS,
QUARRY STREET,
HAMILTON.
BRANCH SHOP—EAST KILBRIDE.

SHARP,
Photographer,
7 and 9 LOW PATRICK STREET, HAMILTON.
CARTE DE VISITE FROM 5s PER DOZEN AND UPWARDS.

J. M'GHIE,
PHOTOGRAPHER,
HAMILTON.

THOMAS TORRANCE,
BOOT AND SHOE-MAKER,
70 CADZOW STREET,
HAMILTON,

RESPECTFULLY intimates, that he has always a Large and well-assorted Stock of Ready-made Boots and Shoes.

In the Bespoke Department, the greatest care is taken to ensure a Neat and Comfortable Fit, combined with using only the Best Materials, and due regard to the Newest and most Approved Styles.

JOCKEYS and other RIDING BOOTS made to Order.

House Painter & Decorator,

JOHN JOHNSTON,
11 MUIR STREET,
HAMILTON.

Painter, | Carver,
Paper-Hanger, | Gilder,
Decorator, | Picture Framer,
Sign-Writer, | Glazier.
&c., &c.

Always on hand, a large and well-selected Stock of

FRENCH AND ENGLISH PAPERHANGINGS,

In Newest and most Modern Designs.

A Large Variety of

Picture-Frame Mouldings.

N.B.—J. J. begs respectfully to call attention to his Special BOOK OF PATTERNS.

| WHOLESALE AND RETAIL | IRONMONGERY | FURNISHING AND GENERAL |

ESTABLISHMENT,
36 CADZOW STREET, HAMILTON.

ROBERT A. PATON

BEGS most respectfully to call the attention of the Inhabitants of Hamilton and surrounding district, to his large and varied Stock of HOUSE FURNISHING IRONMONGERY, which comprises every requisite in this Department. The following are some of the leading Articles :—

Register Grates, Stoves, Fenders, Fire-Irons, Kitchen Ranges, Hat and Umbrella Stands, Iron Bedsteads, Mangles, Washing and Wringing Machines, Coal Vases and Scoops, Baths, Toilet Sets, Dish Covers, Jacks snd Screens, Plate Warmers, Travelling Boxes, Fish Kettles, Pots, Pans, Kettles, Sauce ahd Stew Pans, Lamps, Gasaliers, Table Cutlery, Nickel Silver, Britannia Metal, and Electro-Plated Goods, &c., &c.

A Large Assortment of

Encaustic Tiles for Hearth and Decorative purposes.

All kinds of JOINERS', CABINETMAKERS', BLACKSMITHS', SHOEMAKERS', and other

MECHANICS' TOOLS AND FURNISHINGS,
Always in Stock.

COLLIERY and other PUBLIC WORKS FURNISHINGS
Of all kinds.

NAILS, SCREWS, BOLTS AND NUTS, WASHERS, PAINTS, OILS, GUAGES AND GLASSES, AUGURS, AXES, SAWS, ANVILS, BELLOWS, FILES, RASPS, &c.

INDIA-RUBBER GOODS of every description *ROOFING, SARKING, and BOILER FELTS.*

LAWN-MOWING MACHINES of various makes.

Garden Seats, Rollers, Spades, Shovels,
AND OTHER
AGRICULTURAL & HORTICULTURAL TOOLS.

Fencing Wire, Staples, and Wire Netting.

GARDEN, FLOWER, AND FARM SEEDS.

36 CADZOW STREET, HAMILTON.

JAMES FAIRLEY,
23 TOWNHEAD STREET,
Wholesale and Retail
GENERAL IRONMONGER,
AND
COLLIERY FURNISHER.

HOUSE FURNISHINGS.
GRATES,
   FENDERS,
      FIRE-IRONS,
         &c., &c.

SHOE FURNISHINGS.
AWLS,
   TACKETS,
      HEEL-PLATES,
         &c., &c.

FARM IMPLEMENTS.
FENCING-WIRE & STAPLES,
   NETTING (Galvanized),
      PLOUGH CHAINS,
         &c., &c.

JOINER'S FURNISHINGS.
LOCKS,
   HINGES,
      NAILS,
         &c., &c.

COLLIERY FURNISHINGS.

INDIA RUBBER SHEET & WASHERS,
GUTTA PERCHA,
PACKING & PIT PLAIDING,
BRATTICE CLOTH,
CLOTH FOR ROOFING,
FELTS,
NAILS,
POWDER,
FUSE,
PICKS,
SHAFTS,
SHOVELS,

ROPES,
PAINTS & COLOURS,
CHAINS,
GALVD. SIGNAL CORD.
GROUND FLINT,
OIL SKINS,
OILS,
GAUGE GLASSES,
LAMPS & WICK,
CHIMNIES & GLOBES,
TANKS FOR OIL,
IRON,
STEEL,
SAFES.

&c., &c.

PRICES ON APPLICATION.

GAVIN NAISMITH,

GENERAL AND FURNISHING IRONMONGER,

Tinsmith, Bell-Hanger, and Gas-Fitter,

CADZOW STREET, HAMILTON,

AND

BANK BUILDINGS, CAMBUSLANG.

GRATES,
  FENDERS,
    FIRE-IRONS.

GASALIERS,
  BRACKETS,
    &c., &c.

NICKEL SILVER AND ELECTRO-PLATED GOODS OF EVERY DESCRIPTION.

Efficient Workmen kept for all manner of Gas-Fitting and Bell-hanging Work.

"A HOUSEHOLD WORD."

PERHAPS THAT WHICH HAS MOST CONTRIBUTED TO MAKE

CINNAMOND,
THE HATTER'S,

SIGN OF "THE LARGE GOLDEN HAT,"

HAMILTON,

"A Name to Conjure By" and "A Household Word" over the whole district to almost all who want THE BEST and MOST FASHIONABLE at the LOWEST READY-MONEY PRICES in

GENTLEMEN'S DRESS HATS,	FELT HATS,
GLENGARRY'S,	TAM O' SHANTER'S,
BALMORALS,	DRESS & WOOL SHIRTS,
UMBRELLAS,	WATERPROOF COATS,
SCARFS,	COLLARS, BRACES, &c.

Is in the fact, that only upon

ONE CONDITION

Will he have any dealings with the Various Makers of the Dress and Felt Hats, &c., he sells, and that is

THEY MUST BE THE BEST MAKERS.
AND MUST PRODUCE EXCELLENCE FIRST.
AND CHEAPNESS FOR CASH AFTERWARDS.

If you have not yet found out where you can

Get a Good 7s 6d DRESS HAT for 5s 11d,
Or a Good 9s 6d DRESS HAT for 7s 6d,
Or a Good 12s 6d DRESS HAT for 10s 0d,
Or a Good 3s 6d FELT HAT for 2s 6d,
Or a Good 4s 6d FELT HAT for 3s 6d,
Or a Good 5s FELT HAT for 3s 11d,

THEN *TRY*

CINNAMOND'S,

"SIGN OF THE BIG HAT,"
HAMILTON.

DENTISTRY.

MR NORMAN M'QUEEN,
SURGEON-DENTIST,
33 CADZOW STREET, HAMILTON.

Continues to Insert ARTIFICIAL TEETH on the Latest and most Improved Principles.

All Operations in Dental Surgery, such as CLEANING, EXTRACTING, and FILLING TEETH, carefully Executed.

CHILDREN'S TEETH REGULATED.

FINEST TEETH, - - - - 5s EACH.

CONSULTATION DAILY.

BURNBANK
COFFEE HOUSE & READING ROOMS,

Open Daily to the Public from 6 a.m. till 11 o'Clock p.m.

The Premises contain, on the Ground Floor, the COFFEE ROOM, where Refreshments, including SOUP, STEAKS, CHOPS, TEA, COFFEE, &c., &c., can be obtained at the most moderate prices.

On the Second Floor, there is a large READING and RECREATION ROOM and LIBRARY, admission to which is One Halfpenny, except on Saturday Nights (when there is generally Music and Singing, or a Reading), the charge is One Penny. A small sum is charged for Games, which consist of BAGATELLE, DRAUGHTS, CHESS, CARPET BOWLS, &c., &c. Several Daily and Evening Papers are laid on the table.

On the Top Storey, there is a Comfortable Room, where several Classes and Meetings are held in the evenings—a Mutual Improvement Class for Young Men in connection with the Young Men's Christian Association; also, Classes for Reading, Writing, Arithmetic, Singing, &c., &c., information regarding which can be had from the Manager, Mr George Moffat, at the Coffee-House.

The YOUNG MEN'S CHRISTIAN ASSOCIATION meet in the Upper Room, every Sunday Morning, at Ten o'Clock, and this Room, where there is a good supply of Books, is Open, *Free*, every Sunday Evening, from Six till Ten o'Clock P.M.

Soup Tickets can be obtained at the Coffee House for giving to the Poor.

A BOWLING ALLEY, at the Back of the Premises, is now in course of construction.

Clydesdale College,

(FORMERLY GILBERTFIELD HOUSE SCHOOL)

HAMILTON,

FOR THE

BOARD AND EDUCATION

OF

YOUNG GENTLEMEN

Head Masters:

WILLIAM WOOD,

UNIVERSITY OF EDINBURGH,

(Formerly Ten Years Head English Master, Dollar Institution),

DAVID G. KINMOND, M.A.,

Classical and Mathematical Honours, Aberdeen University,

(Formerly Seven Years Mathematical and Science Master, Dollar Institution; and Four Years Head Master, Londonderry Academical Institution.)

Assisted by an Efficient Staff of Masters—

RESIDENT AND VISITING.

Hamilton Academy.

DRAWING AND PAINTING.

A SELECT CLASS for ADVANCED PUPILS, conducted by Mr R. L. BAIN, Certificated Art Master, meets every *Saturday*, at Eleven o'Clock Forenoon.

FEE—15s per Quarter; Water-Colour Painting, 21s; Painting in Oil, 31s 6d.

Arrangements may be made for Private Lessons at the Residence of Pupils.

BELLEVUE ESTABLISHMENT

FOR THE

Board and Education of Young Ladies.

When desired, Pupils are prepared for the University Local Examinations.

All the Candidates of last session obtained Certificates.

Quarter Days—1st September, 15th November, 1st February, 15th April. Pupils charged from date of entrance. Preparatory Classes formed twice a-year.

PROSPECTUSES ON APPLICATION TO MISS NELSON.

Resident Governesses and Visiting Masters.

William Wallace,

CARRIAGE HIRER & FUNERAL UNDERTAKER,

Douglas and Clydesdale Hotel Stables,

HAMILTON.

BRANCH ESTABLISHMENTS—

KING'S ARMS HOTEL STABLES,
HAMILTON:

BRANDON HOTEL STABLES,
MOTHERWELL.

FUNERALS CONDUCTED IN TOWN OR COUNTRY

WITH A STUD OF

BEAUTIFUL BLACK BELGIAN HORSES.

CHARGES STRICTLY MODERATE.

EXCURSION OMNIBUS, &c., &c., ON HIRE.

Coach Office,
3 and 5 Townhead Street,
Hamilton.

BLANTYRE.

JAMES HAZELS,
TINSMITH, GASFITTER, AND BELLHANGER, PLUMBER, AND ZINC WORKER,

HIGH BLANTYRE.

Force and Hand Pumps. Estimates given for supplying Water and Gas. Paraffin Lamps made and Repaired. Jobbings promptly executed.

ROBERT STEWART,
SLATER AND PLASTERER,
HIGH BLANTYRE,

JOBBINGS PROMPTLY EXECUTED.

BUSINESS INTIMATION.

MR JAMES B. STRUTHERS,
WINE and SPIRIT MERCHANT,
MASONIC HALL BUILDINGS,
KIRKTON DISTRICT, HIGH BLANTYRE,

GRATEFULLY embraces this opportuntity of returning his warmest thanks to his Friends and the Public for their very kind patronage since taking over these Premises. He has much pleasure in saying, that he has lately erected a Neat COMMODIOUS HALL, suitable for CONCERTS, PUBLIC LECTURES, EXCURSION PARTIES, ASSEMBLIES, DINNER and SUPPER PARTIES, &c.

Also, Purveys for SOIREES, MARRIAGES, SUPPERS, PIC-NICS, &c., &c.

The Culinary being under the strict management of Mrs Struthers (who has both Home and Foreign experience), may be relied upon as replete in every respect—

EXCELLENT ACCOMMODATION. ATTENDANCE PROMPT.
CHARGES MODERATE.

WINES, SPIRITS, AND BEER, of the Finest Quality.

DINNERS Provided for Travellers, Daily, if required.

ALSO,
GOOD STABLING AND COACH HOUSE.
TERMS MODERATE

JAMES B. STRUTHERS, Proprietor.

ROBERT DAVIDSON,
WRIGHT AND TIMBER MERCHANT,
AUCHINRAITH SAW-MILLS,
BLANTYRE.

STORE, WAREHOUSE, SHOP, AND OFFICE FITTINGS, A SPECIALTY.

HOT HOUSE AND CONSERVATORY BUILDER.
ESTIMATES AND PRICE LISTS ON APPLICATION.

☞ UNEQUALLED OLD WINES. ☜

"MAC'S" OLD HIGHLAND WHISKIES continue to give general satisfaction, and an increasing demand causes a most careful Blending of the best Malts. Price, 15s to 18s per Gallon.
PURE OLD MALT WHISKY, from 2s 6d per Bottle.
OLD IRISH WHISKY, from 3s per Bottle.
Our FAMED PALE RUM, 18s per Gallon, or 3s per Bottle.
OLD JAMAICA RUM, from 2s 6d per Bottle.
FINE OLD BRANDY, from 4s 3d per Bottle.

Special attention is called to our
AGED PORT and SHERRY WINES, from 14s to 17s per Gallon. Bottles, from 2s 4d to 3s. Octaves (14 Gallons), £8.
RICH CLARET WINES, from 1s 3d per Bottle.

Terms—Cash.

BERNARD & CO'S RICH LIME JUICE, from 1s 4d per Bottle.
MANDER'S DUBLIN STOUT, 2s 6d per Dozen Pints, or 4s 6d per Dozen Quarts
G. RITCHIE & SONS' EDINBURGH PALE and SWEET ALES on Draught.
BOTTLED ALES and STOUTS, 2s 6d per Dozen Pints.

HALL for Marriage, Dinner, and Supper Parties, Club and Society Meetings.

DAVID M'NAUGHTON,
WINE MERCHANT,
"LIVINGSTON TAVERN," STONEFIELD, BLANTYRE,
AND
MAIN STREET, HOLYTOWN.

THOMAS WALKER,
CHEMIST and DRUGGIST,
APOTHECARIE'S HALL, UDDINGSTON.

ESTABLISHED 1869.

PLEASE OBSERVE THE ADDRESS—

"APOTHECARIE'S HALL."

UDDINGSTON.

ALLAN CAMERON,
Plumber, Gasfitter, and Bellhanger,
ROYAL BUILDINGS, UDDINGSTON.

EDUCATIONAL INSTITUTE,
ROSEMOUNT, UDDINGSTON.

LADY PRINCIPAL—MISS YOUNG.

HEAD MASTER—{ MR JOHN CAMPBELL, Formerly of HAMILTON and MADRAS COLLEGE, ST. ANDREWS.

Assisted by Visiting MASTERS and GOVERNESSES.

Miss YOUNG receives a limited number of Boarders, for whom she has excellent accommodation. Children from India or the Colonies may remain during the Vacation.

Board and Education of Young Ladies.
CARLTON HOUSE, UDDINGSTON.

LADY PRINCIPAL, - - - - MISS JOHNSTON.

Assisted by an efficient staff of Experienced Masters and Resident English and Foreign Governesses.

CARLTON HOUSE is a beautiful detached Villa, situated in DOUGLAS GARDENS, the nicest part of the Village, having Hot and Cold Baths, Croquet Lawn, &c.

The Course of Study embraces ;—
ENGLISH, LITERATURE, DRAWING, PAINTING, SCIENCE.
HIGH STANDARD OF MUSIC.
Special Advantages for FRENCH and GERMAN CONVERSATION.

CLASSICS, MATHEMATICS, SCIENCE, and ENGLISH SUBJECTS,........................	Mr J. PORTEOUS. Mr D. MACRAE, M.A.
ELOCUTION,...	Mr W. S. VALLANCE.
FRENCH and GERMAN	Mlle. GIRARDET. Miss JOHNSTON.
PIANOFORTE, HARMONIUM, HARMONY, SINGING, ...	Herr ROTHSTEIN. Miss JOHNSTON and Miss ADAM.
DRAWING and PAINTING,......................	Mr MONTEITH.
DANCING, ...	Mr M. THOMSON.
NEEDLE and FANCY WORK,..................	Miss JOHNSTON and Miss ADAM.

For Prospectuses, and full particulars respecting terms, apply to

MISS JOHNSTON, CARLTON HOUSE,

BOTHWELL.

ESTABLISHMENT FOR THE
Board and Education of Young Ladies,
AT
MERRYLEA, BOTHWELL.

" This DAY and BOARDING SCHOOL is conducted by the MISSES BAIN, assisted by a Resident ENGLISH GOVERNESS (with French and German acquired abroad), and Masters when desired.

The MISSES BAIN receive Boarders Permanently, Weekly, or Daily.

TERMS ON APPLICATION.

CLYDE HOTEL,
BOTHWELL,

WHERE the scenery of the surrounding lands are beautiful and picturesque, One minute's walk from the Caledonian and North British Railway Stations. Furnished with every convenience. Contains Suites of Rooms for Families, Ladies' Drawing-Room, Coffee-Room, Billiard-Room, with Large Hall attached, furnished with an Extra-Grand Piano. Suitable for Pic-Nic Parties. Ladies and Gentlemen visiting this Establishment can rely on every comfort and attention.

SUPERIOR LIQUORS ALWAYS IN STOCK.

POSTING IN ALL ITS BRANCHES.

Charges at this Hotel on the most Moderate Scale.

Bothwell, Jany., 1879.   *Mrs M'BRIDE, Proprietrix.*

LARKHALL.

VICTORIA HOTEL.

MR SHERIDAN,

Having made extensive Alterations and Additions to this Hotel, Commercial Travellers and Visitors will find every Requisite for their Comfort and Convenience.

The Hotel is pleasantly situated, and in a very central position, and every attention is given to Customers.

CHARGES STRICTLY MODERATE.

Posting in all its branches is actively carried on, and Mr Sheridan runs Open and Covered Machines to and from each of the Trains.

RAPLOCH ARMS HOTEL,
CROSS, LARKHALL.

This Hotel has every accommodation for Commercial Gentlemen and Visitors.

Spacious Commercial Room and Complete Posting Establishment.

CHARGES MODERATE.

Conveyance meets all Trains.

JOHN WILSON, Proprietor.

ROYAL HOTEL,
WILLIAM SIBBALD, Proprietor.

Commercial Gentlemen and Visitors patronising this Hotel, will find every Comfort, combined with Moderate Charges.

COMFORTABLE, WELL-AIRED BED-ROOMS.

STABLING AND EVERY REQUISITE.

AN EXCELLENT BILLIARD TABLE IN THE HOTEL.

THOMAS RITCHIE,
IRONMONGER AND SEEDSMAN,
UNION STREET, LARKHALL.

Agent for Myers' Royal Cattle Spice.
GARDEN AND FIELD SEEDS.
AGRICULTURAL IMPLEMENTS, &c.
House, Colliery, Joiner, and Shoemaker Furnishings.

C A R D.

MR THOMAS JACK,
ACCOUNTANT, HOUSE FACTOR,
INSURANCE AGENT, SHERIFF-OFFICER, AND J.P. CONSTABLE,
HAS COMMENCED BUSINESS IN
BRANDON STREET, MOTHERWELL.

From Mr J.'s great experience in one of the most extensive offices in Glasgow, punctual and correct attention to the various departments of his Business may be relied upon.

| *Temporary Office:* | *House, till Whitsunday first:* |
| Brandon Street, Motherwell. | Campbell Street, Wishaw. |

JAMES RITCHIE,
IRONMOMONGER AND SEEDSMAN,
STRATHAVEN.

AGRICULTURAL IMPLEMENTS,
GARDEN AND FIELD SEEDS,
House Furnishings, &c.

FURNITURE.

ALEXANDER GRANT & CO.,

Established 1850.   Established 1850.

Cabinetmakers and Upholsterers,
BEDDING & IRON BEDSTEAD MANUFACTURERS,
Show-Rooms, 54 Great Clyde Street,
GLASGOW.

Works—Fox Street.

BEFORE purchasing your Furniture from those who, by their polished Advertisements, may have led you to believe many absurdities, we should humbly solicit the favour of a visit to our extensive Showrooms, where a beautiful variety of most substantial Furniture (principally of our own Design and Workmanship) is always kept.

The fact of our having, for upwards of **Twenty Years,** carried on successfully, a regular customer trade, is surely a recommendation sufficient in itself to insure the confidence of all.

All purchases exceeding Twenty Pounds will either be stored free until required, or sent home, carefully packed, and carriage paid, within a radius of forty miles.

Please observe the number is 54.

FLOORCLOTHS WONDERFULLY CHEAP.

BEAUTIFUL DESIGNS IN MIRRORS.

EXTENSIVE VARIETY IN CARPETS.

THE TROSSACHS SUIT

LIVERIES.   **UNIFORMS.**

GENUINE SCOTCH TWEEDS
NEWEST PATTERNS
SIXTY FIVE SHILLINGS.

V. C. THOMSON, 65 & 67 UNION ST., GLASGOW.

www.ingramcontent.com/pod-product-compliance
Lightning Source LLC
Chambersburg PA
CBHW032107230426
43672CB00009B/1655